ISTORIANS will find this an informative and controversial view of rural America from 1900 to 1930. David Danbom deals with the impact of the Country Life Movement on agriculture and rural society. One of the few studies of rural America during this period, the book breaks new ground in both its focus and its premises.

Composed of social scientists, bureaucrats, businessmen, bankers, and others interested in rural America, the Country Life Movement attempted to create a better organized and more efficient agriculture. Country Life reformers believed a renovated agriculture would more adequately serve the needs of urban-industrial society, the most important of which was the need for cheap food. The changes the movement proposed for agricultural practices and rural social institutions were comprehensive and revolutionary. Prosperous, contented, and distrustful of urban motives, farmers resisted the suggested modifications. For a time this resistance was successful, but the First World War set events in motion in rural America which altered agriculture and rural society and facilitated the realization of reformers' goals. By 1930 it was clear that rural America was becoming the productive and efficient supplement to urban America which the Country Life Movement envisioned.

▶

THE RESISTED REVOLUTION

URBAN AMERICA AND THE INDUSTRIALIZATION
OF AGRICULTURE, 1900–1930

THE RESISTED
REVOLUTION

URBAN AMERICA AND THE INDUSTRIALIZATION
OF AGRICULTURE, 1900–1930

DAVID B. DANBOM

THE IOWA STATE UNIVERSITY PRESS, AMES

87-307

FOR MY FATHER

RAYMOND C. DANBOM

THE FINEST MAN I HAVE BEEN PRIVILEGED TO KNOW

DAVID B. DANBOM is an Assistant Professor of History, North Dakota State University, Fargo, North Dakota. He was graduated from Colorado State University, and received the Master's and Ph.D degrees from Stanford University.

© 1979 The Iowa State University Press
All rights reserved

Composed and printed by
The Iowa State University Press
Ames, Iowa 50010

First edition, 1979

Library of Congress Cataloging in Publication Data

Danbom, David B.   1947–
    The resisted revolution.

    Bibliography: p.
    Includes index.
    1.   Agriculture—Economic aspects—United States
—History.   2.   United States—Rural conditions.
3.   Rural development—United States—History.
I.   Title.
HD1765   1900.D36   338.1'873   78-27182
ISBN 0-8138-0945-2

CONTENTS

INTRODUCTION

THIS BOOK concerns American agriculture during a crucial period of its development, the first thirty years of this century. During the first two decades of this period, the nation's farmers were, politically at least, uncharacteristically quiet. For twenty years rising prices and appreciating land values brought an unusual degree of tranquility to what had been the Republic's most consistently dissatisfied group in the last third of the nineteenth century. But paradoxically, this period was also one of unparalleled urban interest in the social and economic state of agriculture and of its practitioners, as urban adherents to what was called the "Country Life Movement" examined and anguished over rural ignorance, ill health, social backwardness, economic inefficiency, institutional stasis, and the effect of these problems on the nation as a whole.

The urban-based and urban-oriented people in government, education, the clergy, business, the physical and social sciences, and the media who composed the Country Life Movement were concerned with raising rural America to a twentieth-century standard of social and economic organization and efficiency. For them, organization and efficiency were the ascendant values of the modern age and the keys to national success and even survival. When food prices rose sharply through the first two decades of this century, Country Lifers were convinced that the cause lay in rural disorganization and inefficiency. Their examination of rural society and the agricultural economy convinced them of the correctness of their assumption, and Country Lifers embraced a program calling for the revolutionary modification of rural America. Because this attempted modification aimed at making rural people more organized and efficient, and because organization and efficiency are the preeminent values of our industrial society, I have labeled this effort the "industrialization" of agriculture.

In the attempt of urban America to industrialize agriculture the primary motivation was not to aid the farmer. Urbanites concerned with the countryside usually hoped that organization and efficiency would benefit rural people, but their principal purpose was to make the farmer a productive supplement to the increasingly dominant industrial sector of the nation. The Country Lifers foresaw a rural society far different from the one which confronted them in the early years of the century. They envisioned a society of happy and contented people, of farmers who applied practical intelligence and scientific agriculture in order to bring forth maximum production, of selfless citizens, sensitive to the needs of an interdependent society and obedient to the dictates of that society. They envisioned, in short, a revolutionary change in agriculture and in rural society. The realization of this vision demanded nothing less than the comprehensive modification of rural America, and Country Lifers fashioned sweeping prescriptions for existing rural institutions and economic practices.

The superiority of the institutions and practices they proposed to existing ones was so clear to the Country Lifers that they believed rural people would quickly adopt them. This, however, was not the case. Because farmers viewed them as inappropriate to rural society and because they threatened traditions nearly as old as the American countryside itself, farmers resisted suggested modifications. But the pressures on the countryside were strong. They took the form of laws and institutions that attempted to compel rural change, particularly when World War I put a premium on agricultural efficiency and organization. More subtle pressures were also at work as rapid population shifts, changes in communication and transportation, rural materialism, the economic boom of the teens, and the bust of the twenties conspired to weaken rural social institutions and alter economic practices in the countryside. What this meant was that though their means were not always effective, the Country Lifers' ends were being realized. By 1930 it was clear that agriculture was becoming a highly productive and efficient supplement to the dominant urban-industrial sector of the nation.

This monograph, then, is concerned with a number of things. On one level it deals with American agriculture at a crucial and somewhat neglected point in its history. On another level it is concerned with the urban-rural conflict at a time when urban society was achieving overwhelming dominance in every facet of life. But perhaps most importantly, it concerns industrialization, the basic fact of American history since the Civil War. It examines the values and goals of an industrial society, and its means of realizing them. It deals with the changes in economic, social, and political institutions and practices industrialism demands. And it concerns the impact of industrialism on all of the society of which it is a part, even those segments not directly connected to industry.

I would like to take this opportunity to acknowledge the efforts of a number of people who helped make this book possible. At various stages of its development the manuscript was read by David Kennedy, Carl Degler, Fred Bowser, Hal Don Sears, and Luther Spoehr, and I believe it is a better work because of their very careful and cogent criticisms. In addition, David Tyack, Don Fehrenbacher, Barton Bernstein, James Shideler, Wayne Rasmussen, Gladys Baker, Gilbert Fite, and Mel Piehl were kind enough to take the time to read and comment on portions of the manuscript. Timely financial aid allowed me to undertake this project and carry it through. I wish to thank Stanford University for four years of generous support, the Weter Fund for one year of aid, and the Institute for Regional Studies at North Dakota State University, which provided me with a summer grant through the efforts of Archer Jones and Bill G. Reid. A number of librarians and archivists facilitated my work, particularly Florence Chu of Stanford and Helen Ulibarri of the National Archives. Jane Edwards and Jo Linda Arnold did a fine job of typing the manuscript. I would like to thank the Iowa State University Press, and particularly Merritt Bailey and Suzanne Lowitt, for treating the manuscript with care and respect. I received emotional support from a number of sources. My colleagues at North Dakota State University, particularly Michael Lyons, Albert Melone, Michael Hobart, Larry Peterson, and Parks Coble, all provided encouragement for my scholarly efforts, as did my parents, Raymond C. and Rowene C. Danbom, and my brother, Daniel R. Danbom. Although she never read it, my wife Karen helped make this book possible because she believed in me. My special thanks go to Karen.

THE RESISTED REVOLUTION

URBAN AMERICA AND THE INDUSTRIALIZATION
OF AGRICULTURE, 1900–1930

1

LIVING IN THE COUNTRY: CIRCA 1900

AT THE BEGINNING of this, America's industrial century, one could still reasonably argue that the Republic was agricultural. Certainly, the officially defined frontier had been closed for a decade, Bryan had been beaten, cities were growing rapidly, industrial development was dynamic, and the majority of Americans no longer lived on farms. Yet in many ways the United States was still a farming nation. In 1900, perhaps two in five Americans still drew their livings directly from the soil, and more people followed farming than any other single occupation. As the century began, three in five Americans were "rural" by census definition, and it is not unreasonable to estimate that two-thirds of these lived on farms.[1] And in that same year, 10,381,765 of the 29,073,233 gainfully employed were employed in agriculture.[2] Beyond the tightly clustered industrial cities farms stretched into agricultural counties and counties stretched into agricultural states. In all, approximately 2,800 counties averaging 2,500 farms apiece comprised the American agricultural empire. Their pride and arrogance notwithstanding, the dynamic cities depended on agriculture to feed and clothe them and on farmers to buy their finished goods, and agricultural surpluses in foreign trade were still a necessary precondition for further industrial development. Despite rapid and continuing industrial expansion, when the century opened it remained true that without the farms grass would have grown in the streets of America's cities.

At the turn of the century, 4,969,608 whites and 767,764 blacks, assisted by 4,410,887 farm laborers, black and white, operated the nation's 5,737,372 farms. Of the operators 30.6 percent of the whites and 73.1 percent of the blacks did not own the land they worked.[3] Though opportunities for farm ownership still existed, the relative scarcity of good land had already decreed by 1900 that in most places east of the Mississippi years of tenancy were necessary before land ownership came

3

to the average man with little capital. Good, easily cultivated land was in short supply, even though it was true in 1900 that millions of acres of relatively marginal land still existed which had never been farmed or which had already been abandoned for the promise of greater profits in the next county, state, or region. Even on organized farms most of the land was uncultivated. The average American farm in 1900 had 146.2 acres, of which but 49.4 percent was improved.[4] But continuing land hunger, high agricultural prices, and the relative shortage of productive and easily cultivated land decreed that in the first twenty years of the new century millions of acres of prairie would be broken, mountain valleys would be opened, lowlands would be drained, forests would be cleared for cultivation, and farmers would bring more of their own land into production. Between 1900 and 1920 nearly 120,000,000 acres were added to the national land area in farms.[5] Thus, American agricultural expansion continued in the twentieth century, but the halcyon years of abundant land, mass ownership, and the social, economic, and political practices those engendered would never be duplicated.

Despite the changes in land supply, despite commercialization, technological innovation, and industrialism, American rural life in 1900 was in broad outline similar to what it had always been. Of course, farmers differed from one another. Region, race, ethnicity, wealth, and tenure status were but a few of the factors which divided and subdivided farmers. Yet the sharpest contrasts in 1900 were not within agriculture, but between rural-agricultural society in general and urban-industrial society. Economically, socially, and politically the American farmer and his family lived in a preindustrial age and embraced the values of that age. Industrial innovations in economic practices, social institutions, and political forms had little direct meaning for the farmer or for his way of life, and he was dubious of their merits. Living much as he always had, the farmer usually believed that way to be good and he hoped to continue it.

I

The first fact that strikes the observer of agriculture in the early years of the century is the universality of hard work. Farmers and their families worked from dawn to dusk, without a thought of vacation, throughout the year in order to feed themselves and bring in crops. Such difficult labor was necessary because of the farmer's attempt to achieve commercial success while at the same time retaining maximum self-sufficiency. Most farmers were, as they had always been, commercial agriculturalists producing cash crops for a world market. The ideal of the self-sufficient yeoman ignored the reality that farmers needed to sell crops to pay taxes and mortgages, to buy machinery, hardware, and clothing which they could not produce, and to purchase the seductive consumer products of industrial society which they increasingly desired. The involvement of farmers in commerce did not mean, however, that turn-of-the-century farms resembled the outdoor factories of modern agribusiness. Most farms were general farms, producing many of the products the family consumed as well as cash crops for the market. In addition to laboring on the commercial crops, then, the general farmer also worked in the vegetable gardens, poultry yards, dairy barns, orchards, woodlots, and smokehouses which helped the family minimize its economic dependence on the outside world.

The number and variety of tasks facing the farmer meant that for much of the year he worked from dawn to dusk. The long annual round of plowing, planting, cultivating, and harvesting faced every farmer and, depending on the crop, consumed most of his year. Winters were less strenuous, but cows still had to be milked, stock had to be fed, tools and buildings had to be repaired, and ice and wood had to be cut. Many farmers reserved the winter for the strenuous work of clearing land, removing rocks, and pulling stumps. In sharp contrast to most industrial workers, moreover, few farmers enjoyed the benefits of much machinery. The average farm had less than $131 worth of machinery in 1900, so the vast bulk of the work was still done with draft animals and primitive farm equipment.[6]

Country life was even harder on the farmer's wife. Unlike her husband, she almost never had hired labor to aid her in her tasks. When the work of the farm was the hardest, as at harvest, the farm wife's work was also hardest, but the winter months did not allow her to slacken her pace. The routine of housework continued the year round, without slowing, unmitigated by even the most minimal of modern household conveniences. While a technological revolution was transforming the middle-class urban home and housewife, the farm wife still struggled with the inconvenient tools used by her grandmother. Nor did farm modernization necessarily benefit rural wives. "Although a constantly improving collection of farm machinery lightened the burdens of the husbandman, the drudgery of the housewife's dish-washing and cooking did not correspondingly lessen," wrote Hamlin Garland. "I fear it increased, for with the widening of the fields came the doubling of the harvest hands, and my mother continued to do most of the housework herself."[7] In addition, farm women were often expected to work even more directly in the business end of the farm. Such things as vegetable gardens, poultry, and butter making were regularly considered to be in the housewife's province, and poverty, labor shortages, or ethnic customs often forced women to work in the fields at crucial times of the year. It perhaps surprises urban people today, as it did then, that farm women endured their drudgery without rebelling. But farm women only dimly perceived the possibilities of a less demanding life-style, and rural society offered women virtually no palatable alternatives to housewifery. Most importantly, work was a way of life for the farm wife, and she recognized that without hard work from every family member the family and the farm might not survive. "I doubt if it ever occurred to our parents that their twelve-to-fourteen-hour days, seven-day weeks, fifty-two-week years might be considered drudgery," reminisces Ted Olson. "They had always worked; they assumed that work was a condition of life."[8]

Although they usually did not work as hard as their parents, rural children shared the rigors of pulling a living from the soil. Children could be economic assets to the farmer, and he seldom avoided using them. "We got plenty boys," noted one of Willa Cather's characters; "we can work a lot of land."[9] At four or five a child could feed poultry or weed gardens, and by ten or eleven a child could be doing the same tasks as his parents. At its best child labor on the farm was "an apprenticeship,"[10] but at its worst it could be cruel drudgery which robbed childhood of its carefree character and misshaped rural children physically and intellectually. Child labor was one of the elements of farm life which sometimes embarrassed rural people and which urban people seldom understood. "Many a time a shudder has passed through the mother heart of me," wrote a Platte City, Missouri, woman in 1909, "at the sight of some little fellow struggling with the handles of a plow, jerking and stumbling over cloddy ground from daylight till dark. Boys 'making a full hand,' 'helping Pa.' "[11] And yet few parents were consciously cruel. As Hamlin Garland wrote of his father, "as he had always been an early riser and a busy toiler it seemed perfectly natural and good discipline, that his sons should also plow and husk corn at ten years of age."[12] When parents had been children they had worked too, and the family could ill afford to feed those who would not contribute labor. Certainly, children expected to work and many were proud of the contribution they made to the family. Even the National Child Labor Committee was forced to admit that "there are hundreds of children all through the country who find chores and caring for animals a good deal more vital and interesting than sitting on a school bench all day with a book."[13] Of course, some parents undoubtedly wished they could do without their children's labor, but farm life was hard for everybody, and unless all contributed what they could the family and the business with which it coincided might fall.

American rural society in 1900 operated in a precarious atmosphere. No public agency assured the farmer that his farm would be saved and his family fed if he died, or broke his leg, or if his barn burned, or his crops failed, or prices fell. There was, of course, a strong sense of neighborliness which extended material and spiritual succor to those in distress. But neighborliness failed to mitigate the large disasters of weather or price which did not stop at one farmer's fenceline. Moreover, rural people were proud and self-reliant individuals, and while they were quick to offer aid to neighbors in distress they were reluctant to ask for reciprocation. This compelling mix of self-reliance, pride, and personal responsibility made constant and pervasive labor all the more necessary.

Hard work was a necessity, then, and rural people elevated it to a virtue as well. The good farmer and the good man was the one with the "Clean corn, shocked stalks, mended fences, oiled harness . . . the obvious results of hard labor."[14] Rural society and rural religion conspired to exalt the moral importance of hard work. "To be a shirker and slacker on the farm is to suffer rural social reproach," concluded early rural sociologist Charles Josiah Galpin in 1918. "Work is the rural virtue."[15]

The compelling work ethic helped to shape rural social and intellectual life, as well as the way in which rural people viewed some of the by-products of advancing industrialism. The increasing leisure orientation of modern society, for example, was regarded with suspicion by people who believed that if work was a virtue, play must surely be a vice. Also the demands of organized labor for shorter hours and better pay found little support in the countryside, and the very rich were often viewed by farmers as profligate and parasitic plutocrats.

For all of the farm family's hard work it was poorly rewarded, at least in material terms. It is difficult to discover exactly what the average farmer earned. Farmers themselves usually did not know how much they made in a year, and many did not even know whether they made a profit. Some farmers did not see more than two or three dollars in real cash in a year, and in many places the barter system remained an important means of transacting business. The farmer's confusion about his income, moreover, was reflected in confusion among the experts. Yet most students of farm income agreed that though the farmer could reasonably be considered middle class because of the size of his investment,[16] he saw less cash and had less income than the average urban middle-class worker. In a pioneering study in 1916, E. A. Goldenweiser noted that "The average farm family makes approximately as much for its labor as the average industrial family, but owing to the lower cost of living on the farm and to the interest earned by the farm investment, the average farm family occupies a much more secure economic position than does the average city family." Goldenweiser added, however, that such marginally middle-class urban people as clerical workers, government employees, and policemen all made more than farmers.[17] This is not to say that some farmers did not make a good deal of money. There were numerous examples of rural enterprisers who got rich on two or three wheat, or flax, or cotton crops, and other farmers got wealthy just on the unearned increment in land values. Moreover, there was vertical social mobility in the countryside, and few were the counties in which an example did not exist of one who started as a tenant or even a laborer and through hard work, luck, sharp dealing, or intelligent cultivation, retired as a landlord owning several farms. There was advancement in the countryside, but shrinking opportunities and the absence of the dynamism of urban economic growth decreed that most upwardly mobile farmers probably rose more slowly to lower positions than did their urban fellows.

Farming had long been recognized as an occupation of maximal labor and minimal remuneration, but in the popular mind these detriments had been countered at least in part by the perception that rural living was physically superior to urban living. Yet urban observers in the early part of the century concluded that rural health was not markedly superior to urban health, and rural standards of diet and sanitation lay far below modern urban standards.[18] Rural childbearing and child-nurture practices, for example, were relatively primitive, with most rural women giving birth at home, many with the aid of a midwife only. As an integral part of a functioning economic unit the new mother did not enjoy the leisure of long periods of rest before, or confinement after, giving birth. Child-nurture practices, moreover, were crude, and investigators reported babies less than six months of age being fed such things as corn, pork, coffee, green fruit, and fried potatoes. A Florida farmer wrote of having "seen mothers give snuff to nursing babies," and though this was surely atypical, laissez-faire rural child-nurture practices made it hard to question the writer's veracity.[19]

By modern urban nutritional standards, the farmer's diet was not superior to that of his infants, though it was not necessarily inappropriate for people who did a great deal of physical labor. Relative to city people, farmers ate too much fried food, too little fresh produce and milk, and too many starches. Two rural sociologists discovered that in Minnesota "Pork, potatoes, and gravy together with butter-bread, and coffee, are still the main diet of the toiling farmer," and, though corn was substituted for potatoes and wheat bread in many areas, this was the basic rural diet throughout the nation.[20] Nor were other rural conditions necessarily conducive to good health. The hard physical labor of farmers sometimes led to uneven muscle development and "flattened chests, spinal curvature, [and] weak arches of the feet."[21] Moreover, farmers seemed to have an aversion to fresh air and sunshine, a factor that made their homes pools of stagnant, unhealthy air surrounded by the beneficial fresh air provided free by nature.[22]

Despite the persistence of these health problems, however, the primary contributor to rural disease was the unsanitary privy and its cousin, the contaminated water supply. Unsanitary disposal of excrement and contamination of water supplies led to hookworm, dysentery, malaria, and typhoid, the most serious physical maladies in most rural districts.[23] A remarkable United States Public Health Service study of 51,544 farm homes in 15 counties throughout the United States revealed that "only 1.22 per cent were equipped for the sanitary disposal of human excreta," and that 68 percent of the drinking water sources were "obviously exposed to potentially dangerous contamination from privy contents." Moreover, many rural people appeared to be ignorant of basic sanitary principles. Of 2,512 people interviewed, less than half indicated knowledge of the cause of typhoid, while the rest either confessed ignorance or blamed such things as fate, green fruit, hard work, frogs, worry, oysters, and church attendance for the disease.[24]

Rural health, diet, and sanitation had not deteriorated, they simply had not changed. In the industrial cities change fathered change and innovation forced more innovation as the nation leaped into the industrial century. But urban dynamism was not easily transferred to the countryside, and the way farmers lived remained relatively unaffected by the industrial age.

II

As was the case with the conditions of labor and health at the turn of the century, the American farm family was much as it had always been. Unlike the agricultural family in nations where land was in short supply and medieval customs survived, the American farm family was conjugal and isolated. Land was relatively abundant in America, and few sons were willing to wait for fathers' deaths to come into ownership. Moreover, the psychological and economic stresses involved in living on an isolated farmstead with parents and parents-in-law no doubt dissuaded many from thoughts of extended family living. Finally, life on the farm was hard, and many parents looked forward to renting the farm to their sons and moving to the village with its central heat, gas or electric light, running water, and sociable town square. The rural familial landscape, then, was marked by millions of conjugal households, each pursuing its living individually with relatively limited economic or social contact with others.

Economic exigencies and the American practice of individual land settlement conspired to make the family the preeminent social, economic, and educational institution of rural society. It was in these millions of tiny commonwealths that everything important in life took place. Here the family's living was made by the entire family. Help might be bought or borrowed from laborers or neighbors, but in the final analysis success or failure was a family success or a family failure. The family was the primary economic unit, and its economic fate could not be attributed to one person. Here also was the primary seat of recreation and enjoyment, where men, women, and children spent the bulk of whatever leisure time they had. Here the sick and the retarded were cared for, as were the incompetent. And here, amid physical conditions urban people usually found primitive, unsanitary, and unhealthy, future citizens were born, raised, taught morality, and closely instructed in the important lessons of living and making a living. Of course, most farm families were neither socially nor economically self-sufficient. Rural people did have social and economic contacts with one another and neighborhoods did undertake joint projects of various sorts. But the American pattern of agricultural settlement did render the farm family much more self-sufficient than either the American industrial family or the European farm family.

The relative isolation of the farm family and the social and

economic baggage it was forced to assume both strengthened it and subjected it to intense pressures. The rural family was a largely "self-
sufficient institution depending less for its sanctions on religion than appears to be the case in the more urbanized localities,"[25] and this self-
sufficiency both inculcated familio-centrism and set families apart from
one another socially.[26] Intense social and economic familio-centrism undoubtedly created significant psychological pressures in rural homes.
There was truth to one observer's contention that the farm "family lives
in such close and compulsory contact in necessary activities that its
members are constantly rubbing elbows psychologically and spiritually in
the home."[27] This close contact conspired with the inexorable economic
demands of the farm to necessitate the repression of individualism within
the rural family. Although it might have been true that "democracy is
the unquestioned order" between families, it was also true that "Within
family groups in the country regions autocracy is the rule," and that the
autocrats were the males who headed the families.[28] Undoubtedly this
male domination and the repression of individualism that accompanied it
contributed further to the psychological stresses of rural life.

In the area of rural family relations one of the sharp contradictions
of farm life becomes apparent. Farmers were widely viewed as individualists because their environment and occupation left them isolated,
self-reliant, and personally responsible for their businesses. And yet, the
same environment which inculcated rural individualism decreed that "the
farm family was a highly coherent group in which individualism was
hardly respected," particularly when reflected in displays of independence by children.[29] Though significantly independent in relation to the
rest of society, the rural family was highly interdependent internally.
Because they potentially threatened the efficient functioning of the family
unit, manifestations of youthful independence often met stern repression.
It seems, therefore, that individualism, a rural trait both praised and
damned by outside observers, was enjoyed by adult males only.

Because they had grown up in families like those they formed, rural
women probably viewed male domination as normal, and perhaps as correct. But women faced other psychological pressures, some of the most
serious of which were engendered by isolation. While men went to town
to buy or sell, and children went to school, the daily demands of the
home limited severely the social contacts of many farm women. As late
as 1923 a Federal Children's Bureau investigator found a woman living
only three miles from a town who had not seen another woman in a
year,[30] and rural sociologist John M. Gillette "came upon an instance in
an agricultural state of a housewife who had not been beyond the confines of the farm for over three years. Her round of duties was her sole
interest." Gillette concluded: "It is remarkable that she and thousands
like her are able to withstand the strain and keep from succumbing to an
overwhelming depression. Perhaps only the sensitive and the imaginative
fall easy victims to melancholia."[31] Of course, rural people did go insane

and did commit suicide, but most merely accepted isolation as one of the inevitable conditions of farm life. Rural isolation and familio-centrism, like most facets of farm life, were usually viewed through urban eyes, and were thus often seen as socially or personally dangerous. But farm people grew up in families just like those they formed, and what seemed socially aberrant to outsiders was natural and normal and even desirable to them.

The relative isolation of the rural family from outside contacts and influences and the even greater isolation of the rural community as a whole had social effects that went far beyond the family itself. In the case of the family, isolation fostered self-reliance and independence while contributing at times to social awkwardness, selfishness, eccentricity, ignorance, stubbornness, and an unwillingness to cooperate with others. In the case of the rural community, particularly in the long-settled areas of the country, isolation fostered "dialects, brogues, peculiarities of dress, eccentric wedding or burial ceremonies, and unique mannerisms."[32] Additionally, isolation strengthened the ancient traditions and superstitions which marked rural people as intellectually and economically preindustrial, and made them difficult to change. Remarkably, most farmers in 1900 apparently interpreted their environment through "notion or tradition" rather than through "cause to effect."[33] Moon farming, for example, a system of planting, harvesting, and slaughtering based on the phases of the moon, was as ancient as agriculture itself and was still followed by many—perhaps most—farmers, particularly in the older agricultural regions.[34] Farmers were commercialists in theory but they remained traditionalists in practice. "The conditions of agriculture so far as the application of science to the tillage of the soil is concerned is conservative," noted the Presbyterian investigators of eight Pennsylvania counties. "The methods of traditional farming are modified only by the effect of the railroads and of the blind, economic forces which have influenced the farmer against his will."[35]

Isolation affected politics as well as the rural society and economy. In politics rural isolation was reflected in the intensely local orientation of most farmers. Much rural localism resulted from the fact that the state and federal governments at the turn of the century did little directly either to or for farmers. In normal times farmers were primarily concerned with issues that directly impinged on them—issues of school policy, social control, and most importantly, direct taxes, most of which were locally generated.

It was true that farmers participated in state and national politics as voters, and it was also true that rural protest movements flashed up from time to time and made demands on state governments and even on the national government. But the lightning rise and equally rapid demise of the Grange and Populist agitations of the late nineteenth century were less indicative of farmers' political sophistication than they were evidence that farmers were unaccustomed to operating in the larger governmental arenas and were uncomfortable doing so. Protest movements lacked staying power, and by and large farmers in the first twenty years of this century did not comprise an interest group capable of planning and acting on its own behalf on the national level in any sustained fashion. When good times came to the countryside rural individualism disintegrated the tenuous political organizations born of hardship, and isolation retarded the development of the political sophistication necessary for farmers to analyze intelligently their relative social and economic position.

The fact that rural society was relatively isolated should not imply that the average rural area was a perfect "island community," in Robert Wiebe's phrase.[36] The rural community bought and sold in the larger society, it participated in that society's functions, crises, and history, and immigrants dropped into it while emigrants fanned out from it. And yet the rudimentary state of communications, the isolation and self-sufficiency of the family, local control of institutions, and the relative absence of means of social control all tended to buffer rural America and minimize the local effects of change in the larger society. This isolation did not make American farmers ignorant and degraded peasants. Most of them were commercialists, but their methods, ideas, and institutions were preindustrial and changed slowly, in large part because of their relative isolation.

III

Second only to the family as a significant social unit in the countryside in 1900 was the neighborhood. Indeed, the rudimentary facilities for transportation in rural America decreed that most rural lives were bounded by the neighborhood and the local village. In the words of a later commentator, in 1900 "the end of the neighborhood was almost the end of the world."[37]

Although all of rural America was formally divided into counties or parishes and much of it was divided into townships, these arbitrary units failed in most cases to reflect the true social divisions of the rural community. Instead, neighborhoods of only a few square miles and a handful of families were the bases of the rural community. Neighborhoods were alike only in their smallness and their informality. Charles Josiah Galpin estimated that the rural neighborhoods in Walworth County, Wisconsin, averaged three to five square miles and fifteen to thirty families each, while Cornell sociologists contended that the average neighborhood in Otsego County, New York, had but two and one-quarter square miles and twelve and one-half families. After a painstaking study John Harrison Kolb of the University of Wisconsin identified fully 121 neighborhoods in rural Dane County alone.[38] Not only were there many neighborhoods, but they were difficult for outsiders to identify. When urban reformers turned to uplifting the countryside in the years before World War I difficulty of identification became a major obstacle. Though rural people knew the neighborhood in which they lived and what the bordering neighborhoods were, ascertaining neighborhood configurations was a difficult and time-consuming task for outsiders. One of the primary difficulties in neighborhood identification arose because many were not united by any common characteristics or institutions. Neighborhoods had originally been defined by topography, nearby hamlets, ethnic or state origin, racial configuration, economic interest, religious preference, or a combination of these and other elements. Moreover, neighborhoods were often bound by common churches, schools, or economic institutions, like creameries, mills, or cotton gins, and such social amelioration and control as existed in the countryside operated primarily in the neighborhoods. The forces of horizontal mobility and economic change, however, sometimes altered neighborhoods to the degree that they no longer had a definable raison d'être. Irrationally, people continued to cling to neighborhood identifications long after their original meaning was forgotten. Hence, it was not uncommon to find neighborhoods that had changed ethnically and had lost or divided their social and economic institutions and functions but which were still embraced as important social units by the inhabitants.

If neighborhoods were united by numerous rational and emotional circumstances, so too were they often split by diverse factors. Demographic changes, ethnic or racial conflict, litigation, materialism, political controversy, and religious schism were only the most important of many factors that disunited and sometimes even disintegrated rural neighborhoods. And yet the neighborhood, even if it lacked a practical meaning, was important to people with few identifying institutions, and they usually did not allow it to die unless they faced extraordinary difficulties.

An institution of major importance in the rural community, and one often coterminous with the neighborhood, was the country school. In 1900 the school of rural reality did not match the little red schoolhouse of American myth. Small, cramped, ill-ventilated, and unsanitary by urban standards, the one-room school bespoke the relative poverty and traditionalism of rural America.

In 1910 an estimated 6,689,970 students, or 37.6 percent of the nation's public school pupils, attended 212,380 one-room schools.[39] Nearly every one-room school was rural, and almost no rural school had more than one room or one teacher. Although the average school was composed of about thirty students distributed through eight grades, many were much smaller. Investigators estimated that one in four schools in rural Iowa had ten or fewer students, and in some states an even higher percentage had miniscule enrollments.[40] While overcrowding was common in impoverished areas, particularly in the South, in other sections it was common to find "districts where three or four families supplied all the pupils."[41]

Although most urban schools had made tremendous advances in their building, health, and sanitary standards and in their physical plants by the turn of the century, most rural schools remained largely what they had always been. Government studies confirmed the common impression that relative to urban schools most rural facilities were poorly built, poorly lighted, poorly ventilated and heated, and unsanitary.[42] Hamlin Garland's boyhood schoolhouse was typical:

> [It] was merely a square, box-like structure, with three windows on each side and two in front. It was painted a glaring white on the outside and a depressing drab within—at least drab was the original color, but the benches were greasy and hacked until all first intentions were obscured.
> A big box-stove, sitting in a square puddle of bricks, a wooden chair, and a table completed the furniture. The walls, where not converted into black-boards, were merely plastered over, and the windows had no shades. Altogether it was not an inviting room.[43]

In what were by urban standards poor schools, with poor equipment, ill-trained and highly transient teachers attempted to teach students spread through eight grades the few lessons they did not learn at home. Boys and girls often barely older than their senior charges taught reading, writing, simple arithmetic, history, geography, and civics, primarily through the recitation method. Ted Olson remembers that "Study and recitation proceeded simultaneously. While a Sodergreen or a Wennerholm was stumbling through the capitals of the . . . states . . . the youngest Olson sat with eyes shut, stuck in the multiplication table. . . . The scrape of pencils on slates told of others working out more complicated problems, or trying to diagram sentences. It was good training in concentration."[44] Storms, harvests, plantings, and illnesses all interrupted the school year to the point where making educational progress was difficult. Not surprisingly, rural attendance lay far below urban attendance. In 1910 the average rural school year was 137.7 days long, while the average urban term lasted 184.3 days. Moreover, the average daily attendance in the cities was 79.3 percent, while rural attendance stood at 67.6 percent.[45] For well-trained teachers the situation would have been difficult, but country districts faced increasing problems in drawing such instructors. Rural districts could not meet urban pay scales or duplicate the freedom and independence city systems and city life gave teachers, so too often rural districts had to choose from among the too young, the underqualified, and the incompetent. Once an avenue of upward social mobility for ambitious rural young people, by 1900 country schoolteaching was coming to be seen as a mark of failure. Most of the students in rural schools absorbed the rudiments of education, but few did much else. Few students finished the eighth grade and almost none went to the practically nonexistent country high schools.

Despite its many failings, however, the rural common school had numerous attractive features from the countryman's perspective. In the first place,. it was very close to the people physically, and in settled regions few students lived farther than one and one-half to two miles from the school. Moreover, the one-room school taught what most rural people wanted it to teach. To urban educators with a broad view of the function of formal education the rural curriculum seemed limited, but unlike the city school, the one-room school aimed only to supplement society's principal educational institution, the rural family. In addition, many country schools served as social centers for the rural neighborhoods, and the spelling matches, frolics, and oyster suppers held there were important both as social diversions and as integrative functions for the rural neighborhood.

Most important, however, rural America was dedicated to its tiny schools because they were controlled by the neighborhoods under a system of neighborhood democracy. On the surface, local control did not seem to be the rule. State departments of education or public instruction existed in every state, and most of these prescribed the curriculum, the textbooks, the length of term, the language of instruction, and the qualifications of teachers. County superintendents theoretically enforced these prescriptions. In those states, mostly in the South, where the county was the smallest governmental unit, county superintendents had direct statutory control of the schools. In states where township or district boards of education operated on the local level, county superintendents were expected to work with and through them. That was the theory, but the system of control failed to work in practice mainly because of the weakness of the county superintendents. In the first place, most of the county superintendents were elected officials who sometimes lacked professional concerns and qualifications and who respected their constituents' opposition to outside interference in local school affairs. Moreover, county superintendents seldom had assistance, and it was virtually impossible for one man to ride herd on a hundred or more tiny schools scattered throughout a county. Finally, even if the county superintendent was conscientious, his means of compulsion were limited, and the moral suasion upon which he depended often proved to be a weak reed. Rural people, then, effectively ran their own schools.

Where the county unit prevailed local control was exercised through public pressure, and elsewhere through the elective boards. In most of the North the district board was the true custodian of power over rural schools. Boards were elected by the school patrons from among themselves, and virtually every adult male who wanted to serve usually got the opportunity to do so. Thus it was the school patrons, whether on boards or informally organized, who controlled the schools, hiring and firing teachers, manipulating the length of the term, shaping the curriculum, choosing textbooks, and even determining the language of instruction.

Another important institution in the American countryside was the church, though there are indications it suffered from declining rural zeal in the early years of the century. "There is in all our rural churches a general indifference toward religion," complained a Missouri minister in 1913,[46] and an Illinois colleague discovered 500 abandoned churches in his state and another 1,200 in Missouri. Not only were these churches abandoned, but farmers added insult to injury by "using them for hay barns, corn cribs, [and] tool sheds."[47] Even in young farming regions numerous churches were abandoned, and investigators usually discovered that in any given locality less than half of the churches were gaining membership and substantial fractions of the population did not attend church or hold membership.[48] Despite these danger signals, however, it was still true that farmers and their families were more regular church-goers than city people. Scattered throughout the open countryside were tens of thousands of tiny churches, most with a mere handful of members, trying to survive. Some gained strength from a racial or ethnic identification, but many others, the products of ancient schisms or half-forgotten revivals, struggled along as symbols of community division and religious jealousy. As was the case with the one-room school, the rural church of American myth was much more attractive than the rural church of American reality. Like the rural school, the rural church was usually small, ill lighted, ill heated, poorly maintained, and under-financed. In order to make a living, ministers almost always had to divide their services among several churches, and even then the belief that one should not profit from spreading God's word forced many preachers to farm or do odd jobs to supplement their incomes. Urban observers believed these problems caused most of the best ministers to gravitate to the towns and cities, leaving the country church "a conven-ient laboratory for the clerical novice, or . . . an asylum for the decrepit or inefficient."[49] But despite its many apparent faults the rural church remained attractive to many country people. Rural people clung to their churches because most were completely controlled by parishioners, many provided important components of ethnic or social identity, and all were significant centers of social enjoyment in a society where precious few such centers existed. Like the rural schools, the rural churches entered the twentieth century as localistic and informal institu-tions, reflecting rural individualism in their doctrines, their sectarian multiplication, and their unwillingness to cooperate among themselves.

IV

As was the case with rural social institutions, the pattern of rural govern-ment at the turn of the century reflected the informality, the in-dividualism, the localism, the traditionalism, and the relative poverty of the farmer's life. Relative to urban society, there was little government in rural America, and the government that was there was not highly active.

As self-reliant individuals farmers seldom perceived what government could do for them while always fearing what it might do to them, at least in normal times. Also shaping rural perceptions of government was the farmer's belief that he was society's primary producer, and that parasitic politicians would take every possible opportunity to live off the fruit of his labor. As the nation's most self-conscious taxpayers, farmers suspected most schemes to extend government or to make political offices appointive rather than elective. It was also true that, as individualists, farmers were often unwilling to defer to governmental leaders, thus making state activism particularly difficult. As one Pennsylvania farmer said to an investigator, "We are too thoroughly American to allow any one to boss us."[50] Finally, most rural areas were simply too poor to support much of a governmental establishment even if they would have wanted one.

Of the limited government that existed, the most important to rural people was county and local government. Outside of the postal service, the federal government impinged but little on farmers' lives, and the same was generally true with state government. Although sharp interest in large questions sometimes rose in rural communities, country people were most concerned with local issues. In a few states, concentrated in the South, such powers of protection, control, and amelioration as existed lay with the counties. Everywhere else, however, governmental responsibility for rural affairs was split among counties, towns or townships, and even smaller local jurisdictions. Aside from some minimal powers over roads, taxation, protection, health, the poor, and elections, counties had few powers. Townships had most of their significant powers in the areas of justice and control, as justices of the peace and constables were usually elected from them. Thus, those whose duty it was to enforce the law were usually elected by less than two hundred electors from a very small community. Local control of law enforcement was assured, though there were townships that did not even bother to elect constables or that used the office as a form of welfare for local ne'er-do-wells.[51] In the relatively quiescent countryside the police function was not an important one. On an even smaller local level existed the school districts, and also often road districts, which were tiny administrative units charged with building and maintaining various stretches of local roads. This highly localized system of administration insured local control of most of the functions of government important to rural people. Tiny, self-contained governmental units fell far short of twentieth-century standards of bureaucratic efficiency, but they taught rural people the lessons of democracy, administration, and decision making. In a rare study political scientist Theodore Manny discovered that nearly half of the farmers he surveyed in a New Jersey township had held public office, and there is reason to believe that, outside of those areas where the county was the smallest administrative unit, his figures were not atypical.[52] Rural government, then, was localistic, informal, unprofessional, and unstandardized, and it was democratic in the most basic sense of the word.

The idea that government should carry out broad functions of amelioration was repugnant to farm people. Illness, hardship, education, or failure were all matters to be handled by the family, or if it failed, informally by the neighborhood. The fact that most counties had some minimal facilities which provided care for the helpless did not diminish this sense of private responsibility. Social control rested primarily on the feeble foundation of public opinion, though it is unlikely that many people had to be controlled. In the rapidly growing cities the problems of social stratification, ethnic pluralization, physical congestion, and the provision of basic social services made social control an immediate and important problem. But with the exception of the South, where racial differences made social control an abiding concern, rural people showed little formal interest in it because there was little to control. In most places, as long as people bothered no one, they were generally left alone, and economic exigencies and the fact that one might well live his entire life in the community probably kept many from trifling with their neighbors. These were, after all, property-owning family people, and not urban mobocrats. When one offended the community sense of morality and was unregenerate, however, little of a practical nature could be done. The offender was probably as socially and economically independent as his neighbors, and his lack of vulnerability meant that if he did not defer to his neighbors' opinion he probably could not be changed.[53] If a number of people offended the moral sense of the neighborhood on some burning local question, controversy might tear the community for years, though it was not unheard of for the two camps voluntarily to split the neighborhood and for each new neighborhood to erect its own social institutions. With little effective government above the neighborhood level and few levers of control there, rural America could reasonably be perceived a practical anarchy, a fact which disturbed urban observers. Its lack of formal organizations of amelioration and control meant to many city people that "The country, like an uncharted sea, is mysterious and terrifying."[54] The practical anarchy functioned, though, because of a general equality of property, self-reliance, respect for the rights of others, a high regard for personal character and morality, local racial and ethnic homogeneity, and the fact that everyone in the neighborhood personally knew virtually everyone else.

V

The relative social and economic stasis of rural society was indicative of its decline in relation to the dynamic urban nation with its industrial base. Rural life was changing, but it had not, and it could not, change as rapidly as urban life. "While rural conditions are actually no worse than they were thirty years ago, relatively they are worse," lamented Seaman Knapp, the father of the county agent movement, in 1906. "The cities of the United States have moved forward by leaps and bounds."[55] This relative decline seemed to be most graphically illustrated by the flight of rural people, not only to the New Yorks and Chicagos of industrial America, but to the Gadsdens, Wheelings, and Fargos as well. Burgeoning urban opportunities and material inducements, the increasing difficulty of securing good, cheap land, and in a few cases, farm mechanization, all contributed to the exodus of young people from the land. The perceived superiority of urban social opportunities and intellectual satisfactions also drew some of the young from the farms, and numerous rural districts were left with many old people to support and children to educate, with but few people in the productive age groups to do the supporting and educating. Not only that, but some believed the most likely to leave were the more ambitious and better educated, raising fears that the quality of rural people was being lowered, absolutely as well as relatively.[56] In addition to the farmers and their children, other rural people also fled. The best-trained teachers, preachers, doctors, and lawyers gravitated to the seductive cities, threatening the quality of rural services. Nor were all of those who stayed pleased with conditions in the countryside. One of Garland's heroines complained that "I hate farm life. . . . It's nothing but fret, fret and work the whole time, never going anyplace, never seeing anybody but a lot of neighbors just as big fools as you are. I spend my time fighting flies and washing dishes and churning. I'm sick of it all."[57]

In the face of changes, those who stayed in the countryside held an ambivalent attitude toward the city. Many believed that the material fruits of urban life were greater, and agreed that there was no place on the farms for all the children farmers produced. Rural people were proud of national success as reflected in mines, mills, factories, and cities, and they were proud of the enterprising young who left the neighborhood and shared in that success. Indeed, rural people seemed to expect the brightest young people to make their successes in the cities, and those who chose to stay on the farms were often accused of squandering their opportunities.[58] This attitude was one of the most visible indications of the sense of inferiority rural people felt in a society where values and expectations were increasingly defined by the cities. But despite those facts, rural people often wanted their children to stay with them and they feared the potential influences of the immoral cities on their progeny. Moreover, their admiration for national industrial successes was tempered by fear and distrust of modern social and economic developments. Farmers believed, often correctly, that the townsmen whose possessions they envied cheated, patronized, and laughed at them and at their practices and beliefs. Additionally, they distrusted the urban mob, with its strange immigrants, curious values, and exotic religions, and they were leery about the economic and political bigness and organization that seemed to be so much a part of modern urban and industrial life. Consequently, the American farmer entered the twentieth century both attracted and repelled by the apparent future.

Urban dynamism and ascendancy and rural-urban migration in the early years of the century convey the impression that the countryside, stagnant and demoralized, was simply waiting to die. However, it is significant that despite the supposed attractions of urban life, most rural people stayed on the farms. Not only did most rural people remain in the countryside, but they endured difficult economic privation and often long years of tenancy or attachment to inferior land in order to do so. Of course, a number probably stayed on the farms because they knew how to do nothing else and they feared being thrust without skills into cities. Because of rural isolation there were others who knew little or nothing about the cities or what they offered, and still others who did not perceive the cities' offerings as advantages. One of Willa Cather's characters, for example, admitted that farm work was hard and paid poorly, but he still believed it superior to city work:

> [In the country] what you had was your own. You didn't have to choose between bosses and strikers, and go wrong either way. You didn't have to do with dishonest and cruel people. . . .
> In the country, if you had a mean neighbour, you could keep off his land and make him keep off yours. But in the city, all the foulness and misery and brutality of your neighbours was part of your life.[59]

Others were attracted to agriculture because it was one of the few business fields left open to the man with limited capital and technical expertise. There were also some who believed that farming was a ready means to wealth, and the "Golden Age" of agriculture which spanned the century's first two decades, and which saw rapidly increasing food prices and land values, seemed to lend some support to their point of view. And yet, even in agriculture's best years few people saw it as a highly remunerative occupation, and few rational entrepreneurs believed it to be an occupation of steady and predictable profitability. As one farm spokesman readily admitted, "to the man who regards the mere accumulation of great wealth as the sole or even the chief criterion of success the occupation of farming will present few attractions."[60] Indeed, most farmers were held on the land, at least in part, by nonrational or semirational motives. The close personal relationships with family and neighbors made possible and often necessary by farm life, the farmer's community with the soil, the animals, and nature in general, and the personal independence farm life afforded all transcended economic motivations and helped influence people to stay on the land.

To justify their choice to themselves and to others, and to mask the hard realities of farm life, rural people often embraced a series of sentimental half-truths, symbols, and myths about themselves. In essence, farmers tended to embrace the belief that agriculture was the most basic economic occupation of society and that all others were, to some degree, parasitic. As the most basic occupation, farming gained in the eyes of the farmer a degree of social legitimacy unattained by any other vocation. Although many urban people agreed that agriculture was the most basic and legitimate economic pursuit, most perceived that agriculture was becoming as dependent on commerce and industry as they were on it. But the idea that the nation was increasingly interdependent was rejected by farmers who continued to cling to a myth increasingly separated from reality. Worthy Master N. J. Bachelder accurately delineated the farmer's view on the importance of agriculture before the National Grange:

> The prosperity of other industries is not the basis of prosperity in agriculture, but the prosperity of agriculture is the basis of prosperity in other industries. . . . Immense manufacturing plants and great transportation companies are dependent upon agriculture for business and prosperity. Great standing armies and formidable navies may protect the farmers in common with other people of a nation, but their support comes from the tillers of the soil.[61]

Holding such an attitude, it was not surprising that farmers were dubious about the merits of industrialization even while they were fascinated by it and profited from it. Nor was it surprising that they sometimes felt that the nation was cheating them, taking them for granted, or passing them by. "The farmer raised and took to market things with an intrinsic value; wheat and corn as good as could be grown anywhere in the world, hogs and cattle that were the best of their kind," noted a Willa Cather hero, who lamented that "In return he got manufactured articles of poor quality; showy furniture that went to pieces, carpets and draperies that faded, clothes that made a handsome man look like a clown."[62]

In addition to serving as the nation's only fully legitimate economic unit, the farmer also believed that he was the Republic's political foundation. The farmer cherished the notion that he was the political balance wheel of the nation, a middle-class independent suspicious both of selfish labor and selfish capital, a Cincinnatus ready to defend the Republic from enemies within and without. "The American farmers compose the most conservative and least corruptible class of citizens. . . ," intoned an Ohio farm spokesman. "The prosperity, peace and greatness of our American republic rests with the . . . American farmer."[63] As is the case with many myths, this one was born in an earlier reality, but continued to shape man's response to his changing world. Farmers had been, and still were to a large degree, socially, economically, and politically independent, but they tended to elevate what was a mere condition of life to a virtue. In so doing, they impeded their understanding of their position in the modern world and their development as a self-conscious and self-interested political group.

Seeing himself as the economic and political basis of the Republic, the farmer also saw himself as its social foundation. This myth encompassed the general belief that the farmer's home was the only true

American home, the seat of morality and Protestantism, and the foundation of the American family. "The country home is the safe anchored foundation of the Republic," one myth preserver claimed. "It is the fountain-head of purity and strength, and will nourish and sustain the virtue and wisdom of this nation forever." As it stood in 1900, then, the agrarian myth still decreed that economically, socially, and politically, the farmer was "the noblest handiwork of the creator."[64]

The popular significance of myth, of course, is a difficult thing to judge. The agrarian myth had been around for a long time in 1900, and had undoubtedly lost its meaning for many people, becoming a merely symbolic chanting of ancient formulas. It had been integrated into larger American myths, and had become for some an irrelevant collection of patriotic bromides. Moreover, politicians and businessmen, whose closest contact with the farm came at the breakfast table, solemnly repeated the canons of agrarianism to garner votes or business, further denuding the myth of functional meaning. And yet there is reason to believe that the myth of the moral superiority of the American farmer penetrated, to some extent, virtually every agricultural class and served to justify an existence that was difficult to justify rationally. One good example of the importance of irrationality in keeping people on farms can be seen in the *Industrial Relations Commission Report* of 1916. In one hearing, W. T. Davis, an aging white tenant farmer from Coleman County, Texas, recited a familiar tale of hard work, poverty, ill health, and uneducated children, all the products of agricultural life. But despite his problems, Davis wanted his children to become farmers, and when asked whether farming promised a contented life he answered, "yes; a legitimate life, a happy life, a useful life, useful to humanity, useful to all developments of every nature."[65] Such was the power of myth in American agriculture.

VI

The opening of America's industrial century found American agriculture economically, socially, and politically preindustrial. Wherever one looked on the rural landscape he found contradictions and enigmas. While a few farmed thousands of acres with mechanical efficiency, others planted by the moon, and still others grew commercial crops of worldwide importance by semifeudal arrangements. Distant wars or economic failures potentially affected the farmer every day, yet he remained the American most locally oriented. Part entrepreneur and part Jeffersonian yeoman, the American farmer was at least half anachronism. Self-satisfied, temporarily prosperous, and independent, farmers were reluctant to change time-honored economic, social, or political practices and institutions. Traditional, inefficient, independent, and unorganized, the American farmer faced a future which placed a premium on change, efficiency, interdependence, and organization.

2

CRITICS

COMPARED to the rapidly changing urban and industrial sector of the nation, agriculture at the turn of the century was economically, politically, and socially static. As the century dawned it was clear to perceptive observers that industry and commerce were rapidly replacing agriculture as the nation's economic foundations. It was also likely that industrial expansion would contribute to the ascendancy of urban cultural and political power.

Ironically, this era of emerging industrial supremacy also witnessed heightened urban concern for agriculture. Between 1900 and 1920, in fact, the interest of urban people in agriculture was probably more intense than ever before or since. Although the social thinkers, scientists, businessmen, and government officials who composed what came to be called the Country Life Movement realized that industry would dominate the future, they also recognized the necessity of supplementing industry with a vibrant and productive agricultural sector. They regarded an economically efficient, socially progressive, and politically stable agriculture as a necessary underpinning for industry and for the emergent industrial nation. Thus, the concern of several national and largely urban-centered groups for the nation's future forced a close study of American agriculture and the people who practiced it. This study revealed to the critics' satisfaction that nothing less than a complete revolution in agriculture and rural life was necessary, and the Country Life Movement developed to achieve this end.

I

Just as rural people were ambivalent about the cities, urban people were ambivalent about the country. For as long as cities had existed, their residents had held sharply divergent views of the nature of country people. In part this divergence reflected questions of the relative importance of different economic occupations or the relative quality of life-styles. But in the United States at the turn of the century it reflected very basic differences over the nature of American society, the shape of American values, and the future of that society and those values. To the farmer's urban friends he was the prototypical American, the independent, self-reliant, natural, productive, middle-class yeoman, the rock of republican government and the conservator of national morals. As such he was an important counter to the industrial cities and to the disturbing social and political trends his friends perceived in those cities. But to the farmer's urban detractors he exemplified the worst in American society. To them he epitomized the crudeness, waste, ignorance, and degeneracy of society. He also symbolized the worst of the selfish, destructive, unrestrained individualism with which many Europeans associated the United States. Just as the unrestrained individual in business, labor, and politics had to be checked in the interest of national progress, these people believed, so too did the unrestrained individual on the farm.

Taken on its own terms this debate was somewhat misleading, because it was less about the nature of farmers than it was about an image of America and American values which farmers seemed to embody. As a debate over the nature of society and its values, this ancient controversy intensified around the turn of this century, when urban and industrial development raised the questions of what America was, what it was becoming, and what it should be, to new importance. The long-standing debate over the farmer became part of a larger debate over whether the United States should hew to its traditional values in the face of changing social realities, or whether it should modify its values to conform to an urban-industrial future which made social and economic planning, organization, and control possible, important, and perhaps necessary.

By 1900 urbanites had lined up on both sides of the ancient urban-versus-rural argument. Both sides were composed of the same sorts of people—editors, popular writers, socially conscious ministers, educators, social scientists, politicians, and popular social thinkers in general—and each was primarily concerned with the nation's social and political future. One side hated and feared the cities, while the other hated and feared the countryside, but each composed an important part of the impulse that came to be called the Country Life Movement.

At least three distinct types of urban people embraced the countryside. First, there were sentimentalists and nostalgics whose praise of the countryside was a species of symbolic homage paid to a life which they understood imperfectly. Other urban people embraced a type of agrarianism for purposes of economic or political advancement. Praise of the farmer was a time-honored form of flattery which garnered rural, and some urban, votes and dollars for city-based manipulators. Additionally, however, numerous social thinkers, many of them urban people and few of them farmers, displayed a form of agrarianism as a means of criticizing the social and political changes attendant on the growth of the industrial city in the late nineteenth and early twentieth centuries. Though some of the most prominent of these people, like Liberty Hyde Bailey and Kenyon L. Butterfield, were academic agriculturalists, they can be called urban agrarians because they directed their appeal to urban people uneasy about the city and life therein. Never very well organized but always highly vocal, the urban agrarians were particularly active in the first decade of the century when city problems and the continuing relative decline of the countryside raised the fears of their urban audience. As realists, most of these agrarians accepted the fact that the nation's future would be industrial and even believed that future to be good. This was the principal difference between their agrarianism and that of many farmers. It was the social and political ills of the dynamic industrial nation—the immigration, the crime, the immorality, the rampant materialism, the irreligion, the political bloc action, the disintegration of the family, and the class conflict—that turned urban agrarians to the countryside for solutions to urban problems, for counterweights to urban people, and for correctives to urban values. For them, rural America symbolized what America had been and was an antidote for what it was becoming.

One of the first articles of faith of the urban agrarians was that the farmer was socially necessary because of his superior physical, mental, and moral health. For the sake of the nation, "A vigorous country population is necessary in order to assure the highest physical health throughout the total body of citizens. It is equally necessary to the finest average character and integrity of the whole people, and also for the richest development of common sense, sincerity, large views, and patriotism."[1] This superiority was the product of the farmer's natural way of life, and urban agrarians understood how urban life and industrial activity separated men from each other, from nature, and from satisfying work.

Agrarians agreed that man reached his highest moral, mental, and physical development in a natural environment, because that environment was simple, real, and isolated, while the urban environment was complex, artificial, and crowded. Cornell agriculturalist Liberty Hyde Bailey, the most popular and vocal representative of urban agrarianism, as well as other popular agrarians, believed that the growth of the suburbs and of the popularity of outdoor recreation indicated a healthy desire on the part of the urban middle class to recapture the simplicity of rural living. But the move to the suburbs could never recapture the real work experiences that only farmers knew, experiences that gave their lives a wholeness others could not achieve. Most agreed with the conclusions of Liberty Hyde Bailey:

> It is very necessary that at least a part of our civilization have contact with real experiences, real situations, with elementary conditions. The tendency of the time is the splitting and the complexing of our civilization and the developing along partial lines. . . . It is very necessary that a good part of our civilization have direct contact with Mother Earth and with types of experiences that bring many native qualities into play.[2]

Most important, the isolation of farm life was instrumental in developing character. It fostered individual self-reliance, immunized rural people against the majoritarianism and conformism of the cities, and allowed the development of thoughts superior to "those that arise from the babble of the crowds."[3]

Urban agrarians believed that farming, in addition to providing the correct relationship of man to nature and to work, made possible the correct relationship of man to man. While the family appeared to be disintegrating in the city it survived in the countryside, continuing to provide the morally sanctioned relationship of man to woman and of parent to child. The countryside, in many agrarians' view, still based relationships on the personal equation, while the cash nexus formed the primary urban bond. The community of rural people with nature and with natural people created for the nation "men and women who are frank, virile, direct, clean, [and] independent,"[4] and who composed the finest specimens of Americans. In their analysis of interpersonal relations in the countryside, the urban agrarians idealized rural living to an extreme degree. In part this was due to the fact that they were more interested in creating a stereotypical antithesis to urban society than they were in providing an accurate description of rural life. The belief that the relative naturalness of rural life made it superior to urban life, however, was held by many Americans at the turn of the century.

Out of this widely held view of the countryside grew a distorted environmentalism which decreed that rural people were always superior to urban people in every way, and that the only way to match them was by moving to the countryside. "Nature sets moral safeguards about those .

who are near to her,'' concluded one writer on the subject of rural character. ''Honesty and orderliness are not the result of precept, but of right conditions of life.''[5] Far from being merely a shibboleth of maudlin sentimentalists or half-baked nostalgics, this belief was shared, at least publicly, by many urban commentators, including a number of ''scientific'' social workers who hoped to reform everyone from criminals and juvenile delinquents to paupers and madmen by giving them a mandatory dose of nature.[6] It is noteworthy that this environmentalism, based on at least a partial acceptance of the agrarian myth by urban people, continues to thrive today despite the decline of blatant urban agrarianism.

Urban agrarianism further held that the farmer's social significance to the nation was exceeded only by his political importance. Seeing bloc action by organized groups, violent conflicts between capital and labor, incipient socialism and anarchism, and unassimilated immigrants all around them, many social thinkers turned to the self-reliant farmers as the saviors of the Republic, particularly when waxing urban radicalism coincided with waning rural insurgency. Popular agrarians saw the farmer as politically significant because he was a third element to balance the violent and avaricious forces of capital and labor. As Kenyon Butterfield of Massachusetts Agricultural College noted, ''In the country there is little of large wealth, luxury, and ease; little also of extreme poverty, reeking crime, unutterable filth, moral sewage. Farmers are essentially . . . middle class.''[7] Urban agrarians saw a crucial role for the farmer in the twentieth century, when ''Anarchy and socialism among the city poor, greed and snobbery among the very rich, will each find an antidote in the content and conservatism of a great farming class.''[8] Urban commentators believed that the farmer was uniquely fitted for the role of ''harmonizer between capital and labor''[9] not only because of his natural superiority, but also because his position as a hard-working small capitalist allowed him to sympathize with both sides.

Many urban agrarians were also hopeful that farmers as a group would defend American values from the new immigrants arriving from southern and eastern Europe. In the words of E. Benjamin Andrews, the eastern-born president of the University of Nebraska, ''the staunchest type of Americans is that country and village population . . . [which is] so little subjected to the undesirable influences of our newest immigration.''[10] The lesson for the American farmer was clear: ''The incoming of the immense army [of new immigrants] . . . places heavier burdens on the conservative, native-born population''[11] to preserve American values.

It was the farmer's independent conservatism which would save the Republic. In 1901 Georgia Commissioner of Agriculture O. B. Stevens thanked heaven that farmers were ''law-abiding, conservative and God-fearing to a degree not often seen in these days of social unrest and gloomy skepticism,''[12] and Seaman Knapp claimed in 1908 that ''farmers are staunch supporters of conservative government. They are intense lovers of home and opposed to radical changes."[13] This reliance on the farmer is remarkable in the face of the sometimes radical agrarian uprisings of the late nineteenth century, but few urban agrarians, though generally quite conservative, ever mentioned Populism or its predecessors. There were ample grounds for the belief that farmers were basically conservative, but it was more a mark of their fear of the city and its people than a sign of their faith in agriculturalists that the agrarians embraced farmers so fervently. The urban agrarians were basically pessimistic about man in general, but their fear of urban man was so compelling that they overidealized rural man. Consequently, even when they mentioned the rural uprisings of the nineties and before, agrarians rationalized and excused them by contending that farm groups were never as radical, lawless, or dangerous as modern labor unions.[14]

The farmer was not only important as a social and political balance to the city and the disturbing elements that composed it, but was considered by the urban agrarians to be instrumental in the continuation of the city and in its future greatness. Although they wavered between ambivalence and hostility toward the cities, their people, and their values, agrarians recognized that the city was here to stay, and they were more inclined to use agrarianism as a foil to criticize undesirable urban social and political developments than as a weapon to destroy the city. Urban agrarians noted, moreover, that the cities would depend on the countryside for their future population, both because of a relatively higher rural birthrate and because rural people had the desirable character traits the city needed. The urban agrarians believed that "Not only is it true that most of our leaders in politics, in the pulpit, in all professions and in the great industries were born and bred in the country; the city is still looking to the country to develop in large degree the leadership of the future."[15] Not only did urban agrarians believe this to be the way things were, but it was also the way things should be. Cities were necessary, but the agrarians believed that they should be led and controlled by men with rural backgrounds and values if the nation was to survive. It was the countryside that would counter the city, and migrants from the country who would tame it.

So for the urban agrarians America's agricultural population was simply the means of criticizing, shaping, and controlling the modern industrial cities. Of secondary importance in itself, rural America's significance for urban agrarians came through its anticipated ability to hold a changing society to a traditional value system. In the rural America of their conception urban agrarians found the decency, character, self-reliance, conservatism, and responsibility they believed the urban-industrial society needed. But those urban people who loved the farm for the values they saw there were countered by others whose perception of rural society led them to hate and fear it.

While there had long been urban people bent on ruralizing the cities, there had also been those city people bent on urbanizing the countryside.

From the time of the Puritans on, the urban attitude toward the American countryside had been ambivalent. For the intellectual ancestors of the urban agrarians the countryside was a garden created and inhabited by God, but for others it was a wilderness, suffused with evil and inhabited by savages. While the first group saw the farmer as the embodiment of the best in America, the latter group saw him as the embodiment of all that was crude, selfish, ignorant, irresponsible, and uncontrolled in American society. Just as urban agrarianism survived the turn of the century, so too did urban antiagrarianism. But by 1900 the latter point of view was no longer the exclusive property of Puritan divines and political reactionaries. Instead, by 1900 antiagrarianism had become the preserve of the fast-rising fields of social science.

Amateur and professional social scientists—a key component of what Robert Wiebe calls the "new middle class"—played an important part in the Country Life Movement, just as they played a significant role in so many other activities during the Progressive Era.[16] Prescriptive, naive, self-confident, and brash, social scientists did not doubt that the public interest could best be served by social and governmental institutions which modified and controlled society according to scientific principles. Today the social engineering they attempted seems manipulative, elitist, arrogant, and even cruel, but that judgment must be tempered by an appreciation of their optimism, their innocence, and their good intentions. Working individually or through government, universities, churches, and private philanthropic organizations, social scientists paid increasing attention to the problems of rural America in the early years of this century. This concern was further reflected in the increasing amount of time devoted to rural problems by organizations like the American Academy of Political and Social Sciences, the American Sociological Society, the National Conference of Charities and Correction, and the National Educational Association. As was true with the urban agrarians, the social scientists' perspective was an urban one, but unlike the former the latter saw the city as ideal and the countryside as deviant. This point of view held by a vanguard social group is indicative of the way in which urban society, institutions, and values were becoming dominant in American society.

In viewing rural America from their urban perspective, the social scientists were struck by the rudimentary nature of rural social and political institutions. Not only did social scientists believe that rural institutions were too weak to respond to rural needs, but they also feared that their weakness allowed many country individuals and communities to isolate themselves from institutional influences. Great believers in the ameliorative and control potentials of institutions, social scientists perceived a direct relationship between institutional debility and social degeneration. Commentators abhorred the primitive nature of rural schools and churches and their limited programs, the absence of rural health, welfare, and police organizations, and the limited and informal character of judicial and governmental systems in the countryside.[17] This "practical anarchy" made social amelioration and control through existing institutional arrangements impossible and both resulted from and contributed to individual and neighborhood isolation, "the great peril of the farming district."[18]

Certainly the urban agrarians were aware that isolation was a double-edged sword and they admitted that it sometimes led to antisocial behavior and the rise of aberrant political beliefs,[19] but they liked to emphasize the self-reliance and the beneficial moral qualities they believed arose from isolated farm existence. Social scientists, however, with their faith in institutions and institutional solutions for problems, emphasized the viciousness, radicalism, and degeneracy they believed arose out of the isolation of rural people from institutional means of amelioration and control.[20]

One group of rural people about whom both urban agrarians and social scientists were concerned was the immigrant population, but this was one rural problem on which social engineers were sharply divided in the early years of the century. Their fear of the hordes of immigrants concentrating in the cities where they lived made many social scientists join urban agrarians in calling for the dispersion of urban immigrants, and they agreed that farm ownership might make immigrants responsible and conservative citizens.[21] Thus, social scientists often supported efforts to place immigrants on the land. Moreover, there were indications that European peasants, with their habits of cooperation and intensive agriculture, were more productive and efficient than American farmers.[22] There was, however, growing unease about immigrants in the countryside, particularly as southern and eastern Europeans began to take up farms in the eastern states. Rural sociologist John Lee Coulter, for example, worried in 1909 that the dumping of the "refuse immigration which is not wanted in the industries" on the countryside might immediately intensify rural problems and lead to major difficulties for the nation as a whole,[23] and sociologist and Presbyterian minister Warren Wilson argued that distribution would endanger the strongholds of Americanism in the countryside.[24] Increasingly, though, as rural sociologists exposed more facts about the laissez-faire nature of rural life and institutions, social scientists began to express the belief that the development of instrumental urban social and political institutions made the city the best place for the assimilation and control of the immigrant. Rural sociologist Alexander E. Cance noted in 1912 that immigrants must "come into touch with the currents of American thought, American methods and American life as rapidly as possible," but that in some cases "rural isolation has tended to perpetuate old country traditions, customs and language; Americanization has proceeded slowly."[25] The question of immigrant placement reveals with particular clarity the way in which social scientists mirrored their adversaries, the urban agrarians.

Like the urban agrarians the social scientists manifested a fear of man, but unlike the urban agrarians they believed that control was easier in the institutionally advanced cities.

Despite their growing worries about the immigrant in the countryside, social scientists were most concerned with native American farmers. As they studied rural America, social scientists convinced themselves that the nation had endangered itself by allowing laissez-faire social practices and weak, unresponsive, and individualistic social and political institutions to continue to function unhindered and unmodified in the countryside.

Social scientists were particularly concerned that the weakness and inactivity of rural social and political institutions had allowed the countryside to degenerate physically, intellectually, and morally, thus threatening the nation with contamination. Most agreed with Harvard social scientist Thomas Nixon Carver, who claimed in 1911: "Where the conditions of life are as easy as they have been in this country up to the present time, even very inefficient specimens of humanity have been able to hold their own against competition. . . . Accordingly one finds, in the out-of-the-way places in different sections of our country, a degree of ignorance, inefficiency, and moral degeneracy which it would probably be impossible to find in any of the countries of Western Europe."[26] The lack of competition was only part of the problem, however, for even in the cities people dropped out or were forced out of the race of life without causing the same widespread degeneracy social scientists believed to be characteristic of the countryside. It was the lack of organized and scientific health and welfare organizations and the general isolation of rural families and rural neighborhoods that allowed ill health, poverty, mental retardation, and moral degeneracy to perpetuate themselves for generations. Exposing rural degeneracy had become an honored practice among social scientists by the early part of the century, largely as a result of Robert Dugdale's 1874 study of *The Jukes*. In 1912, Henry Herbert Goddard mined the same vein with *The Kallikak Family*, and, in *Misery and Its Causes,* Edward T. Devine claimed in 1909 that poverty was more prevalent in the countryside than in the cities. Others went beyond exposure to emphasize the social scientists' belief that rural ills rose from the paucity and weakness of social institutions in the countryside.[27] The degenerate were not the only people who suffered from the absence of ameliorative social institutions, however. Social scientists believed that people had a natural need for social organization and activity, and its relative absence in the countryside, they ventured, lowered the quality of all rural people. "With no broad, rich social life, no general intellectual activity, no religious inspiration, no initiative to political self-consciousness and community action," wrote pioneer rural social worker G. T. Nesmith in 1903, "life in the rural districts tends toward idleness, vulgarity, animality, and drunkenness."[28] Ever the alarmist, Edward

Alsworth Ross quoted an acquaintance who contended that the underdeveloped rural social life—and underdeveloped mechanisms of social control—had dangerous effects:

> The moral conditions among our country boys and girls are worse than in the lowest tenement house in New York. In the cities the youth has interests, something to take his mind off his instincts. Here life in the isolated farm houses during the winter is apt to be lonely and dreary for young people. Nobody to see, nobody going by. What is more natural than that the boys should get together in the barn and while away the long winter evenings talking obscenity, telling filthy stories, recounting sex exploits, encouraging one another in vileness, perhaps indulging in unnatural practices?[29]

Moreover, social scientists believed that the natural social needs of rural people led paradoxically to further rural social degeneration. Farm owners and their sons, thought to be more ambitious and socially interested than the generality of rural population, became disgusted with the rudimentary social institutions of the countryside and left for the cities, renting their farms to tenants. Tenants were believed to be particularly dangerous to the rural community, for they lacked the political conservatism fostered by ownership and the minimal attachment to social institutions held by farm owners. These tenants, social scientists believed, further weakened social institutions and accelerated the flight of owners.

Social scientists, then, were concerned with the state of rural America in the first years of this century. Rampant, uncontrolled individualism, institutional debility, social and individual degeneration, and the rise of tenancy they perceived all disturbed them. Their concern did not derive primarily from solicitude for rural people. Though social scientists in the two decades before 1920 made elaborate professions of the affection and care they felt for rural people, the tone of many of their statements indicates that these feelings were seriously compromised by antithetical emotions of fear and loathing. Their main concern with rural America derived from their fears of the effect of rural developments on urban society.

The urban agrarians were mainly concerned with urban society as well, of course, though they tended to see it as a problem rather than as a solution. But population and tenure changes in the countryside, which were so compelling to social scientists, helped to turn the attention of urban agrarians from the problems of the city to the problems of the country.

The percentage of the population that was rural had dropped steadily, with one exception, in every decade of the Republic's history, and the states of the Northeast had suffered precipitous declines, both relatively and absolutely, in rural population. When the new century saw the percentage of Americans engaged in agriculture drop to forty, however, concern for the future of the nation and of agriculture heightened.

Urban agrarians believed that the country had to stock the city with people and provide value models for urban America, but they feared that rural population was dropping to the point where these functions would become more difficult to perform. They also shared the concern of the social scientists that the people most likely to leave the countryside were farm owners and their sons, leading to rapid increases in farm tenancy, particularly in the highly productive states of the Midwest.[30] Tenancy in the South had been grudgingly accepted as the only feasible way to bring land and labor together and to control the Negro, but it was widely regarded as one of the banes of southern agriculture. The growing importance of this land system in the white, native, food staple areas of the North most disturbed urban agrarians. The tenant's supposed tendency to overwork staple crops and mine the soil was disconcerting, as was his lack of education and his transience. As this indicates, the urban agrarians and social scientists could see little in tenancy that was good. We know now that tenant farmers were not necessarily poor farmers or poor citizens, and that they were not necessarily less educated or more transient than owner-operators. Just as there were all sorts of owners there were all sorts of tenants, and some were clearly the forerunners of modern agribusinessmen.[31] Since the general thrust of the Country Life Movement was toward the development of modern agribusiness, it is ironic that Country Lifers viewed tenancy as such an odious development.

Part of the reason, perhaps, for this monolithic view of tenancy was the popular association of tenancy with Negroes and of Negroes with ignorance, poverty, and degeneration. These assumptions, which indicate much more about the pervasive racism of the Progressive Era than they do about either Negroes or tenancy, probably helped impede these critics of agriculture from viewing tenancy anywhere among any people in a dispassionate manner. But the popular view of tenancy was also shaped by the assumption that land ownership conveyed character, independence, and conservatism, which were necessary for the nation's social and political health. Theodore Roosevelt was but one of many to echo the urban agrarian warning that because his values made him important to the state, "we can not afford to lose that preeminently typical American, the farmer who owns his own farm."[32] The problem for urban agrarians in the face of rural depopulation and rising tenancy was to devise a way to satisfy urban manpower needs while maintaining a strong, self-reliant, landowning farmer class on the land. As Kenyon Butterfield noted in 1906, many of the best rural youth were needed in the cities, but "we want to maintain upon our farms a class of people that represent the very flower of our American citizenship."[33]

The exodus of the farmer from the country, the rise of tenancy, and the national difficulties these developments portended thus contributed to turning the agrarians from the problem of the city to the more basic problem of "the maintenance of the typical American farmer—the man who is essentially middle class, who is intelligent, who keeps a good standard of living, educates his children, serves his country, owns his medium-sized farm, and who at death leaves a modest estate."[34] Generally dismissing the perennial rural complaint that the farm problem was essentially economic, the urban agrarians accepted the notion that the disintegration of native rural social institutions, social solidarity, and social customs had been the cause, rather than the effect, of the flight to the cities and the rise of tenancy. Thus, despite their praise of rural individualism, urban agrarians agreed with the social scientists that social organizations and social institutions were important to people. As he did so often, Cornell's Liberty Hyde Bailey focused the agrarian argument:

> Good farmers are making the farms pay. The financial part of the business is improving. The community feeling, however, seems to be dormant, if, in fact, not actually perishing in many places. We need to give as much attention to the social welfare of the rural country as to similar questions of urban regions.[35]

The agrarians gave several reasons for rural social disintegration and the flight to the cities they believed it caused. Bailey believed that rural social institutions had lost their uniqueness and had become copies of urban institutions, thus losing their meaning for farm people.[36] Others believed that labor-saving machinery had isolated the farmer and had cut him off from the social satisfactions of communitarian economic efforts, while revolutionary changes in transportation and communications allowed him to reject his neighborhood social institutions and embrace those of the towns.[37] Another perceived effect of mechanization was a sharper rural social differentiation which crippled country institutions. Whatever the cause, the urban agrarians agreed with rural sociologist Warren Wilson that "throughout the prosperous and productive farming regions of the United States, which have been settled for fifty years, community life has disappeared."[38]

It remains to be seen whether the rural community had in fact disintegrated as the urban agrarians believed. The urban agrarians later discovered that most farmers were content with the rural community and perceived little change in it. Indeed, most investigators of rural society were disturbed primarily because so little change had taken place there. But urban agrarians were captives of the agrarian myth, and when examination showed that the rural reality did not coincide with their preconceptions, they assumed that change had taken place.

Social scientists shared agrarian anxieties regarding rural community disintegration, but they were less concerned that declension forced people to the cities than that it made it virtually impossible to control the "stagnant, dank, and noisome"[39] people left behind. In neighborhoods composed of landowning farmers public opinion had sometimes functioned as an informal means of social control, and neighborliness had functioned to ameliorate some local social problems. But social scientists thought that tenants were so little attached to their neighbors that public opinon ceased to have any effective police value and neighborliness ceased to function in its ameliorative, or in any other, capacity.[40] Social scientists believed that the decline of the power of public opinion and neighborhood influence was particularly dangerous because nothing existed to take its place. Rural police forces, courts, and means of punishment were all weak, unscientific, and informal, while churches and schools were feeble, individualistic, and largely unable to contribute to the effective control or aid of rural people.[41]

Despite their strikingly different perceptions of rural and urban life, and their different reasons for reaching their conclusions, agrarians and social scientists agreed that the countryside needed immediate social renovation. Social scientists had an implicit faith in the necessity and efficacy of active, professionally controlled social agencies and institutions. They believed that these agencies had both to ameliorate and to control for the social and political good of the nation. For the countryside they prescribed the kinds of activist and instrumentalist agencies and institutions which were rapidly developing in the cities. Social scientists looked to mechanisms of amelioration that would keep the best on the farms, and mechanisms of order that would control rural society as a whole. Thus it was toward the development of urban institutions for rural people that many social engineers turned in the early years of the century.

Because they hoped to make rural life more satisfying and attractive for those who lived there, urban agrarians as well embraced the reconstruction of country social institutions on urban models. Yet urban agrarians had more difficulty reaching this position. Not only were they predisposed to accept and even celebrate the countryside as it was, they were also distrustful of urban agencies and their functions. But even the staunchest agrarian could see rural faults, and rural depopulation and the acceleration of tenancy indicated to him that changes had to be made. The urban agrarians' belief that people left the farm because they were socially dissatisfied led them to grasp social solutions, and the fact that most successful institutional models existed exclusively in the cities led agrarians to accept urban institutional solutions for rural social problems.[42] The implicitly contradictory positions that urban means could be used to achieve rural ends and that institutional means could preserve rural individualism were problems agrarians recognized.[43] But it was an age of organization, of cooperation, and of institutionalization, and despite their reticence agrarians embraced solutions embodying these characteristics.

And so urban agrarians and urban antiagrarians found themselves united in the Country Life Movement, despite the fact that they differed very sharply on the nature of rural America, the nature of the larger society, and the nature of American values. But there were several contact points as well. Both groups believed, for example, that rural problems were social, rather than economic, and that they could be solved by restructuring social institutions. It was also true, despite their professions to the contrary, that neither had very much faith in man. But the most important similarity between urban agrarians and social scientists was that each was involved in the Country Life Movement not because of an abstract interest in the countryside but because each was primarily concerned with the larger urban-industrial society. Indeed, this was one characteristic which bound the entire Country Life Movement.

II

Sharing some of the concerns of the urban agrarians and the social scientists but concentrating on what they saw as economic problems in agriculture were businessmen and agricultural scientists. As was the case with the rest of the critics, most of the people in these groups were urban and were concerned primarily with the urban industrial system and its future. Their concern with the city, and primarily with the feeding of the city, led these people into the Country Life Movement.

The first decade of the twentieth century saw a disturbing trend in American agriculture. After a decade of overproduction and low prices, most sectors of American agriculture enjoyed a decade of relatively static productivity and rising prices. For most crops in the period 1907-1911, the productivity per acre remained essentially what it had been in the period 1897-1901, or even declined.[44] More land came into production, of course, but not enough more to keep food prices low. In the first decade of the century farm production rose 9.3 percent, but a 21 percent increase in population forced staple prices sharply higher. From the period 1899-1901 to 1909-1911, the price the farmer received for corn, wheat, and cotton, the basic products of American agriculture, advanced 36.6 percent, 49.6 percent, and 58.7 percent, respectively, and the price paid by consumers for food jumped sharply.[45] The rising cost of living was quite disturbing to a generation of consumers which grew up in an age of static and even declining prices. It was "one of the most talked-about economic issues" for twenty years, and rising costs were particularly evident in the area of agricultural products.[46] Most prices increased in the early years of the century, but the wholesale price of farm products increased at nearly three times the rate at which the general price level rose.[47] Changed conditions were also reflected in agricultural imports and exports. Exports continued to exceed imports, and in 1907 agricultural exports exceeded one billion dollars in value for the first time in the nation's history. Values were deceiving, however, and the volume of exports, particularly in the category of foodstuffs, was steadily declining.[48] Imports, on the other hand, were increasing, and for the first time the United States imported substantial quantities of meat and grain. In 1899-1901 the value of agricultural imports had stood at 46.3 percent of agricultural exports, but by 1909-1911 this percentage had climbed to

71.5, increasing the unease of many with the state of American agriculture.[49] Urban people were particularly concerned about rising prices and static productivity, and they refused to see that price developments indicated an adjustment by agriculture to changed industrial conditions and a movement toward increased economic viability after the disastrous depression decade of the nineties. Instead, they believed that agriculture was pulling the nation down economically and threatening its very survival. Many agreed with the gloomy conclusion of educators J. D. Eggleston and Robert W. Bruère in 1913:

> When the farmers stop producing an abundant surplus our growing millions face not only lowered standards of living, but in many cases actual want and starvation. When the harvests cease to be abundant the fires of our national life in country and city alike begin to burn low, the productive powers of the nation are checked—the entire economic and social organism suffers a kind of paralysis.[50]

The increased public activity of Malthusians and Back-to-the-Land enthusiasts in the first decade of the century reflected heightened popular concern with the food problem. Their belief that "High prices are but an indication of a mild degree of famine" sparked the Malthusians into action to save the nation from high prices, or at least from starvation.[51] The most engaging solution devised by Malthusians was the Back-to-the-Land Movement, which some believed would save the Republic socially, economically, and politically.[52]

The solution of the Back-to-the-Landers was simply that urban people leave the cities, take up small parcels of land, and farm them intensively, using modern scientific methods. Back-to-the-Landism had for years been the almost exclusive province of rich men who wished to play at scientific agriculture, call themselves "squire," and escape from the summer heat of the cities.[53] But the Back-to-the-Land enthusiasm which rose between 1905 and 1907 envisioned permanent living by common city people on the land. Sharing the urban agrarians' view of nature and agriculture, Back-to-the-Landers advocated "the taking up of farm life by the city person who has grown to realize the worthlessness and the unwholesomeness of the average metropolitan existence" and who wished to live a contented and moral life.[54] Not only would the individual benefit from rural living, but the Republic would be benefited both socially and politically by Back-to-the-Landism. Bolton Hall, whose *Three Acres and Liberty* served as a Bible for most Back-to-the-Landers, implied that the movement would reopen the safety valve shut off when the frontier closed:

> It is not the growth of the cities that we want to check, but the needless want and misery in the cities, and this can be done by restoring the natural condition of living, and among other things, by showing that it is easier to live in comfort on the outskirts of the city as producers, than in the slums as paupers.[55]

Despite the social and political importance all attributed to the flight from the cities, however, the primary emphasis was placed on the economic benefits to be derived from Back-to-the-Landism. The urban refugees were expected scientifically to produce abundant crops for the nation on limited acreage, and the theorists believed that this would both lower food costs and provide handsome livings for the new agriculturalists. The *Independent,* the *World's Work,* and the *Craftsman* all embraced the movement, some experiments were undertaken,[56] and a few utopians even predicted that the day would come when much of the nation would live in agricultural communities, cultivating intensively and working in handicrafts or light industry in their spare time, thus providing themselves with the best of both agriculture and industry.[57]

Despite the excitement engendered over their movement, the Back-to-the-Landers were almost completely unsuccessful. Few city people went to the country, while rural people continued to flow into the cities. Those who did enter farming were often failures in the cities and many continued their failure in rural surroundings. Other Back-to-the-Landers found rural life lonely and dull, with insufficient social institutions, police protection, and health services.[58] Still others bought marginal, or even submarginal land from crafty farmers and failed to return paying crops. But even those Back-to-the-Landers who got good land, were intelligent, and were self-reliant enough for country living found that intensive planting by scientific principles might mean big crops, but it also meant high costs with no assurance of profit.[59] By the early teens the Back-to-the-Land boom had temporarily busted, and it awaited seasons when high food costs or disenchantment with urban society would reinvigorate it. Despite its limited size and short duration, the enthusiasm was important in indicating the depth of concern among some urban people with food prices and the quality of urban life in the early part of the century.

The excitement over Back-to-the-Landism tended to obscure the fact that a number of more realistic Malthusians had never believed the return of urban people to agriculture to be a viable solution for the food problem. Although they agreed that "The American people of the future must either learn the lesson of intensive agriculture, or starve, or fight,"[60] these people generally believed that the farmer was the best person for intensive agriculture.[61] The main problem, as stated by premier Malthusian and pioneer railroader James J. Hill, was in arousing the farmers "to a sense of national economic responsibility"[62] and thus stimulating them to produce more with better methods. In this conclusion they were joined by most agricultural scientists and a significant portion of the business community.

Although some agricultural scientists flirted with Back-to-the-Landism,[63] most agreed that the cause for and the remedy of the high cost of living lay with the existing farmers. In the early part of the century, American farmers produced more per man and less per acre than any other agriculturalists in the statistical world. The relative shortage of labor and abundance of land in the United States led farmers to farm large, acreages poorly rather than small acreages well. This policy had been the child of necessity and had served the nation rather well until the price rises of the early twentieth century forced its reconsideration.

Most agricultural scientists agreed that food prices were rising because rural productivity was not improving. Production increased, but it rose because of the cultivation of previously untilled acreage rather than because farmers were tilling old acreage better or more intensively. This had been the traditional means of increasing agricultural production in America, but the supply of uncultivated agricultural land was dwindling ominously by 1910. Some scientists even feared that productivity, fertility, and the use of machinery were decreasing, and studies appeared which indicated that this was the case in some areas.[64] "The decline of a nation is usually preceded by the decline of its agriculture," warned North Dakota Agricultural College President J. H. Worst in 1909, and it seemed to Worst and others that the decline of agriculture had already started.[65] Whether agriculture was really declining or just marking time, it was not the fault of agricultural scientists. Indeed, by the turn of the century their discoveries and inventions revealed the promise of a future agriculture both extensive and intensive, an agriculture in which better cultivation and seed, crop, and land selection would allow farmers to double crops without expanding acreage or adding hands.[66]

The problem faced by scientists was less one of finding ways of increasing production than of getting farmers to adopt the innovations they had developed. As farmers' institute worker W. D. Hurd sighed, "After fifty years of work by the colleges, the experiment stations, the boards of agriculture, the Grange and other farmers' organizations, and the agricultural press, we find ourselves face to face with the fact that the average crop production of our great staple crops had not increased during that period."[67]

Despite the bombardment of farmers with publications, addresses, and demonstrations from farmers' institutes, state and national governmental agencies, agricultural colleges, businesses, and agricultural papers, "the great body of farmers" held to the "methods that prevailed fifty years ago."[68] Thus, ironically, a species of that same rural conservatism that made farmers socially and politically attractive endangered the very survival of the nation when it took the form of resistance to productive innovations. By the early years of the century agricultural scientists had joined those whose concerns for the nation's future and agriculture's place in it led them into the Country Life Movement.

Staunchly supporting the endeavors of agricultural scientists was a large group of local and national businessmen, who agreed that "The history of farming in America has been farming without intelligence or skill, without method or management, without knowledge or care."[69] Business commentators, contending that efficiency was the watchword of the twentieth century and the key to their industrial successes, joined in the movement to make agriculture conform to a twentieth-century standard of productive efficiency. Railroads, banks, chambers of commerce, processors, and seed, fertilizer, and implement companies all worked on farmers at the local level with publications, demonstrations, and lectures aimed at enhancing productivity, and the formation of business organizations like the National Soil Fertility League reflected the concern of national businessmen with what they perceived as agriculture's problems.[70]

It is true that businessmen claimed, and probably believed, that greater efficiency and productivity would be a boon to farmers, but it is also true that businessmen usually found that their interest conjoined with that of those they were attempting to change. Whether or not greater productivity would aid the farmer, it would aid those who carried and processed the product, those who sold the means to raise it, and those who lent the funds necessary to obtain those means. National businessmen, moreover, were always in favor of high agricultural productivity, and though it might not aid the farmer it did lower food prices, dampen worker discontent, and result in a general "quickening of the wheels of industry."[71]

The primary concern of social commentators was with the social and political future of the urban nation and the industrial base on which it rested, while agricultural scientists and businessmen were primarily concerned with its economic future. In all cases the interest in agriculture was a secondary one arising out of more basic preoccupations. This is not to say that the people who composed the Country Life Movement were not concerned with farmers for their own sakes. Most of them believed that the modification of rural social institutions and economic practices would enhance rural life, making it happier, healthier, more satisfying, and more profitable, but the changes to be wrought were, and would remain, merely means to the ends of the urban, industrial nation. Nobody ever proposed the modification of urban social institutions or economic practices to conform to agricultural needs, and when push came to shove the needs of the urban nation always won out. The human cost rural people were made to pay for social and economic modification was substantial, and even their self-appointed friends were unwilling to present them with alternatives. In a rare moment of insight, part-time urban agrarian and full-time agricultural scientist Eugene Davenport of the University of Illinois acknowledged that the industrialization of agriculture would not necessarily benefit all rural people:

> Many individuals will be crowded out as agriculture exacts more knowledge and skill. . . . The great laws of evolution and the survival of the fittest will continue to operate, and, in the interest of progress, they ought to operate. Progress is not in the interest of the individual, and it cannot stop because of individuals. Everything must surrender to the central idea that this is a movement for the highest attainable agriculture in the fullest possible sense of the term.[72]

Few in the Country Life Movement were as straightforward or realistic as Dean Davenport.

III

The economic preoccupations of all of these groups were reflected by federal elected officials and civil servants, whose national and international perspective gave them worries of their own as they regarded the state of American agriculture.

Highly disconcerting to federal officials, particularly those in the Department of Agriculture, was the inability or unwillingness of farmers to embrace the teachings of scientific agriculture and increase staple production. Longtime Department of Agriculture employee A. C. True admitted that scientific advances were being taken up by few farmers,[73] and when David F. Houston became Secretary of Agriculture under Woodrow Wilson, he contended that "less than 40 per cent of the land is reasonably well cultivated and less than 12 per cent is yielding fairly full returns."[74] The USDA faced peculiar problems, in the sense that the farmers it supposedly represented were receiving relatively high prices between 1900 and 1915 and were generally contented with the economic state of agriculture. Indeed, the high cost of living which disturbed urban consumers translated itself into a 55 percent increase in gross farm income between 1900 and 1910.[75] Particularly struck by this dilemma was James ("Tama Jim") Wilson, Secretary of Agriculture under McKinley, Roosevelt, and Taft, who in the same breath often waxed ecstatic over farm prosperity while bemoaning the fact that farmers were not increasing productivity.[76] Wilson's biographer contends that "Like an inspired prophet he never for a moment wavered in his belief that his mission was to lead the American farmer out of the wilderness. In his farm creed science was to be the guiding star."[77] But Wilson was as much rural politician as scientific prophet, and his reforming instincts were often restrained by his appreciation of rural suspicion of outside interest in times of agricultural prosperity. Secretary Houston, however, noting "not only a relative but also an absolute decrease in a number of our important staple food products, such as corn and meats,"[78] never questioned his president's belief that the primary job of the farmer was to produce more crops, regardless of profits or contrary rural inclinations.[79]

Increasing agricultural productivity was necessary if the nation was to maintain commercial and industrial greatness and realize its full economic promise. And the realization of economic potential was closely related to the maintenance of national power. Agriculture did not operate in a vacuum, but was part of an interdependent and increasingly industrial system. In this system, progress was dependent on the full development of each part. "The farm and the factory must go side by side," wrote the USDA's Plant Industry Bureau Chief B. T. Galloway in 1907, "in order to bring about the greatest progressive, intellectual, and industrial development.''[80] To government officials the factory was clearly progressing, but the farm was not, and the question arose of how long industry could continue to grow unsupplemented by a vibrant agriculture. As Theodore Roosevelt noted, "Successful manufacturing depends primarily on cheap food,''[81] and American food was becoming more expensive all the time.

Government officials were also fearful of the international consequences of static agricultural productivity. Rising staple imports and declining exports were danger signals for the nation's economy. Elected officers and civil servants were already concerned that American agriculture was unable or unwilling to produce a number of raw materials needed by industry,[82] but a more dangerous threat emerged with agriculture's apparently declining ability to produce basic foods and fibers. By raising the cost of production of industrial goods, expensive food endangered their international competitive position. Moreover, the nation still depended upon an agricultural export surplus to give it a favorable balance of trade. Any sustained agricultural trade deficit could spell economic and political disaster for the debtor Republic. USDA official Willet M. Hayes in 1911 delineated the international dangers the nation faced from an inefficient agriculture:

> The wars of the future are not to be wars with arms; they will be economic wars. Their outcome will depend largely upon the ability of the people, not only to produce largely, but to live cheaply; for some of the races of the world with which we are to come into competition live far more cheaply than we do. The training of the people in agriculture is a training of fundamental importance, in that it will fit them better to wage the economic wars of the world.[83]

With national and international political and economic factors forming their frame of reference, government officials agreed that agriculture had to become more productively efficient. Not only would agricultural exports have "constantly to increase, notwithstanding the pace with which the population of this country is increasing,''[84] but they would have to be produced efficiently enough to provide industry with cheap food and to compete successfully with foreign agricultural products.[85] To achieve this end the federal government was willing to support both the economic and the social modification of agriculture, and to support the Country Life Movement, which had that modification as its goal.

IV

The concerns of all of the groups interested in agriculture were represented in the report of President Roosevelt's Country Life Commission. Theodore Roosevelt's concern with rural life reflected the complexity and the contradictions of the man himself. Though a city man, Roosevelt shared some of the urban agrarians' misgivings about cities and the people therein. Likewise, he appreciated the social and political conservatism he believed farmers exemplified. But Roosevelt was no retrograde nostalgic. Indeed, he understood the mutually supportive relationship between economic strength and political power and the way in which industrialization had enhanced national power. He also recognized the interdependence of modern society and the potential for social and economic organization and efficiency therein. It was Roosevelt's perception of present and future social realities that stimulated his interest in conservation, and his concern with country life was a part of that interest. In American agriculture Roosevelt favored the conservation of both physical and human resources. Both were important because they complemented one another, but they were more important because their preservation was necessary if agriculture was to become an efficient supplement to modern urban-industrial society.[86] Like most of the rest of the people interested in the Country Life Movement, then, Roosevelt was concerned with rural America because his primary commitment was to urban-industrial society.

The Country Life Commission, which was formed in 1907 and completed its report before Roosevelt left office in 1909, was composed of people who spanned the spectrum of those concerned about agriculture and its future. Liberty Hyde Bailey, the chairman, was an agricultural scientist at Cornell and the nation's premier urban agrarian. Henry ("Uncle Henry") Wallace, editor of *Wallace's Farmer* and the founder of the illustrious Iowa Wallace family, was simultaneously a nostalgic agrarian and an advocate of scientific agriculture. Kenyon L. Butterfield was an agricultural scientist, a popular agrarian, and the father of rural sociology. Editor Walter Hines Page of the *World's Work* represented the urban business community, and the Commission was completed by the appointment of the nation's efficiency-minded Chief Forester and amateur social scientist, Gifford Pinchot. Later, California farm editor W. A. Beard was added to the Commission, as was Farmers' Union President C. S. Barrett, the only Commission member who had any regular and substantial contact with the nation's dirt farmers.

The sparse representation of farmers themselves on the Commission underscored the fact that agriculture was a national problem with which nonfarmers were particularly preoccupied. As Roosevelt noted in his letter of introduction, static social and economic conditions in agriculture "not only held back life in the country, but also lowered the efficiency of the whole nation. The welfare of the farmer is of vital consequence to the welfare of the whole community. The strengthening of country life, therefore, is the strengthening of the whole nation." The Country Life Commission, then, both to Roosevelt and to those who served on it, was primarily a means of devising solutions for national social and economic problems. The Commission hoped and believed, of course, that their solutions would also aid agriculture, but they were interested in the farmer primarily because they thought he determined the future of the urban nation.[87]

The Country Life Commission formulated the most complete plea to date for a thoroughgoing revolution in agriculture which would pull agriculture up to modern social and economic standards by introducing into it the industrial virtues of organization and efficiency. The Commission admitted that, relative to the past, agriculture was prosperous, but it believed that prosperity was a doubtful indicator of economic possibilities or social well-being in the countryside. In economic prosperity and efficiency, in governmental activity, and in social advancement and development the Commission believed the countryside to be far behind the industrial cities. The countryside lagged in the Commission's view because it had not learned the economic, social, and political lessons learned in the industrial cities. "There has been a complete and fundamental change in our whole economic system within the past century," noted Chairman Bailey, the principal author of the report. "This has resulted in profound social changes and the redirection of our point of view on life. . . . In all the . . . farm occupations the readjustment [to changed conditions] has been the most tardy, because the whole structure of a traditional and fundamental system has been involved."[88]

In the Commission's eyes, the farmer and his family paid dearly for their tardiness in making these fundamental modifications of their way of life. For one thing, the Commissioners believed that economic backwardness and social stagnation drove the best farmers and their children to the cities, further crippling the countryside economically and rendering it sterile socially. Furthermore, the relative paucity of organization among farmers allowed organized interests to have their way in the countryside despite rural opposition. Isolation, farm labor problems, soil depletion, intemperance, juvenile delinquency, poor health, and lack of conveniences were also prices the Commission believed farmers paid for economic inefficiency, social disorganization, and laissez-faire political institutions.[89]

The solutions devised by the Commission for the problems of agriculture were broad and vague. A few specific ameliorative reforms like parcel post, federal road-building activity, and federal public health action were proposed, but the scope of rural reconstruction demanded changes in rural life that were too broad to be legislated from without. For one thing, the Commission called for an entirely redirected education system which would make adults and children more productive agriculturally and better organized and more contented socially. The reconstruction of the country church was also demanded, and the Commission hoped that the church would help stimulate social and economic organization and efficiency, and would attempt to propagandize farmers about the satisfactions of country life. In order to bring agricultural prosperity to a twentieth century standard the Commission urged farmers to buy and sell cooperatively, but it embraced cooperation in a gingerly fashion, and hoped that it would further national ends like product standardization, distributive rationalization, productive efficiency, and rural political conservatism while helping farmers. Moreover, the Commission hoped that economic cooperation would lead to social regeneration, make people more satisfied with country life, and allow them to obtain modern ameliorative conveniences like electricity and telephones.[90]

It was the hope of the Commission, and particularly Bailey, that the proposed revolution in the countryside would be carried out by rural people themselves, prodded by a young, fresh, and idealistic country leadership. The Commission hoped that teachers, ministers, editors, and scientific farmers would sense the importance of social and economic organization and efficiency for the countryside and would introduce them. "Care must be taken in all reconstructive work to see that local initiative is relied on to the fullest extent,"[91] warned Bailey, who joined his colleagues in the hope that country people, if given examples and leadership, would voluntarily reconstruct their institutions and modify their practices to conform to twentieth-century conditions and demands.

Although they disagreed on specifics, most critics of agriculture acknowledged that the better living, better farming, and better business the Country Life Commission hoped would come to rural America demanded nothing less than a complete social and economic revolution in agriculture.[92] Moreover, they agreed with the Commission's analysis of rural ills and agreed on what changes were necessary.

With the completion of the report of the Country Life Commission, the Country Life Movement can be said to have begun. In some ways this is an artificial delineation of the movement's beginning, for urban interest in rural problems had been rising for at least a decade, and all of the matters touched on by the Country Life Commission had already been thoroughly discussed. Indeed, the very formation of the Commission by the politically astute Roosevelt is indicative of the growing national concern with agriculture. But the Country Life Commission did attempt to focus and organize the numerous and seemingly contradictory concerns of a wide variety of commentators on the ills of the countryside. In its report, the Commission arrived at a comprehensive catalog of the weaknesses urban critics perceived in the countryside. It was less successful in devising means of addressing rural problems which were proportional to the problems themselves, but this was a difficulty which the entire Country Life Movement faced. The problems of the countryside seemed huge, but the democratic system and the paucity of institutions in rural America limited the means available for dealing with them. In later years, this basic problem frustrated and angered Country Lifers, but the report of the Country Life Commission helped energize them and focus their efforts. For at least a decade after the Commission reported to Roosevelt, urban interest in the problems of rural life was high.

The Country Life Movement was a remarkable phenomenon for a number of reasons. First, it was remarkable because it was in large measure an urban movement. Earlier movements which attempted to address rural problems had risen in the countryside and had directed their energies at the cities, but the Country Life Movement rose in the cities and was directed at the countryside. This intense concern with agriculture was also remarkable because it rose during a period of high farm prosperity and of consequent rural political quiescence. The period between 1909 and 1914 was called the "Golden Age of Agriculture" because of the high prevailing farm prices, but when compared with the periods preceeding and succeeding it the entire period between 1900 and 1920 could justly bear that title. It will come as no surprise to students of agricultural history that this period of economic prosperity was also a period of relative political calm in the countryside. And yet, as farm prices rose and the farmer enjoyed his unaccustomed prosperity, the concern of Country Lifers with rural problems only intensified. This clearly indicates that the Country Lifers were less interested in the countryside itself than in the effect of developments there on the larger society.

Another thing that made the Country Life Movement remarkable was its vagueness. Its beginning was vague, as was its conclusion. Moreover, there was no major, formal Country Life organization until the American Country Life Association (A.C.L.A.) was founded in 1919. Though the American Country Life Association continued to operate until the early forties, the decline of the Country Life Movement and the founding of the A.C.L.A. were virtually coincident. Contributing to the vagueness of the Country Life Movement was the diversity of its membership. Nostalgics and Malthusians, social and agricultural scientists, preachers and teachers, capitalists and workers, bureaucrats and Back-to-the-Landers, among others, all identified themselves with the movement during its heyday. Indeed, virtually anyone interested in "improving" rural life was considered part of the Country Life Movement, even though the means to the end of rural improvement sometimes reflected the diversity and the apparent contradictions of its membership. Like the ecology movement of the late sixties and early seventies, the Country Life Movement was vague and diverse. But as is true with the ecology impulse, the vagueness and diversity of the Country Life Movement does not mean that it lacked social significance.

In its vagueness and diversity the Country Life Movement closely parallels the Progressive Movement which was operating at the same time. But the Country Lifers parallel the Progressives in other ways as well, and each of the major interpretations of the Progressive Era also applies at least in part to the Country Life Movement. Historians like John Chamberlain and Richard Hofstadter, for example, have seen the

Progressives as throwbacks to an earlier era; as men attempting to perpetuate an increasingly dysfunctional set of values in an industrial era.[93] Some Country Lifers, particularly the urban agrarians of the Bailey wing of the movement, seem to fit comfortably into this interpretation, as one student of the Country Life Movement has noted.[94] It is understandable that historians might see Liberty Hyde Bailey and other urban agrarians as composing the Country Life Movement, because they tended to be persistent and prolific writers and because they did hold prominent positions in country life activities. But to do so ignores both a wide variety of Country Lifers and the subleties and complexities of the urban agrarians themselves. Gabriel Kolko and James Weinstein, on the other hand, see the Progressives as business-oriented conservatives bent on shaping the modern era to their selfish purposes.[95] Certainly, the prominence of businessmen and bankers in the Country Life Movement makes this thesis an attractive one, but there were lots of other people in the movement as well, and even among businessmen and bankers there were important variations. One thesis which fits the Country Life Movement rather well is that advanced by Samuel P. Hays and Robert Wiebe. They see the Progressives as being primarily interested in advancing social and economic efficiency and organization in the United States.[96] When their movement was at its height, no Country Lifers questioned the proposition that the countryside should be better organized and more efficient. Indeed, most of them explicitly stated organization and efficiency as their goals for the countryside, and their pursuit of these goals was constant even if they differed on questions of means. So the Hays-Wiebe thesis applies to the Country Life Movement in broad outline, but even it does not perfectly explain what the Country Lifers were about. The major way in which the Country Life Movement diverges from the basic Hays-Wiebe model lies in the question of the impetus behind the drive for organization and efficiency. In agriculture the drive for organization and efficiency came not from the group to be organized and made efficient—in other words, the farmers—but from predominantly urban people who were not part of the rural community. So what we see in the Country Life Movement is not simply another facet of the Progressive drive for organization and efficiency, but also a manifestation of the ancient rural-urban conflict in which the latter, increasingly dominant in society, politics, and the economy, attempted to impose its values and notions on the former. That these values and notions were the Progressive ones of organization and efficiency does not alter the aspects of conflict, manipulation, and imposition involved.

Indicative of the commitment of the Country Lifers to the values of organization and efficiency was their pervasive criticism of excessive rural individualism. While the nineteenth had been the century of individualism, most critics of agriculture were sure that the twentieth would be the century of cooperation.[97] Cooperation and the consequent subordination of individualism made possible great industrial and commercial enterprises, allowed cities vastly to improve their environments and their quality of life, and benefited capital and labor alike, as well as enhancing national efficiency. While the rest of the nation learned the benefits of social and economic cooperation, agriculture plodded more or less steadily down its individualistic furrow. "Community interests bring to our people some of the best things in modern life," noted agricultural editor T. D. Harmon. "Citizens of villages, towns and cities have learned that the welfare of their many interests are better conserved by planning and working together. Business men find that by mutual understandings and combinations of efforts many things can be brought about that would be impossible in any other way," yet agriculture remained unorganized and individualistic, and hence unimproved.[98]

If agrarian individualism affected no one but farmers and their families it would not have disturbed the Country Lifers as much as it did, but increasing national social and economic interdependence seemed to make its modification imperative. Even urban agrarian Liberty Bailey conceded that "a farm is not a private business in the sense that it should be absolved of responsibility to society and be outside all regulations in the interest of society."[99] What was needed in the countryside was a new, "socially serviceable"[100] individualism, one which would recognize that "There is no divorcing of freedom and duty."[101] The emphasis the "new individualism" placed on duty and social serviceability might make it seem idealistic. But the society rural people were to serve was always defined as urban society, and their duty was always characterized as serving that society efficiently. In addition, the new individualism had its authoritarian aspects, attacking rural self-determination along with selfishness and stressing the importance of obedience and conformity. In a 1904 address, President John W. Cook of the National Educational Association captured the attitude of the critics when he concluded that in the new century the highest individualism would be "that which embodies the highest qualities of all, not the capricious eccentricities of those who covet distinction by their radical differences from their fellow men. It will . . . bend its head in quick assent to the word of national authority."[102]

This new individualism the critics envisioned put a premium on social and economic efficiency. "Efficiency is the demand of the age,"[103] intoned educators George Betts and Otis Hall, and all other critics agreed that rural inefficiency and reticence about progress had harmed the nation as well as rural people.[104] In an earlier period the nation was rich enough to afford rural economic inefficiency and social laissez-faire, but the end of the frontier and the demands of the industrial cities decreed that the United States had "unmistakably reached the period where we must think and plan,"[105] particularly in economic affairs. Few Country Lifers conceived that social and economic efficiency could be harmful to rural people. Indeed, most of them genuinely believed that increased efficiency in all phases of life would be a great boon to the countryside.

This was a naive but an understandable position, given the context of the times. As Samuel Haber notes, with only slight exaggeration, the "efficiency craze" of the Progressive Era was "a secular Great Awakening."[106] It was generally believed—and Country Lifers shared this belief—that increased efficiency would benefit everyone and would hurt no one, and that it would present Americans with a technocratic utopia, both in the economy and in the society. There were a few, of course, who doubted whether change in the countryside could be completely free of dislocation and pain, but the weight of Country Life opinion and the trend of the times overruled these skeptics.[107] The fact that Country Lifers believed that efficiency would benefit rural people, however, does not mean they wanted social and economic eficiency in the countryside for that reason only. Indeed, the countryside was to be made efficient in order that it could more adequately supplement the larger, increasingly industrial society. For the Country Lifers, efficiency in the countryside was less an end in itself than the means to national ends which transcended the rural community.

The best route to efficiency, in the critics' eyes, was through organization. Indeed, most believed that industrialization had proved organization and efficiency to be one and the same. The *World's Work,* edited by Country Life Commissioner Walter Hines Page, believed organization to be one of the primary ways "in which town life and modern life in general have been made efficient,"[108] and it was clear to the critics that in an increasingly organized society unorganized people could not effectively act or be acted upon economically, socially, or politically. As Kenyon Butterfield, one who spent his life attempting to preserve the preservable in rural individualism, conceded in 1905, "organization . . . [is] a test of class efficiency, and consequently a prerequisite for solving the farm problem." Or, as he noted some years later, "Organization is the one essential efficiency."[109]

Economic organization was the form of group activity to which farmers were most favorable, and was one of the forms embraced by critics. Perceptive farmers and farm leaders had long recognized that buying from and selling to organized trusts left unorganized farmers at a disadvantage, and a good many local shipping, storage, processing, buying, and selling cooperatives dotted the rural landscape. Unlike the farmers, however, the critics were interested in more than the economic organization of agriculture for the simple purpose of enhancing the farmer's profits, even though they did recognize the validity of that goal. Among other things, they believed that economic organization would help rationalize the market and food distribution, would help standardize and improve food products, and would lower the cost of food for urban consumers. In short, the most hopeful critics believed that economic organization would allow the nation "to Henry Fordize agriculture in the whole sense."[110] Moreover, economic organizations would have beneficial political effects because they were more easily acted upon than individuals, because they would "teach the farmer to coöperate and to obey,"[111] and, because organizations are vulnerable and have substantial interests to protect, they would be more conservative than unattached individuals.[112]

Rural social organization was just as necessary a means to agricultural efficiency as was rural economic organization. In fact, Country Lifers understandably found it difficult to separate rural economics from rural society. Even those who could separate the two agreed with Garland A. Bricker that "The solution of the rural problem depends upon development along two distinct, co-ordinate, and mutually dependent lines: one has reference to industrial evolution and the other to social transformation."[113] Social institutions were important because they were the only existing way to socialize rural people and introduce them to the demands of the twentieth century. They could develop "the community sense" at the expense of rural individualism and get people "working together," thus stimulating economic cooperation.[114] Social institutions could act as ameliorative and educative agencies, teaching scientific agriculture, keeping good farmers in the countryside, and generally making rural people "efficient and contented," in Secretary Houston's phrase.[115] Finally, by ending isolation and putting people under the influence of social institutions the worst of rural political conservatism and radicalism could be mitigated.[116]

Despite their differing concerns and perceptions, by 1910 most of the critics believed that a social and economic revolution was necessary in rural America. The intertwined problems of individualism and inefficiency had to be attacked by institutional means, and the values of organization and efficiency had to be inculcated. The Country Lifers hoped that the countryside would change itself voluntarily, reconstructing its social institutions, constructing governmental institutions, and modifying its economic practices. Having defined the rural problem and the general solution, the Country Life Movement turned its attention to the specific changes necessary for the industrialization of agriculture.

3

PRESCRIPTIONS

THE COUNTRY LIFE MOVEMENT demanded nothing less than a complete revolution in rural life. "The application of modern science to the practice of agriculture . . . the no less necessary application of modern commercial methods to the business side of the farming industry. . . ." and "the building up, in rural communities, of a domestic and social life which will withstand the growing attractions of the modern city" were the minimum goals of the critics.[1] Their optimism regarding the attainment of these goals did not obscure the Country Lifers' realization of the revolutionary character of their aims. They recognized that the task of the Country Life Movement was "to develop a new rural civilization . . . industrial, political, and social,"[2] and they laid the groundwork for the new civilization with a welter of prescriptions for ailing rural social, economic, and political practices and institutions.

Of primary interest to many critics were rural social institutions, particularly the school and the church. Critics recognized that social institutions could be vehicles for economic change, that they could function as agencies of amelioration and control, and that they were the only agencies under which many rural people were organized. Hence, many Country Lifers saw the modification of rural social institutions as the necessary precondition for the industrialization of agriculture.

I

Reflecting the consistent American faith in the ameliorative and modifying powers of public education, Country Lifers agreed that the social institution most in need of reconstruction was the school. So important was the school, in the critics' view, that upon its modification depended to a large degree the industrialization of agriculture as a whole. It was the duty of the rural school to lead, as well as reflect, the modernization of rural society. By 1900 most urban systems had modified their schools, both in form and in function, to conform to the manifold demands of the industrial age, but because these demands had less relevance for country people rural schools remained essentially as they had always been. By the turn of the century, however, their sense of the imperatives of the industrial future and of increasing national interdependence turned the attention of leading national educators to the problems of the country school.

One of the principal problems Country Lifers perceived in the rural educational system was its weakness in the upper levels. There were very few high schools in the countryside, and children who desired formal education beyond the eighth grade level found that they had to leave home for neighboring towns or cities. Commentators feared that progressive rural parents, disgusted with the lack of secondary educational facilities in their neighborhoods, were permanently leaving the farm to provide their children with educational advantages. Those who fled the countryside seldom returned, and critics believed that the flight of ambitious and educationally dissatisfied parents and children to the towns would intensify rural ignorance, immorality, radicalism, social degeneration, and economic backwardness.[3]

The Country Lifers believed that agricultural colleges were equally inadequate for rural purposes. Since there was at least one in every state, few critics complained that there were too few agricultural colleges. Most agreed, however, that many agricultural schools did not respond to rural needs. The main complaint was that the colleges had removed themselves from the farmers they were supposed to serve by inflating entrance requirements, emphasizing the classical aspects of the curriculum, and encouraging farm youths to enter other professions. United States Department of Agriculture employee Dick J. Crosby repeated a common complaint when he sneered that he had met an agricultural college graduate who could not "plow, or dig a ditch, or harness a horse, or milk a cow."[4]

Although the rudimentary nature of rural secondary education was a constant concern, educators tended to concentrate on the reform of the rural primary school. Even those rural children who had high schools available to them seldom attended, and still fewer students reached college. In fact, it was "the exception rather than the rule for children to complete the eight grades of the rural schools," and educators estimated that less than one in four rural scholars completed the eighth grade.[5] Consequently, the Country Life Movement concentrated its efforts on the social and economic possibilities of the rural primary schools.

Educators agreed that a generation of progress in urban school physical plants, professional instruction and supervision, and curriculum reform had not been matched by rural schools.[6] Investigation showed that the rural school of 1910 was essentially what the rural school of 1880 had been, and that it was thus in a much inferior position relative to the urban school. Unstandardized and locally controlled, marked by primitive physical facilities and unsanitary conditions, plagued by unprofessional instruction and poor attendance, the nation's one-room schools epitomized educational inefficiency to urban educators.

Educators, reflecting their faith in the expert, agreed that weak supervision contributed to most rural educational problems. Schools were unsanitary and unhealthy because supervisors lacked the will or the power to improve them. Teachers were inexperienced and demoralized because supervisors had inadequate control over their hiring and their work. And school terms were short and schools were ill attended because elected supervisors could not or would not force change or enforce laws. Even appointive county superintendencies were understaffed and overburdened, and superintendents were seldom able to visit the average one-room school more than once a year. In practice, what supervision there was in the countryside was carried on by unprofessional local farmers, a fact which appalled educators who wanted to see strong professional supervision to enforce change.[7]

Strong supervision was a necessity if important changes in rural education were to be carried out. One area of rural education which seemed to be in particular need of modification was the curriculum of the common school, which modern educators saw as woefully inappropriate and inadequate.

While urban systems had introduced such curricular innovations as industrial arts, home economics, music, art, and physical education, rural schools in 1910 offered the same courses they had always offered, taught in the same way. Modern educators believed that the courses traditionally taught to children in country schools had "no relation to the life they are to lead." Urban agrarians in particular contended that the rural curriculum fitted children only for white collar occupations, and that it led them to disdain physical labor, and they believed that courses taught by teachers who wanted to go to the city with textbooks written in the cities gave farm youth an urban outlook on life and encouraged them to flee the countryside.[8] This was an ironic conclusion considering the fact that proposed reforms were based on urban experience, but it does underscore the fatal paradox under which the urban-agrarian wing of the Country Life Movement was forced to labor.

Their urban orientation and their perception of the industrial future led educators to conclude that the consequences of the rudimentary rural system of education for the countryside were serious. In the first place, critics contended that the school did not teach efficiently even the basic skills on which it concentrated, and to support their point they noted that the rate of rural illiteracy was twice that of urban illiteracy.[9] Yet this was only a part of their larger perception that the rural school had failed completely as a socializing agency. Rural schools had once been an adequate socializing influence, educators believed, because they had been supplemented by a neighborhood and home life which satisfied rural youth socially and trained them adequately for their future work. The school had failed to change as the society around it changed, however, and its failure to expand its social and technical functions while those of the rural community contracted rendered it economically useless and socially moribund.[10]

Whether all of this was true or not is an open question. Certainly, it is not clear that there had been a general declension in the rural neighborhood or in the rural family, and it is not clear that the country school was any less adequate than it had ever been. Although they were always sure they knew what was wrong with the countryside and how to right it, the Country Lifers worked from a very narrow empirical base. They tended to be urban people with urban standards, their understanding of the rural past derived largely from the agrarian myth, their understanding of the present derived from impressions and a relative handful of dubious studies, and their prescriptions derived from new and inadequately tested social scientific principles. But none of these problems seemed to impede the Country Lifers' confidence in their ability to diagnose and cure rural ills.

Had the supposed shortcomings of rural schools affected only the rural community, it is probable that few people would have been interested in them, but national interdependence and industrial needs made them national problems. Indeed, most farmers believed that rural schools still adequately served rural purposes, and few showed enthusiasm for the renovations proposed by progressive educators. The nation's world economic position and the food and labor demands of the industrial cities decreed that rural schools had to become a force for social and economic efficiency and organization, which sparked rural productivity and held intelligent farmers on the land. Thus, Country Lifers avidly turned their attention to the reconstruction of the rural school.

The premise on which the critics based all of their reforms was the progressive educators' one that the job of the school was to prepare the student for all facets of life. One persistent critic of the country school, for example, contended that to the extent that education led "to a more fruitful life in the home, the state, the church, and other social institutions . . . to more effective work in a worthy occupation . . . education spells *efficiency*."[11] The job of the schools in the twentieth century, then, was to "train for citizenship . . . train men in the art of living . . . aid in preparing for an occupation . . . not merely for the good of the individual, but for the good of society as a whole."[12] In the countryside the need for schools to be socializing influences turning out socially serviceable individuals was particularly compelling. Urban educators attuned to the demands of the industrial future believed that the job of the rural school should be to counter the individualistic current of agricultural society and inculcate the virtues of social organization and efficiency. Their hope was that the rural schools would become social centers for the community, and would through their social and educational functions make adults and children alike socially efficient and organized and contented with rural life. Though important in itself, however, social efficiency was primarily significant only insofar as it contributed to economic efficiency. The good, socially serviceable citizen was the economically efficient citizen, and the primary purpose of social efficiency and organization was as a stimulant to economic efficiency and organization. Educators perceived that the work of the school in industrial society was the preparation of people for an efficient economic life. "The work of the public school is to get a maximum product in efficient citizenship out of the community to which it is assigned," intoned J. D. Eggleston and Robert W. Bruère in *The Work of the Rural School,* "and the distinguishing mark of efficient citizenship in the rural community is skill in the production of food." In addition to stressing the social components of economic efficiency, the critics also looked to the rural school to work directly for economic efficiency through industrial, agricultural, and domestic science training. Since the urban school was rapidly becoming a training center for the students' economic future, the critics believed that it was time to tie agriculture to the rural school.[13] This would insure the economic future of the industrial nation by insuring the productive future of the nation's agriculture.

The educators agreed, then, that the job of the model rural school was to further the industrial Siamese twins, social and economic efficiency, in the countryside. Although this was proposed primarily for national purposes, the critics believed that social and economic efficiency would be a boon to the countryside, leading to social satisfaction and economic well-being.[14] Of course, the critics hoped that school renovation would insure equal educational opportunity for rural children, whose obsolete education handicapped them when they went to the cities. And yet, the changes were conceived primarily for the benefit of the industrial nation, and few critics denied that they had to be carried out, regardless of the consequences for rural people.[15] For national social and economic purposes, then, Country Lifers proposed a number of broad changes in rural school curriculum, method, and organization.

One of the curricular changes proposed by the critics was the introduction of nature study in the rural schools, but like other suggested modifications this one went far beyond a mere tampering with the course of study. Nature study, conceived in the 1870's by William Torrey Harris, was embraced by Liberty Hyde Bailey and his wing of the Country Life Movement.[16] The nature study advocates believed that the most important thing the rural school could do was to keep children on the land and make them love it. Hence, they proposed a course of study which would "teach the children to love the country" by imbuing them with a romantic understanding of the natural environment and propagandizing them about the superiority of agriculture and the problems of urban existence.[17] This would be accomplished through the institution of formal nature study courses and through the introduction of texts and methods of instruction in the traditional subjects which celebrated agriculture and rural life. Since the students would be taught to love nature and agriculture, urban agrarians expected that the new generation of farm children would be more efficient and contented farmers.[18]

Despite Bailey's enthusiastic advocacy of nature study, most Country Lifers believed that alone it would prove an uncertain means of achieving the desired ends of economic efficiency. Less romantic than the urban agrarians, most critics of rural education called for the introduction of practical courses in agriculture, industrial arts, and domestic science in rural schools.[19] Most Country Lifers believed that a directly practical course of study would orient rural youth toward agriculture and would also bear immediate fruit in the form of enhanced rural efficiency. Practical courses would teach children "to do in a perfect way the things their fathers and mothers are doing in an imperfect way, in the home, in the shop, [and] on the farm," and would indirectly influence parents to adopt better methods, leading to greater economic efficiency.[20] Practical education would further insure that in the future the nation would enjoy an agricultural class which was favorably disposed toward the teachings of scientific agriculture.[21] In spite of their economic preoccupations, these educators also believed that social benefits would follow from practical education. Courses in agriculture and domestic science would elevate farming and homemaking, rendering them interesting to intelligent rural youth, and encouraging them to stay in the country.[22] Working together on projects, moreover, would lead rural children to see the benefits of cooperation, thus countering the individualistic orientation of the country school.[23]

The Country Lifers also expected the rural schools to help advance practical education by cooperating with the boys' and girls' club movement. The boys' and girls' corn, pig, canning, tomato, and poultry clubs, which later became the 4-H clubs, were started in the first few years of the century by USDA-affiliated county agents in the South. The agents began these clubs with the aid of local businessmen and school officials in an attempt to influence southern farmers to diversify their crops and thus survive in the face of the boll weevil invasion. Those interested in the club movement soon realized that it could be used to promote social efficiency and political conservatism as well as better agriculture, and club leaders pressed for the modification of rural life along a broad front.[24] As was true with most of the movement to industrialize agriculture, however, the primary interest of the club leadership was economic efficiency, and it concentrated on stimulating production. Throughout its early career the club leadership saw the movement as a means of standardizing crops, increasing production, and diversifying agriculture through children, who at the very least would be efficient economic units when they grew up, and who at the most might influence their parents to become more efficient immediately. Country Lifers thus believed that the schools, which also were expected to emphasize practical education, should cooperate with the club movement.

Nearly every critic of rural education agreed that the one-room district school was too small, too poorly instructed and supervised, too informal, too individualistic, and too independent to institute proposed curriculum changes and undertake expanded functions with any degree of uniformity or hope of success. To educators the one-room, ungraded, neighborhood school was the most striking symbol of rural inefficiency and individualism, and they believed that rural progress was contingent on its destruction.[25]

To take the place of the one-room school educational renovators proposed the construction of consolidated schools, to which pupils would be transported daily. Consolidation of schools and transportation of students were not new ideas. The first formal consolidation had been carried out in Massachusetts after the Civil War, and Iowa educator Henry Sabin had strongly advocated the idea as a cure for rural educational ills in 1897. It was only after the turn of the century, however, and particularly in the years around 1910, that rural school consolidation became a popular panacea for the problems of rural education. Educational renovators believed that consolidated schools, rationalized by grading and platooning, standardized in curriculum, and professionalized in instruction and supervision, would be the most potent means of effecting a permanent modification of rural society and economics.

School consolidation, educators believed, would facilitate efficient instruction in agriculture, domestic science, and industrial arts by competent and professional teachers.[26] By ending individual instruction, stressing the precepts of social serviceability, sponsoring club work, encouraging school government, and instituting planned courses like physical education, consolidated schools could encourage social and economic cooperation and train both the leaders and the followers of future rural society.[27] Moreover, the superior personnel and expanded physical facilities of the consolidated school would make it a social center for the community, and hold out the possibility of adult education and the immediate modification of agricultural practices.[28] The most hopeful Country Lifers believed that with consolidation the rural school would "become the industrial, the business and the economic, as well as the social center of the community."[29] The view was also increasingly expressed, particularly in the teens, that the consolidated school could be used to purify political and personal morality in the countryside. Once control of the schools was removed from the local community and placed in professional hands, the critics believed, rural people could be "saved from their sordid and materialistic selves" by teachers and courses of study which would inculcate the correct social, political, sexual, and personal attitudes in their children.[30]

Educators expected that the work of remaking the rural school would be carried out by indigenous educational personnel—teachers and supervisors—aided by the normal schools, state departments of education, and agricultural colleges. The fact that rural people did not sufficiently "understand their own *needs*" made it imperative that supervisors and teachers, who were more likely than farmers to share the Country Life Movement's understanding of rural problems and solutions, provide the leadership in modernizing education in the countryside.[31] Rural schoolmen themselves were expected to turn for leadership to the "school engineer" in the agricultural and teachers' colleges. These experts, who were the Country Lifers themselves, had the "scholarship, culture, tact, wisdom, energy, consecrated purpose, and business ability" to bring rural schools "to a sense of the possibilities and responsibilities of educating for twentieth-century life."[32] They would aid teachers and supervisors in determining rural needs and in arousing community consciousness to a perception of those needs. Then, the organized community would voluntarily renovate its system of education. Reflecting the early optimism of the Progressive Era, the Country Lifers were confident that once rural people understood the modifications they proposed and the bright new day for rural society these changes would bring, they would rapidly refashion their schools on the industrial model.[33] But the Country Lifers' assumptions about how educational reforms would be put into operation reflected more than just their optimism and confidence. They also reflected the naiveté, the condescension, and the arrogance of the new-middle-class experts in the education establishment. They were sincere in attempting to aid rural people, but their assumption that those people did not know what was best for themselves and that they—the experts—did, shows ignorance, arrogance, and an undemocratic tendency which marred their good intentions. As time went on, the good intentions tended to fade and the unattractive attitudes of educational renovators gained prominence, but that was only after it became clear that many rural people lacked enthusiasm for the uplift the Country Life Movement offered.

II

Another important rural social institution Country Lifers wanted to see renovated was the country church, and many believed that the church could be the most important force in the industrialization of agriculture. Not only did the position of the church as one of the few rural agencies of social control place it in a pivotal position, but some critics perceived that the rural deference to religious authority put the country church in a position where it could readily mold rural practices and attitudes.[34]

And yet the critics also believed that the country church at the turn of the century faced problems that were in some respects more serious than those of the one-room school. Throughout the nation thousands of rural churches stood abandoned, while thousands more struggled along with declining membership and attendance. Like the farmer's school, Country Lifers contended, the farmer's church suffered from primitive physical facilities and inferior leadership, but as a voluntary institution it could draw on fewer resources than could the school. Most churchmen concerned with rural affairs still agreed that "the roots of the religious and moral life of the nation are chiefly in the country church,"[35] but they recognized its problems and expressed the fear that unless the decline of the rural church was reversed the countryside and then the Republic would soon lapse into "paganism and barbarism."[36]

A number of ministers, particularly ministers from country parishes, laid the declension in rural churches to "the decadence of faith" in the countryside, and they blamed rural people for that decay.[37] Most Country Lifers, however, believed that the problems of rural religion derived from the country churches themselves. Noting that the country church was largely populated by women and old people, this group contended that "concerned in too many cases with technical religion, formal piety, [and] small and empty social duties, the country church does not appeal strongly to men with rich red blood in their veins."[38] Others believed that fundamentalism in an age of liberal religion had hurt the rural church, but most critics agreed that the individualism of the rural church had damaged it as a social institution and as a socializing agency.

"With the whole world turning to combined or coöperative action as the basis of efficiency," concluded C. O. Gill and Gifford Pinchot in their influential work, *The Country Church*, "the program of the country churches continues to deal wholly with individuals, and hence remains defective and one-sided."[39] Churchmen perceived that individualism was the bane of rural religion in every way. It led to the sectarian multiplication and overchurching that rendered rural churches small, weak, and inefficient. It was reflected by rural revivalism and rural preaching, both of which appealed to individual souls and implicitly impeded social organization and cooperation.[40] A Presbyterian study of rural churches in Indiana concluded that "The saving of men for heaven is much emphasized, the saving of men for Indiana receives little emphasis, the saving of Indiana for men receives practically no emphasis from the church."[41] When the urban church faced a steady declension after the Civil War many ministers had reached back into the Protestant tradition and had come up with the Social Gospel. The Social Gospel emphasized the duty of men to men and to their communities, and the duty of the church to man in the economic and social here and now rather than in the celestial future. Perceiving that the problems of rural religion had arisen from the same religious irrelevance that had earlier crippled urban Protestantism, most critics prescribed an infusion of the Social Gospel for rural religious ills.[42]

The critics hoped that by adopting the Social Gospel, by celebrating "the ideal of the *good citizen* before the ideal of the *good man*," and by emphasizing "social morality" at the expense of personal morality the churches could satisfy modern rural needs, reassert their social leadership, and incidentally modify rural social and economic behavior.[43] By expanding and changing to meet rural social needs, the country church could become the center of rural society and could both mold and serve its clients' social needs and instincts.

Socially, the rural church was expected to organize rural people and to stimulate "a revival of old-fashioned sociability," providing wholesome gatherings and recreations that would satisfy gregarious country souls and tie them to the church.[44] Churchmen were particularly interested in social programs for young people and tenants, two groups most in need of social control. Organized recreation and group activity, these Country Lifers believed, would hold young people for the church and prevent them from indulging in immoral amusements, and attention paid to the tenant and his family would tie him to the community and discourage immorality. Moreover, social organization and activity would stimulate the satisfaction of rural people with country life and would hold them on the farm.[45] Social control in the restrictive sense of the term was not the sole function of social organization and activity, however. Modernists hoped that the expanded social functions of the church would undermine rural individualism and lead to a heightened sense of social activity and organization among rural people in every phase, and particularly in the economic phase, of their lives.[46]

Part of the Social Gospel idea as applied to the countryside was the expectation that ministers would help to further the modernization of agriculture. Country Lifers hoped that ministers would become agricultural educators, relating their message to the farmer's economic life and encouraging him to become more efficient and increase productivity. Critics of the country church stressed their belief that better farmers were better men and better Christians, and they urged the rural religious establishment to lead the fight for an improved agriculture.[47] Some of this could be done through direct agricultural instruction, but most Country Lifers, with their modern emphasis on specialization, professionalism, and expertise, doubted that most ministers were capable of becoming agricultural educators. Instead, the critics hoped that rural preachers would attempt to make farmers responsive to the scientific agriculture others were pushing. Country Life Movement churchmen expected ministers to emphasize the superior morality of scientific agriculture, productive efficiency, and economic cooperation, manipulating their credulous auditors to embrace the New Agriculture.[48]

As one commentator suggested, as early as 1902, "The clergyman, under this newer and broader interpretation of his functions, is nothing less than a social engineer."[49] As a social engineer who had his hand on every social and economic pulse in the community, the influential Kenyon Butterfield suggested, the country minister could rapidly transform his church into "a social-service church, or an institutional church, or again, . . . a 'country church industrial.' "[50] In this endeavor the rural minister would be joined and led by the critics themselves from their posts in the liberal seminaries and sectarian home mission programs. Ministers were also offered the aid of the YMCA, which by 1910 was hard at work in a number of rural counties pushing the gospel of social Christianity, morality, and social and economic cooperation through its recreational program.[51]

As had been true with the country school, Country Lifers believed that the new functions of the country church could not be carried forward without new forms. New and expanded church programs called for new and expanded church physical plants with facilities large enough to handle the physical burden of being social centers. Moreover, intelligent, well-trained, full-time ministers were required to industrialize the rural church and rural life, and churches had to be large enough to support them. For these reasons, and also in order to unify rural neighborhoods and reduce inefficient sectarianism, a number of critics called for church consolidation and interdenominationalism.[52] This, then, was the vision of the rural church of the future—a church which led society and broke the ground for economic change, presided over by nonsectarian social engineers in bright new social centers. The future rural church envisioned by the Country Lifers was much like their future rural school, reflecting their belief that all rural social institutions had to be modified if agriculture was to reach an urban-industrial standard of social and economic efficiency and organization.

III

The Country Life Movement put forward a plethora of suggestions for the reconstruction of rural society. Most involved the principal existing social institutions—the school and the church—but others envisioned the creation of entirely new social institutions and social forms for the countryside. Movements arose for such varied things as rural social centers independent of churches and schools, neighborhood pageants and organized recreations, local improvement and beautification associations, country theater, and traveling libraries. The backers of each innovation claimed that it would be the one to end rural isolation, enhance satisfaction with rural life, idealize country living, end the flight to the cities, stop rural immorality, and promote social and economic efficiency and organization.[53] Yet all critics recognized that rural social institutions, new or old, could scarcely hope to modify rural society in any lasting way until they modified the basic rural social institution—the family—in its lifestyle, its structure, and its function.

Despite the fact that a substantial segment of the Country Life Movement, including most of the urban agrarians, contended that the mere idealization of rural life by social institutions would be sufficient to hold people on the farms, a more realistic group recognized that idealization would fail to hold people to a life of isolation, hard work, and ill health. Country Lifers believed that the isolation of the farm family contributed to aberrant social behavior, rural insanity, and unhealthy individualism. Hard work and long hours stole childhood from children, drove them from the farms, and prematurely aged adults. Ill health sapped vitality and led to early death.[54] The critics concluded that the renovation of farm and home life was one of the necessary preconditions for the permanent reconstruction of rural life.

Although they worried a great deal about the deleterious effects of hard and isolated farm life and labor on rural men and children, country life observers were particularly concerned with rural women. Discontent among farm wives was most dangerous because the woman was the basis of the rural family and the rural family was the basis of rural society. Agriculture as Americans knew it would disintegrate if rural women became discouraged and rural girls stopped marrying farm boys. Consequently, few suggestions for changes in rural home and family life were made without the farm wife in mind.

Particularly attractive to urban observers were means for easing the toil of rural women. The principal suggestion critics made for the lightening of the farm wife's work load was that rural people acquire household conveniences like central heating, sewing machines, iceboxes, modern ovens, electricity, and hot and cold running water. Since these conveniences existed and some rural people enjoyed them, the critics believed them to be feasible for most farmers and blamed rural traditionalism when they were not rapidly adopted.[55] Country women were also urged to simplify their work and make it less burdensome by cleaning more efficiently, keeping household accounts, cooking simpler meals, and even by joining community laundries.[56] In all of these efforts the Country Lifers urged farm women to seek the aid of county home demonstration agents or other specialists in domestic science.[57] To make the home life happier for the whole family the beautification of homes and grounds was proposed, and critics expected that the telephone, rural free delivery, parcel post, good roads, and automobiles would also contribute to making farm life attractive by lessening isolation and broadening social opportunities.[58]

The improvement of the rural home was seen by many critics as the key to the improvement of rural life as a whole. A more convenient and less isolated home would be more efficient and more socially satisfying. It would be a home in which social and economic change would be more likely to be welcomed and in which children would be raised who would love the countryside and would long to stay there. On the other hand, some Country Lifers questioned whether the reconstructed home would really serve to socialize rural people and keep them on the land. Some urban agrarians feared that improvements in communications and modern conveniences might merely whet the appetites of country folk for urban living and speed their migration to the cities. It was true, as one commentator noted, that "In those communities best provided with modern conveniences the drift cityward is most rapid."[59] Others were concerned that the telephone and automobile would allow farmers and their families to avoid their neighbors, further crippling rural society. Still others believed automobiles would make farmers less efficient by encouraging them to neglect their businesses and to buy cars rather than the implements of scientific agriculture. Finally, a number of critics suggested that farmers were conservative because they were physically isolated, and that once they became mobile they would become radical.[60] The bulk of the Country Lifers, however, recognized that the industrialization of agriculture without the modernization of the home would be impossible, and they went ahead with their campaign for basic rural change.

Country Lifers, working through the United States Public Health Service and the General Education Board, also addressed the vexing problems of rural health. As solutions for the health difficulties of farmers Country Lifers urged such things as powerful state and county health authorities, district nurses in rural schools, and campaigns of adult education regarding sanitation, diet, child rearing, and disease. Concerns for rural health arose in part because critics believed that rural people deserved better lives, but their commitment to the city was at least as important to investigators of rural health as was concern for the country. In the first place, of course, critics recognized that the unhealthy countryside was dangerous for urban visitors.[61] More important, however, as federal health official Allen W. Freeman noted in 1911, "The health of the city depends in a large measure on the health of the country," in the sense that contaminated milk, meat, fruits, and vegetables endangered urban people.[62] Critics also concluded that sick people could not achieve the productive efficiency necessary to provide cheap and plentiful food to the cities, underscoring the fact that the critics were interested first in the farmer as an economic unit which supplemented the larger society and only second, if at all, in the farmer as a human being.[63]

Criticisms of the rural home and of other rural social institutions contained a strong current of dissatisfaction with the rural family. This dissatisfaction reflected the fact that the critics were looking at the rural family from a twentieth century, urban-industrial perspective. The rural family at the turn of the century was, in general, the inclusive social institution it had always been. Unlike the urban family, the family in the countryside was the primary economic, social, and educational unit of society. Its functions were broad, unitary, and general, while those of the urban family were increasingly narrow, disunited, and specific. As its primary economic and educational institution, the rural family was the foundation of rural society. The urban family, on the other hand, left with few economic and educational functions, was increasingly a primitive survival in the urban age with less and less raison d'être. The attacks made on the social institutions of agriculture, coming from an urban-industrial perspective, could not avoid being to a large extent attacks on the preindustrial family. What the critics were saying when they called for renovation of rural schools, churches, and other social institutions was that the farm family alone could not function as an efficient social, economic, or educational unit in the twentieth century. They were saying that in an age of specialization, rationalization, professionalization, and interdependence the rural family could not meet expanded educational and social demands. These had to be assumed, as they had been in the cities, by professionals in specialized agencies. They, and not the rural family, would henceforth be responsible for educating rural children for their life work, controlling their social activities, providing environments for the construction of socially serviceable citizens, and providing health, welfare, and protection. The ultimate vision of the critics, then, was of a rural family much like the urban family, a social unit of custom and convenience, modified in economic functions and stripped of most important social and educational roles.

Just as the industrialization of agriculture demanded changes in the role of people within families and families within society, it also demanded changes in the role of government in society and the relationship between the people and government. Social scientists in particular assumed that change was impossible unless preceded by control, and control was impossible without flexible, activist governmental agencies staffed by professionals. Economic modification demanded expanded state and federal power and the placement of governmental officers in the rural community. Social modification also required expanded governmental functions and the rationalization and professionalization of rural educational, health, and welfare services. Many Country Lifers believed that significant changes in agriculture would be impossible without an active, professionally supervised rural government.

Social scientists were especially interested in the implications for social control of an expanded rural government. This is not to deny that they had great faith in the ameliorative functions of the activist state, but their fear of an unrestrained countryside and their distrust of rural people led them to emphasize the function of control. Imagining poverty, ignorance, degeneration, delinquency, and crime to be rampant in the rural neighborhoods, social scientists stressed the need for formal rural police forces, judicial systems, and welfare agencies in the countryside.[64] In this judgment social scientists betrayed their urban prejudices. The city was good, in their opinion, because it was organized and controlled. It followed logically that those rural neighborhoods most separated from towns and villages were the most degenerate, and most social scientists soon embraced some form of Wisconsin Professor Charles Josiah Galpin's "rurban" idea. Believing the village to be institutionally superior to the hinterland, Galpin hoped to solve the problems of rural anarchy by uniting the countryside with nearby towns and villages in new political units. As political entities, these "rurban" units would be controlled by the towns' governmental agencies.[65]

Although the social scientists were the most extreme critics in their fear of rural anarchy, few Country Lifers could be found who disagreed that the countryside desperately needed more government and more professional administration. Even social thinkers with a highly agrarian orientation agreed that the countryside needed a professional, functional government. They also noted the social problems that had arisen because of weak rural agencies of amelioration and control.[66] They differed with the social scientists, however, in their perception of rural people, and they believed that an expanded government was necessary to allow the rural majority to control a rural minority in a formal, rational, professional manner.[67] These agrarians agreed with social scientists that a breakdown in the unity of the rural community and in the social control powers of rural social institutions demanded more formal means of control.[68] Their fear of the cities led them to reject "rurbanism," but since most of the working examples of activist governmental agencies were urban, they proposed the same agencies for the countryside the social scientists proposed.[69] Once again, then, the agrarians faced the problem of attaining rural ends through urban means because these were the only means available. Nostalgics talked a great deal about developing an indigenous and unique rural society, yet the changes they proposed were invariably camouflaged copies of urban forms, and their critiques of rural government, society, and economic practice usually paralleled those of the other critics.[70] Because they wanted to save preindustrial society, then, even the nostalgics reluctantly embraced the very solutions that they feared might destroy it.

IV

Those critics who emphasized that a social reconstruction of the countyside would lead to economic organization and efficiency in agriculture were countered by another group that wanted to attack more directly the immediate problems of economic disorganization and inefficiency. This group, which was concentrated in the state and federal governments, in the agricultural colleges, and in business and industry, agreed that social reconstruction was a necessary step and important in the long run, but they concentrated their fire on the adult farmer and his shortcomings in production, distribution, and organization. On the other hand, those who emphasized the primacy of social reconstruction also recognized that their success was at least partially contingent on economic advancement. These two main divisions among the critics were, then, compatible, and their slight difference in emphasis should not obscure the fact that they shared preconceptions, personnel, and ultimate aims.

The first priority of the critics who wanted to attack directly the economic inefficiency and disorganization of agriculture was the stimulation of a more scientific, standardized, and mechanized production which would increase food supplies and lower prices. They believed that some way had to be found to inculcate farmers with the spirit of scientific agriculture lest the nation face disastrous consequences. Unfortunately, however, despite years of attempted education through a variety of media, the vast bulk of farmers still hewed to custom in most of their operations. Farmers even seemed to shun machinery, thus severely limiting the scope of their operations. Industrialist E. A. Rumeley noted in 1910 that a farmer had to walk 8.25 miles to turn one acre with a twelve-inch plow, and 1,320 miles to turn a quarter section. Despite what were to Rumeley obvious advantages, however, only one acre in 20,000 was plowed by power machinery.[71] Country Lifers seldom considered that a thoroughly scientific and mechanized agriculture producing standardized products might well make farming much more of a business than a way of life, drive many people out of it, and bring to agriculture the problems of class differentiation and conflict that plagued industry.[72] Few questioned the basic desirability of industrial progress for farm and nation alike, and most shared the opinion that increased efficiency would benefit everyone and would help hold small farmers on the land rather than driving them off. When one of the great technocratic tribunes of modernization, Charles McCarthy, talked about "Henry Fordizing" agriculture, he did not mean that agriculture should be turned into a dehumanizing assembly line operation. Rather, he invoked the name of Ford to suggest the most beneficial and utopian possibilities of efficiency. To McCarthy and his contemporaries, Ford had taken efficiency to its logical and most promising extreme. Because of the innovations he had introduced to the manufacture of automobiles, Henry Ford seemed to have benefited himself, his workers, and the consumers while hurting nobody.[73] What the Country Lifers failed to see was that the demand structure for food, as opposed to automobiles, was highly inelastic, and they also ignored some of the less attractive aspects of Ford's operation, but they were sincere in believing that increased efficiency would benefit agriculture. Even if they had not believed this, however, it is doubtful that most Country Lifers would have behaved differently. Their main concern, after all, was with the high cost of food, and agricultural efficiency was deemed necessary primarily because it would solve that problem, and not because it would help farmers.

Critics who focused on the rural economy realized that if increased productivity was to lower the cost of food it had to be accompanied by an improved system of distribution. The system of distribution of farm products to market in the early part of the century was informal and haphazard. Farmers sometimes shipped products hundreds of miles for low prices while the local demand went unsatisfied. More inexcusable than that, the critics believed, the irrational and uncontrolled system of distribution forced urban people to import food while unbought crops rotted in the fields. To remedy this situation the critics called on farmers to avail themselves of the services of state and federal marketing agencies and to follow crop and price reports and send their produce where and when it was most needed. Even more elementary, however, was the simple physical problem of getting crops to market. Country Lifers addressed this problem by calling for centrally controlled, rationalized, and physically improved public road systems which would allow towns and cities more efficiently to tap their agricultural hinterlands, insure the cheap transportation of abundant foodstuffs, and incidentally lessen rural social isolation and facilitate school consolidation.[74]

The distribution problem was compounded by the problem that most farmers simply were not rational businessmen. Highly tradition oriented, the vast majority of farmers grew the same crops year after year, seldom knowing which were profitable, where they were profitable, and when they were profitable. Few farmers kept accounts, so most had no idea at all of what their return on investment or labor income was, and many were unaware even of whether they were making money or not. For most farmers, in short, agriculture was still much more of a way of life than a business. The industrial nation, however, demanded a more efficient and businesslike agriculture, and Country Lifers forwarded several suggestions for the realization of this goal. The critics hoped that farmers would completely rationalize their business by keeping accurate accounts detailing the income, the outlay, and the time involved in raising everything the farm produced. Farmers would then know what to grow and what not to grow, and whether to diversify or expand. This application of "city business methods to country business problems" would facilitate further rationalization.[75] Optimistic critics even hoped that agriculture could emulate some industries by rationalizing the business to the point where the demand for labor would be stable throughout the year, thus allowing farmers better to attract good and steady workers.[76] In all of these things, farmers were offered the aid of state and federal farm management specialists, agricultural college personnel, and often local bankers and businessmen.

In a rather gingerly fashion, the Country Life Movement also embraced a favorite rural prescription for the economic ills of agriculture—cooperative buying and selling. Some critics were chary of recommending cooperative marketing and purchasing because they believed this would destroy the rural merchant and hence the rural town, but most of those who opposed it did so because they feared the economic and social consequences of united rural action. Critics of cooperation noted that when organized farmers controlled the nation's food supply they could cut it off and force prices upward, and urban agrarians questioned how the rural individualism they wanted to save could be preserved by an activity that was essentially antiindividualistic.[77] As support for all of these arguments anticooperationists pointed to such things as the Planters' Protective Association and the violent night-riding activities that arose between 1905 and 1909 from its attempts to hold Kentucky, Tennessee, and Ohio tobacco off the market.[78] Most critics, however, noted that the twentieth century was the century of organization, and that efficiency without organization was impossible. These renovators answered those who feared the economic consequences of cooperation by noting that it would result in benefits for consumers and for urban-industrial society generally by advancing the teaching of scientific agriculture, hastening crop standardization, and rationalizing the sources of supply.[79] Those who favored cooperation admitted that organization would increase rural political power, but they also believed it would help stabilize political behavior and would make farmers more conservative by giving them interests to protect. Cooperation would also teach obedience, conformity, and deference to constituted authority, thereby mitigating the worst manifestations of rural individualism.[80] By the early teens most Country Lifers had come around to the position of favoring at least some form of rural economic cooperation. Reflecting this trend of thought, the USDA formed the Rural Organization Service in 1913 for the purpose of encouraging all forms of rural organization, including economic cooperation. Because questions arose about the propriety of USDA involvement in the actual work of creating cooperatives, the National Agricultural Organization Society was formed in 1915. The NAOS operated as a semipublic, nonprofit agency which aided farmers who wished to create and operate cooperative enterprises. The NAOS saw cooperation as a panacea both for rural economic problems and for the high cost of living, and its creation indicated how far the Country Life Movement had gone toward accepting economic organization in agriculture.

The Country Lifers who concentrated on rural economic problems believed that their primary job was not to make agriculture more socially satisfying or convenient, but to make it more economically efficient. In contrast to critics who believed that farmers could be made more efficient, more socially satisfied, and more contented through the actions of renovated social institutions, those who concentrated on economics alone were skeptical of the manipulative potential of social agencies. This is not to say that they did not harbor hopes that social institutions would change rural economic behavior, but they feared that this would be a long, slow process. Economic renovators believed, probably correctly, that most people left agriculture or stayed in it not because it was socially disappointing or satisfying, but because it was unprofitable or profitable in relation to alternative economic activities.[81] Additionally, these critics tended to believe that social reconstruction would be more the end of than the means to economic change. "The first step toward a regeneration of rural life is to make it profitable," concluded the *World's Work*. "Social regeneration quickly follows this step.[82] Moreover, rural people controlled rural social institutions, and they would not allow changes in them unless they themselves were changed.[83]

These Country Lifers accepted the idea that agriculture should be made more profitable, but they demanded that this profitability come only through greater rural efficiency. Farmers had traditionally embraced political panaceas or schemes to limit supply in their attempts to solve their economic problems, but their urban critics believed that the adoption by farmers of a twentieth century standard of economic efficiency was the only acceptable cure for economic ills. Among these critics, "Agriculture was viewed as a business and the farmer as a businessman," and they believed that modern principles of science, organization, standardization, and rationalization, if applied to agriculture, would aid the nation and the farmers by making both more efficient.[84] If farmers adopted the same principles of productive efficiency industry had embraced, agriculture would profit as industry had. Consequently, the advocates of the New Agriculture appealed to rural materialism by emphasizing the profits increased efficiency would bring to producers. What most Country Lifers failed to see was that the road to industrial efficiency had been paved with the bodies of the socially and economically inefficient. Some saw that "The small farm of today is similar in its organization to the shop of yesterday, and must as surely give way,"[85] but most apparently did not foresee the individual and institutional prices farmers might have to pay for the heightened economic efficiency that would primarily benefit the urban consumer anyway.

V

The Country Lifers who concentrated their fire on the rural economy agreed that adult education in the countryside was necessary. This agreement is remarkable, given the wide diversity of opinion on the question of solutions for rural problems, but it is interesting for another reason as well. The fact that the Country Lifers grasped a tool which had previously been applied mainly to such marginal social elements as illiterates and immigrants indicates both an appreciation of the gravity of the rural problem and a degree of condescension and even contempt for rural people.

Despite broad and general agreement on the desirability of adult education for rural people, Country Lifers had a difficult time choosing the best means of carrying it forward. Rejecting adult education through churches and schools as too slow and uncertain, agricultural scientists, businessmen, and federal and state government officials searched for an effective means of changing the economic behavior of rural people.

Seemingly, there were already abundant means of adult education in agriculture. The federal and state governments had departments of agriculture which disseminated information on scientific agriculture in printed form to farmers, often without charge. Agricultural colleges and experiment stations often did the same, while conducting movable schools, correspondence courses, and farmers' reading courses to push the New Agriculture. Perhaps in part because their advertisers often were those with vested interests in scientific agriculture, most farm newspapers embraced and heralded it as well. Most states sponsored farmers' institutes which travelled around the countryside during the summer, offering farmers a Chautauqua-like program with heavy doses of practical agriculture and domestic science. State and county fairs also heralded scientific agriculture, and railroads, implement companies, banks, and chambers of commerce sponsored demonstrations and publications designed to bring new developments to the attention of the farmers. Despite this intense and in some cases long-range activity, however, farmers' methods did not change appreciably. "For fifteen years agricultural colleges, experiment stations, state organizations and railroads have been endeavoring to educate the farmer in scientific agriculture," noted Abilene, Kansas, editor Charles Moreau Harger. "According to the statements of men familiar with the accomplishments, only one farmer in ten has paid attention to the teaching."[86] Despite the attempts to change farmers, they remained traditional and conservative producers. And despite the critics' statements that the farmer would soon be a scientific businessman applying industrial principles to his economic activity, it was clear that in the early teens he still regarded the farm as "a home and not a business establishment" and followed traditional agricultural practices.[87]

The problem was that the existing agencies of adult education in agriculture were just not doing the job. In the first place, colleges, experiment stations, and institutes were all understaffed when the magnitude of the job of education was considered. Moreover, technical agricultural bulletins were sent only to those who wanted them, and few farmers asked for them. Even those who did take bulletins found them ponderous, narrow, overly technical, and often inapplicable to local conditions.[88] Most farmers in most areas took farm papers, but that did not necessarily mean they embraced the scientific agriculture advocated therein. Farm papers were wide ranging and appealed to general interests, and farmers subscribed to them for a variety of reasons. In a 1913 study, Carl W. Thompson and G. P. Warber noted that 84 percent of the farmers in the Minnesota township they studied took farm papers, but that "there is a pretty general sentiment against so-called 'scientific farming schemes,' promulgated by station bulletins and farm papers."[89] Critics believed the county fair to be even less useful for purposes of adult education, and they complained that many had degenerated into mere opportunities for rural vice and immorality.[90] Despite optimistic hopes for their success in the early years of the century, farmers' institutes also failed to have much effect on rural economic behavior. Their quality varied greatly from state to state, and they often suffered from poor instruction, rural apathy, inadequate facilities, and a failure to reach rural counties and neighborhoods off the beaten path. Moreover, rural people often tended to regard them as social gatherings, and failed to absorb such useful technical instruction as there was. Perhaps most important, there was no way for institutes to follow up and influence farmers to try the new methods discussed.[91]

The critics attempted to meet the problems of the agencies of adult education in agriculture in numerous ways. Attempts were continually made in the years before World War I better to coordinate farmers' institutes and secure better instructors for them, to simplify agricultural bulletins and make them more relevant to the average farmer's needs, and to reenergize the county fair.[92] But observers recognized that all of these agencies suffered because they depended upon rural volition for their success, and no amount of tinkering would alter that basic fact. As the early teens approached, the critics increasingly agreed with the conclusion of farm institute veteran John Hamilton that "if no better system of dissemination of agricultural information is devised than that which has existed in the past it is manifest that agriculture in this country will progress far too slowly to meet the demands for food and clothing by our rapidly growing population."[93]

The best solution available for the problem of adult education in agriculture seemed to lie in farm and home demonstration work. Begun by Seaman Knapp in 1902 in Texas, farm demonstration was a revolutionary form of adult education in which farm experts, placed in the local counties, worked directly with farmers for more and better production and marketing of farm products. Instead of following the pattern set by the other mechanism of adult education and simply telling farmers about new methods, the agents showed farmers the methods and supervised their adoption. Thus the agents had what none of the other means of agricultural education had—the ability to supervise farmers and to follow up on instruction. The southern agents, supported by combinations of local businessmen and farmers, national philanthropists, and the USDA, concentrated their efforts on stimulating crop diversification and home self-sufficiency as a counter to the rapid spread of the cotton boll weevil. Farm demonstration agents worked with adult farmers and their sons, while home demonstrators attempted to advance home efficiency through farm women and their daughters. By 1912 there were 639 county agents supervising over 100,000 adult farmers and 67,000 boys' corn club members, while 159 women agents led nearly 24,000 girls in canning and poultry clubs.[94] In addition, the movement was spreading into the North and West, often through the support of local business leaders. Not only were the numbers increasing, but the results were impressive. A survey of 1,001 Mississippi, Alabama, and Georgia farmers indicated that while only 15 percent had received aid from county agents, over 90 percent of them had used the agents' suggestions. On the other hand, of the 2.4 percent who had attended farmers' institutes only one in four used the information gained there.[95] This was a striking indication of the efficacy of the demonstration method of agricultural education. Moreover, the county agent, heralded as a "trained social engineer," could be used to further rural institutional modification.[96] Seaman Knapp and his early colleagues saw instruction in scientific agriculture as only a part of their mission. Knapp was proud that, along with agricultural education, "there is much instruction [by county agents] along the lines of rural improvement, the better home, its equipment and environment, the county roads, the school at the crossroads, rural society, etc.," and another writer was pleased to report in 1910 that the agricultural agent "teaches economy, order, sanitation, patriotism, and a score of other wholesome lessons."[97]

By the early teens several bills aimed at institutionalizing the county agent system on a national scale had appeared in Congress, but all had foundered on the rocks of farmer apathy, North-South conflict, distrust of federal power, and the opposition of agricultural colleges and experiment stations, which feared a loss of power over agricultural education.[98] Despite this record of failure, few groups actually opposed agricultural extension and a number supported it. The American Federation of Labor was an early supporter, and the National Soil Fertility League, composed of "four hundred and seventy associations, chambers of commerce, boards of trade, [and] business men's associations," and including "nearly all the leading transportation companies in the United States and large numbers of financial institutions and manufacturing concerns," was created to lobby for extension and even claimed credit for writing the original Lever bill.[99] Businessmen were very enthusiastic about industrializing agriculture because they believed agricultural efficiency would benefit farmers, local businessmen, and national businessmen.[100] Businessmen had long been active in extension endeavors of their own, and though they believed them valuable, they were more than willing to have the government take over the work. The railroads had been particularly active in agricultural education, as had been implement companies,[101] and by the early teens numerous local bankers and businessmen and national concerns were staunch supporters of the county agent idea.[102]

Finally, in May of 1914, timely compromise and presidential support combined to push an agricultural extension measure, the Smith-Lever bill, through Congress. The bill set up a voluntary program through which federal matching funds were provided on the basis of rural population to states and counties desiring the services of county farm and home demonstration agents. The most fervent support for the bill came from the impoverished South, which believed that county agents were saving it from the boll weevil and would fashion the New Agriculture for the New South. Aside from the southerners, however, few congressmen pretended that agricultural extension was intended primarily to aid farmers. Few would have disagreed with the conclusion of a later commentator that "the original idea from which the county agent arose was that the people as a whole needed a more efficient agriculture to the end of cheaper foods and fibers. Help to the individual farmer and the industry as a whole was only incidental."[103]

An examination of the debate over the Smith-Lever bill supports the thesis that the purpose of adult education was to get farmers to increase production and thus lower the cost of living. Senator Furnifold Simmons of North Carolina, for example, claimed that adult education was necessary because "in this country . . . we are not producing much more than enough to supply our own population," and Nebraska's Gilbert Hitchcock added that "the purpose of educating the farmers is to reduce the cost of living by reducing the cost of food."[104] A number of urban congressmen agreed. Representative Martin Madden of Chicago contended that "the population of the city of Chicago is interested in successful farming. It is interested in reducing the cost of living." Adolph Sabath of the same city and Edward Townsend of Newark, New Jersey, vigorously echoed Madden's endorsement of the bill.[105]

This is not to imply that Congress was involved in a conspiracy to manipulate farmers into producing cheap food for the sole benefit of the cities. A number of congressmen hoped that adult education would allow farmers to lower their cost of production and pass the savings on to urban consumers. This was an attractive notion, since it promised to benefit everyone, but it was also an unrealistic one which ignored the fact that supply and demand, rather than the cost of production, determined agricultural prices. Other congressmen contended that increased efficiency, reflected in increased production, would aid farmers as well as consumers.[106] This argument also promised something for everybody, but the severe economic inelasticity of most farm products made it questionable at best. Whatever arguments were used by the bill's proponents, they seemed always to return to the necessity of lowering the cost of living. Whether the bill would aid farmers or not, the benefit to the urban consumers was the most persistent strain in the debates.

There were congressmen who questioned the bill, often recounting in the process the rural belief that increasing production and falling profits usually went hand in hand.[107] Some congressmen were also irritated by the implicit condescension of the bill and its implication of rural stupidity.[108] Moreover, northern congressmen were unenthusiastic about the bill because of the apathy of their farm constituents regarding it. North Dakota's Senator Asle J. Gronna claimed that he had "yet to find the first farmer who has asked for this appropriation," despite an extensive inquiry.[109] Farm papers supported extension, of course, as did some farm organizations, yet most farmers, particularly in the North, were generally apathetic and seemed to agree that the county agent would be just another useless burden on the rural taxpayer.[110] As was the case with their representatives, farmers failed to comprehend the potentially revolutionary import of extension.

Rural misgivings notwithstanding, the absence of a crystallized rural opposition, the fact that the program was voluntary, congressional concern with a large number of important national and international issues, and a number of crucial compromises allowed the Smith-Lever bill to pass both houses of Congress on voice votes. Thus, the Smith-Lever Act, which Woodrow Wilson correctly called "one of the most significant and far-reaching measures for the education of adults ever adopted by any government," the purpose of which was to "insure the retention in rural districts of an efficient and contented population" became law with little fanfare and less national attention.[111]

VI

With the passage of the Smith-Lever Act the potential means of revolutionizing agriculture were complete. Teachers, ministers, and county agents were expected to be the principal emissaries of the New Agriculture, carrying the promise of a renovated country life to farmers and their families. New and expanded social and governmental institutions and altered economic practices would be the components of the new country life, but the whole was much larger than the sum of its parts. The future country life of the critics' vision was so revolutionary that it bore little relation to rural America in 1900. In place of the laissez-faire countryside, with its individualism, informality, localism, and inefficiency, the Country Lifers hoped to build an agriculture which conformed to modern industrial standards of social and economic organization and efficiency. The Country Life Movement, stripped of all pretensions, was nothing less than the demand of an ascendant urban-industrial America, backed by an increasingly activist state, for an organized and efficient agriculture that would adequately supplement it socially and economically.

The critics of agriculture were optimistic that rural people, when led by the missionaries of the new country life, would readily change their social and political institutions and their economic practices. With guidance, they would quickly perceive the advantages efficiency and organization would bring. It was not until they learned more about rural America that the renovators discovered how attached countrymen were to their inefficient little institutions and how stubbornly they clung to their outmoded economic practices.

4

ACTION, INACTION, AND REACTION

THE DECADE before America's entry into the First World War witnessed an enthusiastic and optimistic attack on what the Country Life Movement saw as the social and economic shortcomings of agriculture and rural people. Country Lifers believed countrymen to be inefficient and unorganized to a degree unacceptable in the twentieth century. Invoking urban-industrial standards of social organization, economic efficiency, and governmental activism, and reflecting modern notions of the role of social institutions, the meaning of education in society, and the future social role of the family, critics of agriculture found much in the countryside that shocked them. They demanded revolutionary changes in rural social institutions and economic practices—changes which they usually believed would aid the countryside but which were aimed primarily at making agriculture and the people who practiced it efficient supplements to the developing industrial nation.

Leadership in the drive for rural regeneration came from County Lifers in their positions in colleges and universities, churches, philanthropic organizations, and in the governmental bureaucracy. In the rural community itself, leadership was supposed to come from the local representatives or allies of the new-middle-class technocracy—teachers, social workers, ministers, editors, businessmen, bankers, and county agents—who were expected to be attuned to the imperatives of organization and efficiency. This conception of the way change should take place was highly elitist, but the Country Lifers were able to find ways to dress themselves up as democrats. For example, though change would not come through popular volition or even popular approval, County Lifers contended that it was democratic because it was done for the people.[1] Thus, "the trained man, the expert, the superior man" was "an agent of democracy" despite the fact that he paid more heed to popular needs than to popular wants.[2] But the Country Lifers were not content to assert that the expert was merely a different kind of democrat; to them he was a superior democrat, one whose leadership was "imperative in an efficient democracy."[3] His superiority as a democrat derived not only from the expert's special skills and knowledge, but also from his broader perspective. "The expert must be a real democrat," intoned Kenyon Butterfield in 1917, when the war sharpened and legitimized the Country Lifers' conception of democracy. "His obligation is to the great society, not to any small or exclusive group of society; or if he work with such a group, always as the ambassador of the mass, the protagonist of the common weal."[4] Under the Country Lifers' conception of expertise, then, the role of the local expert was to advance democracy by molding the rural community in the interests of the larger, increasingly industrial society.

The Country Life Movement recognized that the organization and efficiency they hoped to bring to agriculture and rural society would not come overnight. There were many rural counties, communications were poor, rural people were isolated, and, because they had not yet been enlightened by Country Life experts, they tended to cling to outmoded institutions and practices. But it was an index of their optimism or their arrogance that Country Lifers believed rural people would readily adopt changes once they understood them and the improved life they would bring. Whether this indicated a paradoxical faith in people for whom the Country Lifers had a good deal of barely concealed contempt, or whether it showed overarching confidence in their own ability to manipulate and persuade is not clear. But it is clear that the Country Lifers were ill prepared for the unfavorable reception their innovations received in the countryside.

I

One of the primary goals of the Country Life Movement was a renovated rural educational system with a curriculum that would advance social and economic organization and efficiency. There even seemed to be some demand for educational restructuring arising from the agricultural community itself. Schoolmen in contact with farmers or farm organizations had long agreed that, though they were vague on the details, rural people "ask for something practical" in the school curriculum.[5] The inarticulate yearnings of farm parents, moreover, were underscored by the calls of some organized farm groups for practical training in the common schools.[6]

Yet when the time came to institute practical courses of education, rural resistance was often sharp, and what farmers defined as educational improvement seldom corresponded to the critics' broad definition of that term. Among other things, farmers tended to believe that the practical courses suggested were useless and wasteful. Agriculture, domestic science, and industrial arts could all be learned at home as they always had been, and rural pride was undoubtedly wounded by the implication that the practical lessons of life were being taught imperfectly in the family. The fact that homemaking and farming were learned at home and were so much a part of daily life made it difficult for rural people to see them in terms of education at all. "Education means ability to read, write, spell, and figure" to rural people, noted a Wisconsin school official, and not the ability to plow, plant, cook, or sew.[7] Not surprisingly, less obviously practical curricular reforms like nature study and physical education also met rural opposition. "We believe it to be much better for the pupils to be proficient in the usual elementary studies," concluded Hubbardstown, Massachusetts, school board member Allen S. Woodward, "than to dabble in too many fads."[8]

Farmers who were dubious about the value of new courses of study also suspected the motives of those pressing them. Practical education courses coming from urban educators led many farmers to suspect that the city's primary aim was to lower food prices, as indeed it largely was. When urban educators claimed that curricular reforms would help keep the young in the countryside farmers answered that these reforms would freeze them there by unfitting them for other occupations. Before long it was clear to all but the most naive that "the demand for education in agriculture comes as a whole more from educators, business men, and others . . . than it comes from the average farmer."[9]

Though they certainly did not expect the amount of rural resistance they encountered, Country Lifers did expect farmers to be reticent about reforming the curriculum overnight. They expected local teachers and school officials to assume leadership in renovating courses of study. In this hope educational reformers were particularly disappointed. In the first place, most rural schoolteachers were unprepared to teach subjects like agriculture and domestic science, even if they had the facilities to do so. "While much in the way of suggestion may be given in the country schools touching the subject of elementary agriculture, it *is* unreasonable to expect large results where the teachers have had no scientific training in this subject," concluded Iowa State Superintendent of Public Instruction John F. Riggs. "Such training, not one in a hundred of Iowa teachers has had."[10] Efforts were made to remedy this situation through extension and the revamping of teacher-training courses, but normal institutions generally lacked both the facilities and the will to supply the countryside with meaningful numbers of adequately trained teachers.[11] Not only were country schoolteachers unable to become leaders in curricular reform, they were also often unwilling to do so. Lacking the sophistication of progressive educators and isolated from the main currents of educational thought, rural teachers often doubted the utility of curricular innovations or saw changes as threats to themselves. Country schoolteachers reflected their rural patrons much better than they manipulated them, thereby proving to be inadequate missionaries of the Country Life Movement.

But even when they had the ability and the desire to institute practical curriculum reforms teachers faced tough going. Almost completely powerless in the communities where they worked, reform-minded teachers found it virtually impossible to buck the tyranny of public opinion. If she tried to slip a little agriculture, homemaking, or nature study into the curriculum the schoolteacher was likely to be confronted by an angry patron who "sent his children to school to learn something useful."[12] Nor were there many people to whom she could turn for aid. In the face of opposition the best the teacher could hope for was a neighborhood schism in which the community was divided and her job was endangered, all for some marginal tinkering with the curriculum. There were, of course, agricultural organizations that publicly supported curricular reforms, but their championship of change was often rhetorical and meant little on the local level. The California Grange, for example, was vocal in its support of practical education in the common schools, but at the 1915 convention it was revealed that in the previous year only one of forty-six local Granges had undertaken any reform activities in the local schools. By the war years most country life reformers agreed, "It is idle to claim . . . that country teachers are leaders,"[13] but it is an index of their tenuous grasp on reality that they had ever believed those ill-trained, powerless, and dependent teachers could really be efficient missionaries of industrialization.

Furthermore, even where supervisors, teachers, or patrons successfully introduced practical courses into the curriculum, the innovations were usually not as successful as educators hoped they would be. The common school curriculum was already crowded, and teachers had trouble finding sufficient time for new courses. Moreover, teachers often discovered that their charges had such a weak grasp of the basic educational skills that diluting the standard curriculum was folly.[14] Teachers also found that early courses in agriculture, home economics, and nature study were often poorly conceived, uninteresting, and expensive, and that textbooks did not capture students' interests.[15]

In the face of failure educators redoubled their efforts to cajole or to force the rural school to reform the curriculum. States passed laws requiring or otherwise inducing instruction in agriculture and homemaking, and with the Smith-Hughes Act of 1917 the federal government joined in that effort.[16] But the lack of government in the countryside and the practical autonomy of the one-room school diminished the effectiveness of compulsion. "For many years we have been endeavoring to secure instruction in agriculture in the rural schools," concluded Wisconsin education professor G. A. Works in the third annual report of the Wisconsin Country Life Conference in 1913. "The cases where much has been accomplished are the exception rather than the rule." Statistics confirmed Works's gloomy summary. As late as 1919 a Bureau of Education survey of 3,278 rural teachers in relatively progressive Nebraska showed that only 21 percent taught vocational or homemaking courses, and of these 71 percent thought the subjects burdensome.[17]

Of course, educators did not expect great progress in curricular reform until consolidated schools were introduced. Consolidation would facilitate the hiring of better-trained and more professional teachers who, removed from community control, would work under a rationalized, graded system which would allow them to specialize. But if rural people were opposed to curricular reform, they even more staunchly resisted school consolidation. One of the principal reasons for rural opposition to consolidation was its cost. Not only did farmers believe that consolidation would raise taxes, they also feared that the school's removal from the neighborhood would cause their property to depreciate.[18] More important, farmers opposed the transportation of their children to school, a significant consideration in times when roads and conveyances were still very primitive.[19] In the few areas where consolidation was welcomed controversy flared over whether the new school should be located in the open country or in the local town.[20] Rural people were most concerned, however, that consolidation would mean the loss of local control and would undermine the rural neighborhood.[21] With consolidation the rural neighborhood faced school control by appointed officials or control shared with other, perhaps incompatible, neighborhoods. In the face of rural opposition critics were forced to admit that " 'the little red schoolhouse' is evidently dearer to many than advanced theories of education," and that, even where it was possible, "the discontinuance of a school is very rarely accomplished without strong protest from school patrons."[22] Educators sometimes wondered whether they were making any progress at all, for rural people matched their aversion to consolidation with a continual clamor for even more and smaller one-room schools.[23]

Like curricular reform, consolidation was often more successful in theory than in practice. Transportation continued to be a problem, and organizing and managing enlarged physical plants with expanded functions was difficult. Most important, early consolidated schools did not often bring the promised improvements in instruction, curriculum, learning, and social organization and enjoyment.[24] Neither less expensive nor more efficient than the one-room schools, many consolidated schools rapidly lost what support they had, and one educator even asked whether, in the case of consolidation, "the interests and welfare of the pupils have not been sacrificed for the sake of carrying out an idea."[25]

To an even greater extent than was true in the case of curricular reform, rural teachers were powerless substantially to advance consolidation. Although Country Lifers expected them to be the cutting edge of rural consolidation sentiment, teachers themselves were reticent about consolidation because they feared it would bring higher professional standards and cost them their jobs. There were, of course, teachers who attempted to press for consolidation, but their powerlessness and hostile public sentiment frustrated their efforts. At least with curricular reform there had been organized agricultural interests which had lent the proposed renovations rhetorical support, but in the case of consolidation even this modest approval was usually lacking.[26]

The failure of voluntary renovation and of teachers as missionaries depressed educators concerned with rural problems. "A little gain has been made in consolidation, but not a marked gain," lamented Ohio Common School Commissioner John W. Zeller in his annual report to the governor in 1909, "and the friends of centralization as a system for the solution of the rural school problem are very much discouraged." At least Ohio could point to some progress. A Wisconsin school official reported in the mid-teens that two decades of agitation had failed to effect even one consolidation in his state.[27] Some educators called for financial encouragements for consolidation, but schoolmen were increasingly attracted to compulsory legislation giving school officials complete power to consolidate, to remove school questions from the ballot, or forcibly to close schools that fell below a given enrollment.[28]

Despite a handful of successes and continuing utopian predictions of success, it was clear to most educators by the mid-teens that the attempt to reform rural schools through voluntarism had failed. It was an index of their frustration that educators increasingly gave vent to attacks on farmers as "conservative, unprogressive, jealous, penny-wise, and lacking in any proper conception of the value of good educational conditions."[29] Yet the failure of voluntary reform did cast doubt on the myth that most people who fled the countryside did so because of dissatisfaction with rural social institutions. Educators were forced to concede that most country people were generally satisfied with their one-room schools, even when they recognized shortcomings. The main dissatisfaction with rural institutions lay not in the countryside, where they continued to carry out the functions rural people expected of them, but in the cities that were trying to change the countryside. Urban educators convinced themselves that the renovation of the rural educational system would be good for farmers, but their primary yardstick was always a national one and their paradigms were always urban. The Country Lifers concluded that rural people did not understand the world or their place in it well enough to perceive, even with the aid of educators and their missionaries, its needs and their own needs, and the critics thus justified their increasing attraction to compulsion.[30] Actually, the shift from voluntarism to compulsion was a comfortable one for many in the Country Life Movement. Most of the Country Lifers had always assumed that they knew what was best for rural people, and their contempt for rural people had often shown through. For many in the movement, voluntarism was more a tribute paid by social engineering to American traditions than a solidly held commitment. For these, shedding the mantle of voluntarism was easy.

In the efforts to reform rural schools and in the rural response to those efforts we can see in microcosm the pattern of failure of the Country Life Movement as a whole in the decade before the nation's entry into World War I. First, it is clear that the Country Lifers were ill-served by an excess of optimism. Overly optimistic about the responsiveness of rural people, the potential efficacy of proposed changes, and the power of local school personnel, the Country Lifers were bound to be disappointed. In one sense this excessive optimism can be seen as a part of the ebullient optimism of the Progressive Era in general. But it also sprang from a lack of comprehension of rural America on the part of the urban-based critics. Since they perceived the world through urban glasses, it is not surprising that Country Lifers expected farmers to accept their analyses of rural problems, expected them to be responsive to urban-inspired solutions, expected these solutions to be relevant to rural society, and expected professionals in the countryside to have the power, inclinations, and vision of their urban counterparts. In part, the Country Life Movement's misperceptions can be blamed on rural people. In the case of education, for example, some rural people did complain about their schools and they did seem to want something different. This was surely a minority sentiment, but it did provide some basis for Country Lifers' optimism. But even this surface sentiment masked an undercurrent the Country Lifers would have felt had they known rural America better. Despite their appreciation of some rural problems, rural people in general were highly defensive about their society and its institutions. This defensiveness is quite understandable in an era in which the nation, its values, and its institutions were becoming increasingly urban and industrial, but Country Lifers seldom perceived it. Not surprisingly, this defensiveness was heightened when rural people faced proposals for change coming from the socially and psychologically aggressive urban-industrial society. The rebuffs they received should have led Country Lifers to a heightened understanding of rural people, but this did not happen immediately. Indeed, in the years before World War I Country Lifers usually responded to rejection by denigrating rural people and calling for compulsory change. This, of course, made country people even more defensive and distrustful, widening the gap between them and the Country Life Movement and completing the pattern of reform failure.

II

Regenerating the rural church through the introduction of the Social Gospel and making it a vehicle for the industrialization of agriculture proved an even more difficult task than renovating the country school. One of the first and most difficult stumbling blocks on the path of change was the controversy over the appropriateness of the Social Gospel. The Social Gospel had originally been devised to revitalize urban churches by making them relevant to urban-industrial problems and the problems and duties of Christians in urban-industrial society. When applied to the comparatively individualistic and self-sufficient rural society Social Gospel solutions lacked the relevance they enjoyed in urban centers. In the cities themselves there was sharp disagreement over whether the role of the church was to save souls or society, and most rural ministers found Social Gospel solutions particularly inapplicable to their problems. They were especially concerned that if they followed the suggestions of Country Lifers the rural church would lose its unique social role and its divine mission. "The main work of the church must not be simply to furnish enjoyment and pleasure, good roads and methods," warned Wisconsin minister A. J. Aasgaard at the First Wisconsin Country Life Conference in 1911. "I am willing to speak a good word for those things, but the thing we want is the moral and religious basis for the development of the heart and the soul life and the church must do that and no one else will." Another minister derided those churches of the Country Lifers' vision where the "chief concern is to make roads as 'a way of salvation,' 'to raise fat pigs for the glory of God,' to 'clean up dirty privies,' to turn the house of worship into a dance-hall and the preacher of the Gospel of Jesus Christ into the director of the dance."[31] Still other clergymen, like many of their parishioners, distrusted the motives of the country life reformers. A Manhattan, Kansas, minister wisely cautioned in 1916: "To feed the flaming passion for big crops is not the task of the country church, and if it stoops to this it will ultimately become the farmer's worst enemy."[32]

Refusing the proffered role of economic leadership, the country church also rejected the suggestion that it become a community center offering social leadership and recreation to the rural neighborhood. Belonging primarily to fundamentalist sects and generally accepting the maxim that enjoyable activities were probably sinful, rural ministers were much more likely to battle things like dancing, card playing, and baseball than to try to co-opt them. "The church takes a decided stand on many of the forms of social activity," Paul Vogt noted in his 1914 study of two Ohio counties, "doing little to provide social life and at the same time condemning what exists."[33] Churchmen who contended that social activities would bring outsiders into the church confronted the further problem that the church had to be changed by its members, and that they were the people in the community most likely to be satisfied with it.

The fact that parishioners' and pastors' prejudices usually coincided held the church to its traditional functions.

The idea that churches should consolidate to save themselves and carry out expanded roles was as ill received in the countryside as the idea that they should modify their functions. Far from being distressed by them, rural parishioners seemed comfortable with their tiny churches, circuit-riding ministers, and primitive physical facilities. Moreover, denominationalism was strong in the countryside, and if it had lost much of its doctrinal significance it had often gained enhanced social importance.[34] Even if they could afford it, then, rural people seldom looked to church federation as a solution for religious problems. The few churches that did consolidate often found that their problems had increased. Federated churches were ripped by disputes over property, ministers, doctrine, and denominational matters and often disintegrated in the turmoil.[35] By the mid-teens it was clear that church consolidation was advancing even more slowly than school consolidation.[36]

By World War I most reform-minded churchmen were very depressed about the stasis of the rural church, and many despaired of ever changing it substantially. The most active major sect in rural church renovation had been the Presbyterians, who used home mission funds to promote innovation, held institutes for rural ministers, stressed the rural calling in seminaries, and made social surveys. But the most powerful rural sects held back from the Presbyterian campaign. Despite some minor activities by the Methodists, neither they nor the Baptists showed much interest in changing the country church, and the powerful Lutheran and Catholic ethnic churches ignored the reform appeal. Denominational fundamentalism fostered a distrust of Social Gospel ideas and denominational rivalry led to suspicion of Presbyterian empire building, so the major sects remained aloof from the cause of church reform in the countryside. In addition to denominational differences and suspicions, however, it became clear that the country church had never been a very promising vehicle for rural change. The one-room school, despite all of its faults and the conservatism of its patrons, was or could be made answerable to authorities outside of the community. Education in America was a public function, and as long as this remained true local schools were potentially modifiable by larger governmental bodies. But the country church was a private institution which was almost completely self-controlled and could only be modified voluntarily. Consequently, when the rural church refused to become an agent of industrialization there was little for Country Lifers to do but abandon it and look elsewhere for help.

III

Consistent with their resistance to modification of churches and schools, rural people also generally opposed expanded governmental functions and political consolidation. The contention of social scientists that activist agencies would end rural anarchy, rationalize charity, regularize justice, and provide necessary welfare services was rejected by farmers wary of taxes, distrustful of government, and of "the opinion that the local community can deal with its social problems quite effectively enough in its own way."[37] Particularly unattractive to farmers were the related proposals of community consolidation and rurbanism. Neighborhood loyalties and the social factors that often reinforced them impeded community consolidation, and the sharp and often bitter social, economic, and political differences between town and country led both to shy from the political unification rurbanists favored. No matter how disappointed social and political scientists were with the rural political structure and its functions, country people were apparently satisfied. Theodore Manny's revealing study, *Rural Municipalities,* showed that in the twenties the farmers he investigated were pleased with their political divisions, distrusted government, and opposed both rural incorporation and rurbanism, and there is little reason to believe they felt differently earlier. By the late teens realistic social scientists were forced to agree, "Among the country people themselves there is no demand for better local government."[38]

The Country Lifers were, in some cases, truly mystified by rural people, who sometimes even resisted changes that would be clearly beneficial to them. This was true with public health, an area in which Country Lifers, often with the best of motivations, attempted to bring reforms in sanitation, diet, child care, and disease prevention to the countryside. But this altruism was countered by rural people who either failed to perceive the problems, were too proud and defensive to admit that problems existed, opposed expanded government, or, as with so many proposed reforms, distrusted the motives and disliked the condescension of health workers.[39] Advocates of good roads also faced a degree of rural opposition they did not expect. Good roads enthusiasts believed that their reform would improve the economic position of agriculture and broaden rural social horizons, but farmers feared high taxes, the loss of local control of local roads, and the disproportionate benefit that good roads would afford to urban users.[40]

In their usually well-meant attempts to lighten the farm wife's load by making farm homes less isolated and more convenient, urban critics were also rebuffed. There were, of course, farm women who agreed their lives could be improved and drudgery could be minimized if only their husbands were more sensitive to their needs. "If there is one place where the American farmer excels," sneered one Michigan farm wife, "it is in getting the utmost out of his wife and family," and a West Virginia woman agreed that "the majority of the men folks are not very liberal toward the women folks of the farm."[41] But most rural women jumped to their husbands' defense, noting that improvements were difficult and expensive and that farmers usually did their best to provide their families with comfort and convenience.[42] "The greatest trouble with the farmers' wives," concluded a Louisiana farm wife, "is a constant play upon their credulity by so many writers tending to convince them that they are neglected, ill-treated and physically weak."[43]

One of the primary reasons for the unenthusiastic reception extended to the country life critics by the countryside was the fact that the suggested renovations had been devised in the cities and looked suspiciously like urban uplift to farmers. As DeKalb, Illinois, county agent W. G. Eckhardt noted in his June, 1915, report, "Farmers, as a whole, resent exceedingly those forces which are at work with missionary intent trying to uplift them." Most rural people were probably satisfied with most aspects of rural society, but even those who saw the need for social reconstruction resented outsiders who were pressing for the same things.[44] Farm people had a strong sense of pride, and they became defensive when critics emphasized the primitive nature of rural social institutions, economic methods, political organization, or health and home practices. Rural people found the fact that the uplift sentiment came primarily from the cities particularly galling. Worthy Overseer T. C. Atkeson of the Grange was but one of many who resented urban criticism:

> I confess that so much talk about 'betterment' and 'uplift' in connection with the farmer class makes me just a little bit weary. Suppose we try a little of the 'uplift' business upon our senators, congressmen, and legislators, governors, trust magnates, stock gamblers, railroad wreckers, and rich malefactors. . . . It might be well for the National Grange to appoint a 'Commission on City Life' . . . to report on the conditions of city life and 'what needs to be done.' . . . The farmers of the United States are all right, and the only thing that 'needs to be done' is to give them a 'square deal' before the laws of the land, and they will work out their own salvation in their own healthy and manly way.[45]

In a sense, this attitude reflected a degree of rural smugness and self-satisfaction. But more important, it was a defensive reaction to the encroachment of urban ideas and institutions on the countryside, a reaction born of pride and a very rational distrust of the cities and their motives. There were rural people who agreed that the countryside had problems that had to be solved, but they distrusted the solutions that came from outside agriculture and were irrelevant to it. "Professors, bankers, railroad presidents, lawyers and what not have criticized and deplored the farmers [sic] lack of financial progress, civic pride, and social attainment," wrote an angry farmer to David Houston, ". . . without in the least realizing that their education, occupation and environment makes them unsympathetic and unjust investigators of a class who's [sic] . . . problems must be lived . . . in order to be appreciated."[46] Farmers demanded that progress come out of agriculture itself, and the clumsy attempts at social engineering from the city not only angered farmers, but probably impeded those in the community who agreed that renovations were needed in rural America.

In the *Report of the United States Country Life Commission,* Liberty Hyde Bailey had warned that leadership in rural renovation must come from the countryside itself. Bailey was one of the few Country Lifers who adequately appreciated the importance of rural pride. But even if those in the rural community had been willing or able to assume leadership, the fact that the criticisms of rural society and the proposed renovations came from the cities still would have wounded rural pride and raised rural defensiveness and distrust. "Farmers," notes Murray Benedict, "were inclined to complain about the hardships of their vocation but they did not want nonfarmers to talk about them."[47] Thus the Country Lifers faced a problem which was perhaps insoluble. They believed it was necessary to raise rural consciousness about problems urban people recognized more clearly than did farmers and point to solutions that often seemed irrelevant to or inappropriate for rural society. And all of this had to be done in such a way as to preserve rural pride and not arouse rural defensiveness or distrust. Even for those with wisdom exceeding that of the Country Lifers, this task would have been most difficult. For the Country Lifers it was impossible.

IV

The cast of industrial missionaries to rural America was completed when the Smith-Lever Act institutionalized the county farm and home demonstration agent system. Supporters of extension envisioned these men and women agents reorganizing rural society, instructing rural children in the ways of advanced agriculture, and making scientific farmers and homemakers out of their parents. The hope that agents would work to renovate rural social institutions, however, was soon dashed. Although there were agents who engaged in various endeavors of social reformation, particularly school consolidation and curricular reform, most lacked the time, training, or inclination to involve themselves in such acrimonious and time-consuming affairs.[48] Early agents were more interested in agricultural club work for boys and girls, and most made at least some efforts in that direction. But club work, too, was often time-consuming and only marginally rewarding. The original idea behind the work was that agricultural clubs would help advance agricultural education in the schools and would train young people to be more efficient future farmers and homemakers. Almost immediately, however, club enthusiasts perceived that club work could be the "entering wedge" to reform and standardize on-going farming and animal-breeding practices.[49] Despite the enthusiasm of many agriculturalists and some impressive successes, club work did not usually measure up to the expectations of its sponsors. Opposition of parents, apathy of children, poor planning, and the lack of responsible local leadership combined to limit the effectiveness of club programs.[50] Perhaps most important, however, agents seldom had the time adequately to supervise a county-wide club program in addition to their other duties, and by the mid-teens many counties were hiring special agents to concentrate solely on club work.

Despite their concern with these other areas of rural renovation, county agents were always most interested in educating adults to be better farmers and homemakers. This was what they had been trained for, and it was in adult education that agents expended most of their efforts. But before they could begin renovating the economic practices of agriculture, the agents faced the immediate problem of interesting farmers in the work. Businessmen and bankers had been far more important than farmers in securing the passage of the Smith-Lever bill, and few farmers were interested in it at all. Agricultural extension was billed as a reform, but it was the kind of reform in which rural people were least likely to be interested. Reforms traditionally attractive to the countryside were those aimed at the banks, the middlemen, the railroads, and the trusts of the industrial cities, where farmers believed the sources of most of their and the nation's problems could be found. The Smith-Lever measure was an urban thrust which implied that the farmer's problems and the nation's problems arose in the country rather than the city and were directly or indirectly caused by the inefficiency of agriculture. Not surprisingly, many farmers were unenthusiastic about the bill and failed to perceive it as a reform. Many others were not even aware of the Cooperative Extension program. In 1917, H. L. Andrew's first year as agent for Auglaize County, Ohio, his "Narrative Report" repeated a complaint common among agents that "the farmers did not know what a County Agricultural Agent was, and what his duties were. . . . There was no sentiment for the work," and others agreed that initially "the great problem of the county agent . . . is to interest the farmer."[51]

Although rural ignorance was a thorny problem, agents soon discovered that knowledge and interest did not necessarily insure success. Farmers understandably perceived agents as foot soldiers of scientific agriculture, and most were distrustful of science or felt threatened by it when it was applied to farming. There were, of course, a few farmers who were interested in scientific developments in agriculture, and most farm papers and organizations at least publicly contended that farmers could learn from the experts. Yet most agriculturalists agreed with Pennsylvania farmer W. F. McSparren, an articulate critic of scientific agriculturalists and their motives, who commented in the 1908 Vermont *Agricultural Report* that "the farmer who is conservative in his adoption of new notions and practices in the conduct of his business will have fewer disappointments and losses than the enthusiast who accepts all that is spoken and written as true and applicable to all conditions and circumstances." But even when government-sponsored innovations worked in the neighborhood farmers were slow to take them up, contending that the government backed experiments with capital that was not available to the farmer who tried the experiment and failed.[52] And of course experiments did fail, or prove too expensive for farmers to copy, or too complex for farmers to understand, and agents did give bad advice, all confirming the wisdom of rural conservatism. Extension leaders envisioned an agrarian utopia in which the farmers and the agents grew just the right crops from tested and improved seed with rational methods and regularly brought forth two blades of grass where one grew before. Farmers, however, were skeptical about this dream, and they were reticent about abandoning proven methods. The old ways did return crops, and if they did not always yield large crops neither did they often lead to failure.

So the early agents ran against the coarse grain of rural conservatism. The father of Claude Wickard, Henry A. Wallace's successor as Secretary of Agriculture, was probably typical. To him, " 'book farming' was taboo. College teachers who taught agriculture were considered crackpots. Farm magazines were read with extreme skepticism. . . . And all of this was capped by an inherent rural antagonism to change of any sort."[53] As local representatives of scientific agriculture, agents and those who cooperated with them were often the victims of much derision. "The average boy 10 or 12 years old on the farm knows what . . . will grow and what will not grow. If farmers had to depend on what these college boys preach they would be worse off than they are now," hooted a Nebraska farmer who reflected a popular rural prejudice against scientific agriculture and its missionaries.[54]

Already distrustful of scientific agriculture, farmers were bound to be offended when people they believed lacked practical experience presumed to suggest different methods of farming. "We now have a young man saddled on us, at an expense of about $3000 per year, to tell us how to farm,—while he sits in a livery rig to do it," complained a Minnesota farmer, and an Ohio man noted that farm advice was particularly "irritating because said in a patronizing way."[55] Farm women were even more offended than their husbands by outside advisers, and they gave home demonstration agents a particularly frosty reception. "I am wondering what the Department of Agriculture proposes to do for us," was one Wisconsin farm wife's bitter question. "Perhaps they may send out some city women to teach us how to cook. We will resent that." Her warning was quickly confirmed by home agents who received sharp rebuffs in their attempts to enlighten farm women on the modern ways of diet, health, sanitation, cooking, cleaning, canning, and child rearing.[56] Of course, demonstration officials and agents believed that rural people had an incorrect conception of the function of extension, and they strove hard, as one agent put it, "to eradicate the idea that I was here to show each individual farmer how to farm."[57] Agents wanted farmers to believe that their job was to help rather than instruct them, but the fact that their job was in large part to instruct farmers impeded the agents' propaganda campaign.

Farmers also distrusted agents because they believed that the aim of extension was to get farmers to increase production. Leery of the USDA's motives, one California farm wife stated the case succinctly:

> There is a question in my mind as to what to 'aid' us farm women means to you. Is it that you wish us to increase farm production, and are contemplating sending us a lot of pamphlets to 'help' us make more butter, raise more vegetables, supply the markets with more eggs than we do now . . .? If that is what your 'service' to us would imply, I decline it with thanks.[58]

She was, of course, largely right. "The aim of the whole agricultural movement is to maintain and increase the production of the land," admitted prominent agricultural scientist E. H. Jenkins in 1914, and the principal measure of county agent success was whether and how much the agent had increased local production.[59] This was, of course, because the motive behind extension was to raise farmers to a level of efficiency at which they would adequately supplement the industrial nation by supplying it with large amounts of cheap, standardized, and improved produce. "What the Government has done to help the farmer has been done still more to help the city man . . . ," noted Gifford Pinchot in 1918. "What the city man wanted was cheap food. Therefore, what was done for the farmer was directed almost without exception toward helping or inducing him to grow cheap food."[60] The problem encountered by the agents was that most rural experience ran against the wisdom of increasing production. Farmers were no more concerned with the well-being of city people than city people were concerned with the farmers' well-being, and they were understandably distrustful of urban calls for increased production. "Farmers are constantly admonished that the most important economic demand of the time is greater production," noted the *Farm Journal* in January, 1914, "but there is nothing in past experience to indicate to the farmer that he would benefit by an increase in his crops." Throughout the nation farmers noted that big crops usually lost money, and they wondered why the federal government was so intent on increasing production. The Grange and others warned that increasing production was dangerous, particularly when middlemen stood to gain the most from such a move, and at least one farm leader noted that if the government had the right to force down farm prices by making farmers more efficient, it should also make industry more efficient and lower the prices farmers had to pay.[61] Agents answered farmers' objections about extension motives in several ways. Some merely attacked farmers as lazy and claimed it was their duty to produce as much as possible, while others attempted to prove that big crops yielded big returns.[62] The agents' most popular defense was that big crops could pay more when accompanied by innovations lowering the per unit cost of production, and some appealed to rural greed by noting that individual large crops paid well when most farmers continued to grow small ones.[63]

This last appeal touched a basic fact about farmers which agents attempted to exploit. Despite the apparent agreement among farmers that overproduction was dangerous, and despite the warning farm organizations and a few farm papers issued against it, individual farmers could be attracted to large crops, particularly when they believed that their fellows would be returning small ones. Indeed, it was an indication of the farmer's perverse individualism and perhaps even selfishness that the very warnings against overproduction stimulated him to produce more. Assuming that his fellows would not increase production, the individual farmer was often willing to do so to increase his profits. And when the individual wanted to increase production, the agent was there to help him. What this meant was that the same rural individualism which exasperated Country Lifers in so many of their endeavors facilitated the realization of their ends, at least in this case. In the area of production, rural individualism and materialism sometimes eroded the very rational rural distrust of urban motives.

Agricultural production did nudge slowly ahead in the early- and mid-teens. Sometimes tentatively and conservatively, farmers seemed to be responding to the high domestic demand and to the unnatural market situation created by the First World War in Europe. It is doubtful that the county agents had much to do with this increase. They were sometimes available to advise farmers who wished to increase production, but the volition for that increase probably derived more from high prices than from anything government and its emissaries had to say. Indeed, the increase in production came primarily through means the extension personnel found unattractive. Farmers, it seemed, were returning larger crops by bringing more acres into production, not by applying scientific principles to their work. Hence, the per acre yield of most crops remained static, an indication of continuing inefficiency in agricultural production.

Increased production, whether achieved through intensive or extensive means, might still solve the immediate urban problem of expensive food. But the food supply increased much more slowly than the food demand as warring Europeans vied with hungry urbanites for American foodstuffs. By the mid-teens the famine Malthusians had predicted for America seemed to have nearly arrived. Between 1909–1911 and 1914–1916 American wheat imports leaped by over 550 percent and corn imports jumped by nearly 6000 percent. In the same period the market prices of wheat and corn advanced 30.6 percent and 42.1 percent, respectively.[64] Despite their best efforts, extension personnel had been unable significantly to change farm practice or supply cheap food to urban consumers.

Rural skepticism regarding the agents' economic motives was reinforced by the close relationship which emerged between county agents and local businessmen and bankers. In a sense this nexus cannot be blamed completely on the agents, for when they arrived in their counties many were shunned by everyone but merchants and moneylenders. On the local level businessmen were often the only people interested in agricultural extension, and the county's share of the agent's salary was often subscribed by local capitalists or appropriated by the county under pressure from them.[65] Merchants' enthusiasm for extension rose primarily because they hoped to make money out of scientific agriculture and because they shared the agents' assumption that the farmer's problems were caused by his own inefficiency. On the other hand, agents entering new counties were always careful to confirm that they had business support, for businessmen could pressure farmers to cooperate with agents, and agents who alienated business faced short careers.[66] In their zeal to garner the aid of commercial people, however, agents sometimes forgot their original purpose and spent time begging businessmen to support them or even undertaking business projects, such as helping erect chambers of commerce and similar commercial clubs.[67] Businessmen and agents often found themselves in a mutually satisfactory situation, with the former supporting the latter and urging the farmers to do likewise, while the agents carried the commercial perspective to the farmer and were careful that their projects did not offend businessmen.[68] This relationship was comfortable for agents, bankers, and merchants, but farmers often regarded it with suspicion. After all, businessmen expected to profit from the arrangement by selling equipment, lending money, carrying produce, and by rationalizing markets and distribution. Not surprisingly, farmers questioned any movement allied with their age-old economic adversaries in the towns. To attempt to counter rural suspicions county agents pressed for understanding and cooperation between businessmen and farmers and joined business in trying to convince farmers that the capitalists had their best interests at heart.[69] As B. F. Harris, publisher of the *Banker-Farmer,* implied, rural businessmen and farmers could both be seen as small, interdependent capitalists struggling to survive in an economy increasingly dominated by massive, urban-based capital aggregations. But farmers continued to shy from what Harris saw as a natural alliance of rural enterprisers, and they continued to distrust merchants and bankers and the county agents identified with those groups.[70]

A further barrier to extension success was the difficulty county agents encountered in organizing rural people. Organization was one of the ends of the industrialization of agriculture, but it was also an indispensable means to the other end—efficiency. To help achieve the broad goals of social and economic efficiency, county agents, with the enthusiastic backing of the USDA, set about organizing the countryside.[71] From the agent's perspective organization was important primarily because it made his job easier. "Christ was able to obtain only

12 Apostles and it might take a County Agent many years to convert an [sic] County of Individuals," noted one Wisconsin agent, "but with groups he need work only a few years and he can revolutionize the agriculture of a county." Others agreed that social efficiency, in the form of organization, was the best means to potential economic efficiency because it facilitated the large-scale teaching of the principles of scientific agriculture.[72] But organization was also important in insuring the survival of the agent. Agents soon realized that organized minorities were often more powerful than unorganized majorities when it came to securing county funds for the work or raising them privately. Organization thus became so important to agents that by the mid-teens in some states agents were not even placed in the field until an organization had been formed in the county to support them.[73]

But getting rural people into organizations was not an easy task. Not only did racial, ethnic, sectarian, political, social, and neighborhood differences and poor communications work against organization, but rural self-reliance and independence also retarded the formation of activist social or economic groups. "The farmer's success has in the past depended very little upon his mental adaptability to other men," concluded Thomas Nixon Carver, the head of the USDA's Rural Organization Service. "He has had to control the forces of nature rather than the forces of society."[74] The farmer's self-centeredness and his consequent social awkwardness and lack of interest in socially or economically active organizations were facts that underlay many of the agents' early difficulties.[75]

Another problem the agents encountered in their organizational endeavors was finding local people willing or able to lead the county farm organizations, but this was just a facet of the larger problem that farmers, as self-conscious individualists, were unwilling to be followers. As the influential *Breeder's Gazette* lamented on September 28, 1916, "The country can never develop and retain great leaders until at least a considerable proportion of the people are willing to be followers." Agents attempted to solve rural leadership problems by doing the work themselves, appointing the leadership and giving it orders, or by turning leadership positions over to the merchants and bankers in the farm bureaus.[76] None of these expedients really worked very well, and they often had the effect of deepening rural suspicions regarding the government, its agents, their motives, and the organizations they formed.

The difficulty agents faced in organizing farmers raises the question of why they failed to utilize the organizations already in existence in the countryside. The fact is that despite the Country Lifers' continual complaints about the lack of organization in the countryside, "When the county agent arrived on the job, he found as a rule fairly good social organizations of farmers in most of the states, such as granges, farmers' clubs, and the like."[77] For a time some agents apparently attempted to work with these groups, but they soon found it necessary to form their own organizations.[78] The reason why agents formed their own groups goes to the very heart of their purpose and underscores the unique and urban-oriented nature of that purpose. The agents formed their own groups because, in the countryside, "There was little, if any, organization, the primary purpose of which was increased efficiency in production."[79] Most existing farm groups did not agree with the agents' assumption that rural problems derived from rural inefficiency. That was an urban—not a rural—analysis of agricultural difficulties, and the agents found it necessary to form entirely new groups which would accept their new point of view. Despite their complaints about rural individualism, then, it was rural distrust of agents' motives and lack of sympathy with their purposes which formed the key impediment to their organizational endeavors.

The organization of farmers, then, was one of the agents' most difficult assignments. But pressing ahead, with the aid of businessmen and a few scientifically oriented farmers, agents bucked widespread opposition and generalized suspicion to bring forth groups—usually called farm bureaus—whose purposes most farmers probably opposed. The organization of a farm bureau did not assure the agent of success, for it faced the same problems of leadership, representation, purpose, and social involvement that plagued every other farm organization,[80] but the farm bureau did give the county agent a place, no matter how tenuous, in at least a segment of the rural community.

This emphasis on rural resistance to county agent work should not obscure the fact that some agents were successful in much of what they tried. Even in the poorest counties a few farmers could be found who believed that agriculture was primitive and should become efficient and organized, farmers who were scientifically oriented and eager for advice. Hence, some agents had extraordinary success and became important men in their counties.[81] Even those who distrusted and disparaged the agents sometimes found them useful. Serious doubts about the motives of the federal government did not prevent farmers from calling on agents for help when they were threatened by individual problems of production. So farmers sometimes found themselves in the paradoxical position of suspecting the extension program in general while using the individual agent. But many agents faced the situation one veteran extension worker remembers from Minnesota, where "the county agent was a sort of 'illegitimate child,' fathered by unhallowed business and left on the farmer's doorstep, certainly not wanted by many farmers."[82]

As outsiders in a hostile or indifferent environment, agents often found it necessary to act with much more circumspection than they might have liked. The lack of rural response to their projects forced many agents to devise plans of work more acceptable to farmers, and sometimes even to undertake projects suggested by farmers themselves, thus often adding detours to what their supervisors hoped would be a straight road to greater productivity. Because of the limitations of their training, most of the agents still undertook projects designed to increase agricultural efficiency. But agents in tenuous situations tended to emphasize projects which would increase economic efficiency (increased income relative to expenditures) rather than those which would increase productive efficiency (increased production per acre and/or per man). This emphasis tended to find more favor with farmers, and a faction within the USDA had long advocated it, but it did not provide the direct route to greater production the Country Lifers had hoped to see in the agents' activities.[83]

Ironically, the farm bureau was one of the things responsible for bringing the county agent under farmer control. Although agents formed bureaus to give themselves an independent power base, they sometimes discovered that they became captives of the bureaus, particularly when the agents, the bureaus, or their members alienated other farmers, other groups of farmers, or, on rare occasions, businessmen.[84] Some agents found themselves tied to the bureaus, taking bureau orders, carrying out bureau programs, and shunned by nonmembers.[85]

Extension personnel generally adjusted to this situation and accepted it. Insofar as the relationship was seen as one in which the "program of work is determined by the local people with the advice of experts," it was accepted and even celebrated as exemplary of the much pursued marriage of democracy and technocracy.[86] Extension Director H. C. Hochbaum of Idaho complained that local people "do not accept the problems we should like them to accept," but even he admitted that "the people have a right to determine for themselves just what help they want."[87] Given the fact that the program was voluntary, this represented a realistic acceptance of the situation. And the agents who were captives of bureaus also seemed to accept the relationship as the correct one.[88]

It would be a mistake, however, to assume that all or even most agents became captives of the farm bureaus, or to assume that capture led to revolutionary alterations in agents' programs. Although M. C. Burritt of Cornell found as late as 1919 that "In a few cases the local associations have too large a control for the best interests of the public partner," he also discovered that "In too many instances the public institutions dominate the partnership."[89] And even where agents were captives, their talents remained oriented towards increasing efficiency and their client groups shared with them the assumption that the problems of agriculture derived from its inefficiency. Although capture sometimes led to shifts in emphasis, the most significant factor in the agent-bureau relationship remained this shared assumption about agriculture and its problems.

But all of these mitigating factors were not clear to the Country Lifers. From their immediate, short-term perspective, the operation of the county agent system in the first years after 1914 was something less than an unqualified success.

It had given its urban supporters hope by advancing to some degree the twin goals of efficiency and organization. But it had not been able socially to regenerate the countryside or adequately to increase the production of food, and in some areas agents had been captured by their own farm bureaus or by existing farm organizations. As developments unfolded, the USDA found itself in a particularly uncomfortable position. Happy that some farmers were beginning to accept the agents, federal officials also shared the concerns of their larger constituency that the agents' presence had not advanced production fast enough to noticeably slow the rise in food prices.[90] By the years of the First World War, then, the agents had achieved a qualified degree of success, but their tenuous hold in the countryside and their declining popularity among urban critics made their situation insecure at best.

V

By the mid-teens most realistic County Lifers were forced to agree that, insofar as industrialization was concerned, the countryside was "unresponsive and even apathetic. It views with suspicion the gospel of social betterment for the country."[91] There were, of course, a few regenerated communities that had embraced all of the panaceas the city had to offer, but their lonely existence was more likely to remind critics of the magnitude of their failure than to give them hopes for ultimate universal success. "In spite of glowing reports of what has been accomplished in exceptional cases and special localities, those who would teach [the farmer] are in despair and he is simply annoyed by their efforts to uplift him."[92] As World War I approached, increasing numbers of critics conceded reluctantly that the voluntary phase of the industrialization of agriculture had failed.[93]

Initial attempts at industrialization had failed in part because the missionaries lacked the independent power to effect change. Again and again social engineers were stymied by rural independence and by popular control of important institutions. It rapidly became clear that, under the circumstances, change without the cooperation of the countrymen was impossible, but cooperation was not forthcoming. This is not to say that farmers did not recognize any problems in agriculture. But they traditionally held that agriculture's problems lay not on the farms but primarily in the larger society, where the oppressive trusts, banks, and middlemen held sway. As for the problems indigenous to the rural community, farmers tended to see them as trivial and, to some degree, as inevitable consequences of an otherwise admirable way of life. The revolution Country Lifers foresaw contemplated immense modifications in rural society and economic practice, modifications that threatened the neighborhood, its institutions, and the traditional role of the farm family. Whatever difficulties they acknowledged, rural people sternly resisted a leap in the dark that threatened to alter the very institutions through which they controlled their lives and defined themselves. They were particularly unwilling to adopt what seemed to them inappropriate urban solutions for rural institutional difficulties.

By World War I critics of agriculture found themselves in a dilemma. The failure of voluntarism presented them with the equally distasteful alternatives of letting the countryside alone or compelling it to change. Urban agrarians, always reluctant renovators, gravitated toward the first option or joined other critics who hoped to give voluntarism another try. But more and more critics, noting spiraling food prices, contended that the nation could no longer afford the luxury of social and economic laissez-faire in the countryside. Some sentimentalists "may resent the idea that rural folk are to be exploited for national welfare . . . ," conceded American Sociological Society President and General Education Board head George E. Vincent in 1917. "[But] the national point of view spares no individual, class, or function."[94] Among a growing number of critics, then, compulsion was justified and even encouraged, though before the war came it was unclear what the opportunity for compulsion and the means to effect it might be.

5

CONFLICT, CONTROL, AND CHAOS

THE STRENGTH AND BREADTH of rural opposition to change called forth several reactions within the Country Life Movement. Some favored a continuation of voluntarism, suggesting that changes should be better explained to farmers or should be modified to satisfy rural objections. But as prices spiraled upward and farmers continued to resist stubbornly even the most innocuous changes, other frustrated Country Lifers embraced the position that farmers were ignorant and degenerate people who could not be trusted to control their own lives and their own institutions.

Ever since urban people had begun seriously to criticize agriculture and rural life the imputation of rural ignorance had lain just under the surface. Farmers felt this implication and were stung by it, even when it did not reach an explicit level. Country Lifers usually took care to praise the farmer as a moral, social, and political paragon, however, for they were aware that without his cooperation change was impossible. But by the mid-teens social scientists, who usually expressed candidly their negative feelings about rural people, were producing numerous studies which seemed to indicate widespread rural degeneracy.[1] Regard for the farmer also declined among urban consumers, who were already suffering from inflated food prices when the disastrous cropping season of 1916 raised them so high that numerous observers called for an embargo on the export of food. Between 1916 and 1917 the wholesale price of corn jumped 40.5 percent, the price of wheat leaped 56.2 percent, and the potato price advanced 131.1 percent.[2] Farmers noted that price increases in large measure reflected weather-influenced declines in yields, but consumers tended to blame profiteering by self-seeking producers. As a result of these factors, urban people increasingly accepted the conclusion that farmers were ignorant, degenerate, and totally selfish anarchists.

Others did not embrace this extreme view, expressing instead the more common Country Life Movement notion that the food shortage was attributable to agricultural inefficiency and disorganization rather than rural cupidity. Theodore Roosevelt, for example, laid the food shortage to the fact that the farmer "still works by methods belonging to the day of the stage coach and the horse canal boat, while every other brain or hand worker in the country has been obliged to shape his methods into more or less conformity to those required by an age of steam and electricity."[3] But the question persisted of why agriculture remained disorganized and inefficient despite years of outside effort directed at changing it. Unwilling to question the accuracy of their critique or the appropriateness of the solutions they proposed for rural problems, most Country Lifers tended to blame their initial failures on rural people. Thus the vicious attacks of social scientists were less an aberration than a reflection of the general direction in which the Country Life Movement was heading. The marriage between democracy and technocracy which voluntary renovation would have effected was unconsummated. Unwilling to question technocracy, Country Lifers turned increasingly toward means of circumventing democracy. In this effort they were encouraged and reassured by their appreciation of the larger good of the interdependent nation. Although they might appear autocratic on the local level, the social and economic engineers remained democrats because of their devotion to the national good.

From the urban perspective, then, rural individualism and inefficiency continued to work against national needs and demands, and this recalcitrance became increasingly dangerous as war clouds lowered. "Present conditions and tendencies in the open country can [not] safely be allowed to go uncontrolled," concluded rural sociologist Paul L. Vogt, echoing an intensifying refrain.[4] But delineating the means of control was more difficult. Some critics continued to call for the traditional rural agencies of social control to "teach the virtues of obedience, subordination . . . and the nobility of self-sacrifice in the interest of the community."[5] But if the voluntaristic phase of the industrialization of agriculture had proved anything it had proved that rural institutions were too tightly controlled by their satisfied patrons to allow them to be very satisfactory vehicles of change. The best hope for the rapid alteration of rural America lay with expanded governmental control, but here also the survivals of democracy frustrated the demands of efficiency. Angry with rural people and unable to find immediate solutions for the problems involved in trying to change them, Country Lifers entered the war years frustrated, pessimistic, and impatient with rural resistance to change. "An omniscient, omnipotent, and benevolent despot could reorganize the nation promptly, put each of us in his proper place, assign tasks, appeal to the requisite motives, and make our common life a marvel of team play. No wonder we sometimes long for Plato's philosophers to come and take charge of us.'' But, continued sociologist George Vincent's lament, ''we are doomed to grope our way slowly toward a far-off ideal of national cooperation.''[6] Yet almost at the very height of their pessimism about industrializing agriculture, the war appeared to hold out the promise of just the sort of benevolent despotism for which Vincent and other industrializers longed.

I

As was the case with American society as a whole, the nation's entry into World War I caught Agriculture unprepared. Farmers had not responded well to the preparedness appeals of the previous years, and in April, 1917, projected production for the remainder of the year was not appreciably greater than for the year just past. Moreover, the fact that the nation entered the war in the spring meant that in many areas additional planting could not be done and crops in the ground could not be changed. Short production, short labor, poor distribution, and rural inefficiency were serious problems that beset the government in general and the United States Department of Agriculture in particular in the spring of 1917.

The fact that agriculture was unprepared for war did not mean, however, that all of the agencies concerned with it were unprepared. As David Houston noted in November of 1917, the nation ''was not fully prepared for war in any respect; but it was fortunately circumstanced in the character of its agricultural organization and the number and efficiency of its expert agencies.''[7] The extension system was one part of the USDA which was functioning efficiently and which was potentially valuable in the task of mobilization, and in the early weeks of the war the government worked to keep existing agents in the field and to place new ones in counties which lacked them. The immediate result of this activity was to save the jobs of many agents and to reintroduce the program in areas where it had been terminated.[8] Congress also recognized the potential importance of the agents to agricultural mobilization, and in the Food Production Act of 1917 it provided funds to place emergency agents in counties where the system did not operate. As late as June 30, 1917, only one in two counties had farm agents and but one in four had home agents. But mostly because of the emergency funds, 2435 of the nation's 2800 counties had farm agents and 1715 had home agents by June 30, 1918.[9] This rapid expansion was beset with some difficulties, but it would have been impossible were it not for the fact that the extension system was already in operation.

The primary aim of agricultural mobilization was to stimulate production, but it soon became apparent to agricultural officials that the government's greatest rural problem might be the farmer's indifference or even opposition to the war. Farmers and farm organizations had generally opposed America's entry into the war for a variety of material, ethnic, ideological, and personal reasons, and rural resistance to preparedness measures had been strong. Nor did opposition cease after war was declared. Resistance to the war was particularly strong in German ethnic enclaves in the countryside, but it was by no means confined to them. There are indications, for example, that southern Anglo-Saxon farmers were strongly antiwar.[10] Local farmers were "failing their country and mine both in word and deed at her time of peril [and] it was heart sickening," complained one Kentucky agent, reflecting the sentiments of many of his colleagues. "Oh, how I longed to smash the soap box orator (in some cases one of my demonstrators) who aired his views in the country store that we were no freer than Germany."[11] Despite widespread opposition that sometimes erupted into violence, however, the main problem with rural people was their apathy regarding the war. Indifference rose in part from ignorance about the war and its causes. More often, rural people had difficulties understanding how the war related to them. As isolated, individualistic, locally oriented people, farmers were understandably slow to see how the war might affect or even interest them.[12] The war was probably the best example to the government of the way in which rural social inefficiency and disorganization impeded the rapid realization of the goals of the activist state. Economically, socially, and politically organized, impinged upon by mass communications and vulnerable to mass appeals, dependent on and susceptible to economic pressures, urban people were relatively pliable for national policy purposes. But for the farmer the situation was far different. "The truth was that the farmer was late in awakening to enthusiastic war spirit," admitted Kansas editor Charles Moreau Harger in 1919. "Partly it was due to his environment. As he drove up and down the dusty furrows, he heard no bands playing, no parades passed along country highways, no street orators stirred his emotions. In a sense the rumbles of war were remote."[13] That same rural independence which many saw as the political safeguard of the Republic endangered the activist state when the times demanded rapid mobilization of resources. "The rural population furnishes a constant stabilizing element at times when . . . landslides in public opinion are imminent," sociologist Carl C. Taylor noted in his book, *Rural Sociology,* in 1926. But he continued: "There are times when it is desirable, and even necessary, that the whole national population be woven into a single public. Such an instance was the World War period. At such times the attitudes of the remote rural sections are slowly mobilized for the task."

The outcome of the first Liberty Loan campaign illustrated rural opposition to the war or at least rural immunity to war fever, and it also pointed out the difficulties involved in mobilizing the rural population. Opposition or indifference to the war, rural misunderstanding or distrust of bonds, the absence of effective means of compulsion, and the ineffectiveness of "the ordinary mass methods of advertising and education" conspired to make the first Liberty Loan a relative failure in the countryside.[14] While it was rapidly oversubscribed in most towns and cities, numerous rural areas hardly contributed at all. In the end the government estimated that only two percent of farmers bought the first Liberty Bond.[15]

The lack of rural war enthusiasm, as strikingly revealed by the failure of the first Liberty Loan campaign, thrust new duties on the county agents. Already responsible for economic mobilization, the agents were soon given important duties in social and political mobilization as well. The agents received their new duties not because they were peculiarly fitted for carrying them out, but because problems existed in the countryside and they were virtually the only federal employees there. As Robert Cuff notes in his study, *The War Industries Board: Business-Government Relations during World War I,* the federal bureaucracy was weak everywhere when the war began, and the countryside was no exception to this general rule. Indeed, aside from postal employees the county agents were the only federal workers in most counties. But equally important was the fact that private organizations which could undertake war work were also sparse in the institutionally underdeveloped countryside. Important social and political duties, then, came to agents because they were there rather than because they were especially fitted to handle them. Necessity forced these federal representatives to undertake functions of organization and control unrelated to their basic agricultural purposes. Within a very few months and with few questions as to the propriety of their functional modification, county agents were acting "to meet the exigencies of the [wartime] situation and to bring the farmer into social control."[16] As the main governmental representatives in the countryside, county agents soon found themselves working with and for such governmental or quasi-governmental agencies as the Treasury Department, the Red Cross, the YMCA, the War Department, the Food Administration, and the local councils of defense and safety.[17] Thus, the problems created by the lack of rural government were addressed by a tremendous expansion of the duties and the powers of people who before the war had been nothing more than semiindependent local functionaries.

As more and more duties were given to the county agents some found themselves unable to devote adequate energy to their primary job of stimulating food production. People who were called upon to sell war bonds, councils,   survey   food   supplies,   advise   draft boards, and allocate scarce farm materials were sometimes forced to neglect their usual duties. Particularly in primitive areas, where little organization of any kind existed, agents often found themselves so freighted with war work that it was impossible for them to work in agriculture.[18] Others jumped with relish into war work and seemed to forget their more mundane functions. A Negro agent in Mississippi, for example, saw his primary duty as keeping black farmers from going to the city, while two South Dakota agents involved themselves in organizing vigilante groups called "Home Guards."[19] An agent in McPherson County, Kansas, worked to propagandize draftees on army life and the war, and one Wisconsin agent even organized a military company of local men and dispatched it to the service. Other agents concentrated on Americanizing immigrants or quashing "traitors within our borders."[20] Bombarded with requests and orders from numerous federal and state agencies and often caught up in the excitement of new duties, then, it was not surprising that some agents forgot their original purposes.

Despite their new and exciting involvement in social manipulation and control, the primary concern of most agents still lay with the stimulation of production. *"Our food production has not kept pace with the growth of our population,"* noted an early war pamphlet. "This fact caused anxiety to agricultural experts even before the outbreak of the war. Now, when we must supply food not only to ourselves but to our allies, it is the gravest aspect of a grave situation."[21] But farmers viewed short food supplies with less gravity than did others. In some places, of course, "The response of the farmers to the appeal to grow more food was very generous and patriotic."[22] But many farmers were suspicious of government appeals to expand production through mechanization, farming of marginal land, or opening of new cropping areas. Originally, farmers tended to view appeals for greater production with the same caution, pessimism, and distrust with which they had always viewed the production schemes of the government and its Country Life allies. On its own part, the government did little to still rural fears. It simply asked farmers to produce more crops, while failing to guarantee them the means of production or remunerative prices.[23] Rural distrust in the North reached its height early in the war when the government fixed the price of the nation's most basic wartime commodity—wheat—at $2.20 per bushel. The price of wheat was fixed in part because, in the words of Federal Farm Loan Board member Herbert Quick, "We shall have in this country a political revolution, if not something worse, unless the question of the furnishing of foods to the people at the lowest possible price is taken up early and carried through to success."[24] Herbert Hoover, the head of the Food Administration, contended during as well as after the war that the fixed price for wheat was designed to encourage production and that it actually saved the farmer from "complete disaster."[25] But Hoover was at least as concerned with the cost of living as he was with farmers. He perceived the need "to ameliorate prices, for unless we can do so we must meet a rise in wages with all its vicious circle of social disruption at a time when maximum efficiency is vital to our safety."[26] Whatever the main purpose behind price fixing was, it angered farmers who expected wheat prices to rise as high as $5.00 per bushel in an uncontrolled market. As a result of the government's action, farmers switched from wheat to corn, fed wheat to hogs, or held it off the market.[27] Eventually, the fixed price of wheat proved profitable to most farmers, though it is not clear whether it stimulated production as the government claimed. The 1918 harvest was 44.7 percent larger that the 1917 harvest had been, but it was still more than 10 percent under the 1915 yield.[28] Whatever effect it had on production, however, the wheat price fixing reaped distrust for the government among Northern farmers.

The appearance of rural reticence in regard to increasing production and lack of enthusiasm in regard to the war called forth a vigorous urban reaction. Urban commentators, and some rural ones as well, complained that farmers were selfish, pro-German materialists who placed their personal preferences above national needs. It might have been an urban "principle that at a time of national crisis private preferences . . . must be sacrificed to the public interest," but farmers seemed unwilling to surrender their selfish interests for the commonweal.[29]

Facing continuing rural suspicion of themselves, heightened rural distrust of the federal government, and increasing rural alienation from urban people, it would seem that county agricultural agents were confronted with an impossible task as they attempted to increase food production. But not all currents flowed against them. In the first place, the agents soon learned to appeal to rural self-interest rather than to rural patriotism. Sensing the farmer's lack of enthusiasm for the war, agents stressed the fact that greater productivity benefited the farmer during wartime by allowing him to take advantage of an unnatural market situation in which supply never exceeded demand. As soon as the farmer recognized that big crops meant big receipts his economic conservatism and his suspicion of government motives began slowly to recede. But perhaps the most important element working on the side of the agents was the fact that the wartime emergency usually gave them effective control over the means of production—labor, seed, fertilizer, machinery, and the money to procure them.

The procurement of adequate farm labor during the war emergency was one of the primary problems addressed by the agents. Getting and holding skilled and reliable farm labor in the face of increasingly seductive urban social and economic conditions had long been a problem in agriculture. But the outbreak of war turned what had been a stream into a torrent as thousands of laborers and laboring sons fled the countryside.[30] Not only did thousands of men enlist in the armed forces, but thousands more quit the farms to avail themselves of the industrial opportunities the war presented. The tightening labor situation was exacerbated when the draft began to operate in the countryside. Skilled agricultural labor was supposed to get exemption preference, but this advice was often ignored by local boards. The USDA was soon flooded with complaints that the draft was denuding counties of laborers and tenants, and that merely maintaining production, let alone increasing it, was difficult.[31]

The agents were valuable in attacking this critical labor shortage. In most counties agents took control of labor procurement, and they met the problem in a variety of ways. Some tapped the resources of the towns for unskilled and sometimes voluntary adult and child help, some contracted for floating labor from other areas, some erected labor exchanges and issued work-or-fight orders to transients, and some relied on all of these methods and others besides.[32] Their job of procuring labor also gave the agents at least advisory powers regarding the draft and soldiers' applications for furloughs, markedly increasing their power and standing in the countryside.[33] Of course, expanded powers over labor included great potentials for social control, and agents and their business and conservative agricultural allies were soon engaged actively in combating radical labor groups like the Industrial Workers of the World (IWW) and in forcing down wage rates.[34]

The agents also held significant powers over other factors of production which were in short supply, including seed, fertilizer, machinery, and capital. Under the Food Production Act of 1917 the president was given authority to control and allocate seed, fertilizer, and implements. The government never found it necessary to use the far-reaching powers granted by the bill on the national level. However, in certain selected areas seed and fertilizer were allocated by the government, and in these areas it was the agents who did the allocating.[35] Even where the agents did not enjoy formal control over the means of production, farmers found them useful in helping secure the things needed to produce crops. Agents enjoyed a superior ability to secure what the farmers needed because they had more contacts, they served as advisors to merchants and bankers extending credits to farmers, and they had greater knowledge about what was available and how to get it. Thus, farmers found that even when they lacked formal control agents were in a better position than farmers to locate and procure what the farmer needed at prices he could more easily afford to pay.[36]

The agents' expanded war powers helped put them in a position of importance and security few of them had enjoyed before the outbreak of hostilities. For the first time in the history of the extension movement significant numbers of farmers needed agents more than agents needed them. The war brought the government representatives new respect and attention from farmers. At the same time, the war allowed a great advance in the extension goal of making agriculture more productive. In a situation in which maximum productivity was crucial, it is not surprising that those farmers who were the most efficient and the most scientifically oriented were also the most likely to receive adequate machinery, labor, and seed, while the more primitive farmers were penalized. Hence, the agents were able to aid those who were already likely to be their allies while their enemies failed to enjoy the full benefits of wartime agriculture. This was not reflective of a conscious extension policy of punishing opponents, but rather of the simple expedient of maximizing production by aiding the most efficient. The goal of making agriculture more productive was further advanced by the fact that the unnatural wartime market situation made things like productive efficiency, scientific agriculture, and mechanization more respectable among more farmers than they had ever been before. Farmers were finally ready to produce more, and the agents were there to help them do so. The unique market situation and the agents' power, then, combined to advance significantly the cause of productive efficiency during World War I.

The cause of organization was also advanced by the war. As the USDA's George E. Farrell noted in 1926, "The war experience emphasized the importance of organization in country life."[37] This lesson came home to the government in the early months of the war, when the paucity of rural social and economic organization impeded the state's efforts to extend social control, stimulate production, and mobilize rural society. "Agriculture is not so well organized as are other lines of business," admitted Missouri Secretary of Agriculture Jewell Mayes in his Annual Report of 1918," and consequently can not be mobilized so rapidly." Hence, one of the primary duties of the agents was rapidly to organize their counties. Even more than it had been before, the concept of organization in wartime was one which emphasized control of the farmer. As a later commentator noted, "the government desired to have organization in the farming communities through which it could know what the farmers were doing and communicate to them its wishes regarding agricultural production."[38]

For the most part, agents' organizational efforts were highly successful. Throughout the nation farm bureaus, home bureaus, and boys' and girls' clubs were started and those already in existence were expanded. In many cases the membership appeals were patriotic, but neither agents nor farmers ignored the facts of self-interest in wartime. The government and the farm bureaus were even more closely identified during the war than they had been before, and local bureaus often shared the emergency functions the county agents had been given. Wise farmers found bureau membership very much in their financial, social, and political interest. "The assistance given the farmers in obtaining deferred classification for their skilled farm help by the Farm Bureau has taken a great deal of the Agent's time of late," noted Dallas County, Iowa, agent H. E. Codlin, "but has been a big boost to the Farm Bureau work. It has greatly aided many farmers in realizing that the Farm Bureau can be of real value to them individually as well as [to] the Government."[39] Thus, the bureaus molded farmers supporting the government and the agents into a unified group, and they facilitated the realization of the government's productive goals. They also often became agencies of direct social control, acting as or with councils of defense and public safety to force local obedience and conformity to government demands. The wartime expansion in the number of farm bureaus did not alter their character. They remained conservative, business-oriented organizations which relished their wartime opportunity to suppress radical groups like the Socialist party, the IWW, and the Nonpartisan League through the special powers they and the agents had been granted.[40] Of course, by enmeshing local people in the sociopolitical aspects of war work the bureaus undoubtedly contributed to social divisions arising in the community over issues of loyalty and control, but local divisions tended to further government purposes by tying substantial segments of the rural population ever more tightly to federal authority. Divisive activities ripped many communities and served to heighten the suspicion some rural groups held regarding the government and its motives, then, but there can be no question that the war greatly forwarded the organization of the countryside and aided the most efficient producers.

The tremendous progress made by the agents during the war should not obscure the fact that resistance to them continued. Substantial segments of the rural populace remained suspicious of the agents, their allies, and their motives for all of the old reasons.[41] Additionally, agents often faced the opposition of Germans, Irishmen, Russian-Germans, and other ethnic groups which "considered the County Agent a sort of Government detective stationed in their midst to report on conditions."[42] Traditional rural resentment of the Extension Service's implication of farmer ignorance also flared during the war, particularly when the government forced emergency agents into areas where they were unwanted. "I have no doubt that the time will come when demonstrators will be sent out by the department to teach the farmers how to blow their noses," sneered Colorado Senator Charles S. Thomas, who agreed with the conclusion of Utah Senator William H. King that the wartime extension program was "paternalism gone mad."[43] The detractors of extension contended that high prices would sufficiently induce the farmers to produce adequate crops. "You do not have to hire some shoemaker or corn doctor to go on a farm and demonstrate to a farmer the need for raising crops," concluded Congressman Martin B. Madden of Illinois, a strong supporter of the extension idea a few years before, "he knows how to do that himself."[44]

Despite this continuing opposition to the agents on traditional grounds, their adversaries often found it wiser to attack them on the patriotic grounds that Extension Service personnel were unjustly deferred from the draft. Although the USDA was never able to make deferred status for county agents an airtight national policy, it was usually able to get them exempted from service by state or local boards.[45] This general policy engendered a good deal of resentment and gave the opponents of extension a patriotic basis on which to assail the agents, and, indirectly, the government. "These days, when we need farm help as we never did before, is [sic] no time to take men from production and possibly exempt them from the draft, as 2,000 employees of the Agriculture Department have been," argued Wyoming Representative Frank W. Mondell, who apparently reflected "a very strong feeling in Congress" against the deferment of agents.[46] Congressional complaints were no more than reflections of local ones. Farmers who had seen their help or their sons sent to war often failed to see why agents had stayed, and as a result farm advisers came under tremendous local pressures to enlist or to abandon their exemptions. Most agents were patriotic and dedicated to the war, and their deferments both embarrassed them and hurt their consciences. Consequently, a number resigned and enlisted.

Agents also faced problems in war work itself that transcended mere resistance. One of the problems that confronted established agents in particular was that wartime exigencies often upset established programs and long-term goals. "While the war was a big factor in making the County Agent's work popular and effective," conceded the agent for Walla Walla County, Washington, "it also was the cause of many wrecked plans."[47] The wartime emphasis on production upset the attempts of some agents to advance efficient agriculture under a rational plan which attempted to maintain price stability. As the USDA's William A. Lloyd later lamented, "Sound rotation practices were scrapped, good farm-management principles were thrown in the discard, and throughout the whole country much of the cumulative influence of extension effort was, at least temporarily, lost" in the effort to increase short-term production at all costs.[48] Other established agents added to this concern the complaint that added war work from nonagricultural agencies prevented them from fulfilling their original purpose, while a few complained that their efforts were frustrated by the fact that there were too many agencies trying to involve themselves in emergency work. The extension program was also hampered by the fact that emergency agents in particular were often ignorant both of agriculture and of rural people.[49] Finding men with technical expertise as well as appropriate personalities for the work had always been a serious problem for the USDA, and the wartime demand exacerbated it.

So the agents faced problems which rendered the wartime extension experience something less than completely satisfactory. Despite the fact that the extension system was already organized and operating, its rapid expansion did lead to some difficulties, particularly in securing competent emergency personnel and in gaining their acceptance in local areas. Even where agents were already in operation long-term plans were upset, regular work was discarded, and their social and political involvements brought opposition to the extension program. Generally, however, it appears that established agents with established bureaus behind them enjoyed successes in furthering their old aims and carrying out their new duties. Emergency agents, on the other hand, who attempted to work in new counties and who did not enjoy established bureau support seemed to have less impact.[50]

Despite some failures by individual agents, and despite some ambivalence about the experience among some others, for the extension system as a whole the war must be seen as a great success. Indeed, Assistant Secretary of Agriculture Clarence Ousley contended early in 1919 that the extension program was "considerably in advance of the progress we could reasonably have hoped to make under peace conditions."[51] When the war came the agents were virtually the only federal employees in local areas, and this placed them in a crucial position. "The founders of the Demonstration Work must have had a premonition of the present world conflict," exclaimed one South Carolina extension official, "which enabled them to lay the foundation for the present work to be done."[52] Although the agricultural bureaucracy did not have the prescience this observer attributed to it, the fact remains that the potential importance of the agents as mobilizers became clear to the government very early in the war. How completely and how well the countryside was mobilized during the war remains a question, but it is clear that insofar as mobilization took place the agents were important elements in stimulating and sustaining it. But even if the agents did nothing more than simply report on local conditions—which they did with regularity and in detail—they served a function which endeared them to the government. By the end of the war, then, the importance of the agents to the activist state was clear, and the position of the extension system in the federal government was secure.

The primary USDA war aim, of course, was not to solidify the position of the extension system in the federal bureaucracy. This was a rather unexpected but quite welcome windfall traceable to the agents' activities. The main war aim of extension was one which conjoined with its long-term goal, the stimulation of a heightened level of agricultural efficiency which would be reflected in increased food production. When food production rose the USDA was understandably quick to appropriate most of the credit. "I can lay down the proposition and sustain it by the records that the . . . increased yield of farm crops . . . is due almost entirely to the leadership of the county agents backed by the Department of Agriculture and the agricultural colleges," Clarence Ousley claimed in 1918.[53] Whether this was in fact true is doubtful. The Food Administration quite reasonably contended, as did agricultural spokesmen in Congress, that high prices were the primary stimulus to increased production.[54] This is not to say that the agents had no part in the increase—after all, when the farmers wanted to move the agents were there to help them—but only that it was not due to their manipulative efforts. The USDA, however, never doubted that the agents were the most important elements involved in sustaining and increasing crop production. Indeed, Ousley went so far as to claim, "If these farmers were left to their own individual initiative, aloof as they are from one another and from the common currents of national information in respect to all these large problems, we would have had a breakdown in agriculture."[55]

Despite the USDA's interest in monopolizing credit for production increases, the question of whether the extension system was successful during the war did not hinge solely on this point. Organization, so closely related to efficiency, was also a long-term extension goal for agriculture, and the development and expansion of the county farm bureaus was an important index of extension success. These local organizations, which in 1920 formed the basis of the American Farm Bureau Federation, presented the government with a number of benefits. Most immediately they gave the government organizations through which to work, thus multiplying the agents' efforts. But it soon became apparent that the farm bureaus identified farmers who were both efficient and patriotic while giving the government a means of responding to those farmers it believed most valuable to the nation. For the first time, the national industrial state had an organization through which it could deal with rural America, and those farmers who embraced the goals of efficiency and organization had a means of dealing with the government and with other economic groups. It soon became clear that the county agents and the organizations supporting them would be important tools for government in its attempts to manage agriculture.

II

The progress made by the extension system in stimulating rural efficiency did not surprise the bulk of the County Lifers, who had great faith in the ability of government to manipulate people. Most of them welcomed the war because they believed it would bring a desirable measure of social and economic control and would reshape a rural character that refused to change voluntarily. Critics of agriculture hoped that the war, either through force of law or force of example, would make farmers work efficiently, organize intelligently, think internationally, see the value of government, and defer to experts. The war would tutor the farmer in self-sacrifice, teach him the lessons of social interdependence, and generally "complete the socialization of the farm."[56] Of course, the Country Lifers were sure that the war would show farmers the benefits of social and economic efficiency and organization. As educator Louis W. Rapeer wrote in *The Consolidated Rural School* at war's end, "The stupendous world war with its unprecedented stimulus to close national organization of railroads, agriculture, and manufacturing, with all their implications of sacrificing individualism to social efficiency, has sent the world, and especially America, a long way toward a desirable organization of all of each nation's forces."

Country Lifers believed that increased efficiency would be paralleled by a rural demand for an expanded governmental role. Rural sociologist Dwight Sanderson claimed in 1919 that "an increasingly complex civilization—even in the rural community—makes it no longer possible for the farm family to live to itself, but that for self-preservation it must look to the social welfare of the whole community with which its life is bound up." Only government had the breadth of vision adequately to see to that social welfare.[57] But the government that would make the countryside socially and economically efficient was not the small, unprofessional, democratically chosen, locally oriented government that existed there, but government by the technocratic experts who envisioned the future in wartime organization. The "traditional ideal in regard to public service in the village must give way, as it is giving way in the larger communities," announced one social scientist in a typical wartime statement, "to the ideal of management by efficient, highly-trained men, competent to handle the business of the community on the same basis as is the management of the best corporations."[58] Only the social engineers themselves clearly understood and could act on the demands of social and economic organization, efficiency, and interdependence. Of course, such ideas violated rural—and once American—ideals of liberty and individualism, but the war had given apparent support for the social engineers' contention that liberty and individualism were code words for social and economic inefficiency, and were thus dangerous to the interdependent industrial state. The social engineers fashioned terms like "new democracy," "new liberty," and "new individualism" to describe the managed future, but each was more "new" than democratic, libertarian, or individualistic. Not surprisingly, the old verities fell under open attack, and individualism and liberty were increasingly identified with the new horror, bolshevism. "Liberty in an unrestricted sense means anarchy, means bolshevism," concluded one educator. "In its better sense it means 'The greatest good for the greatest number.' "[59]

Despite the real progress made in increasing rural social and economic efficiency and organization during the war and the Country Lifers' euphoria resulting therefrom, it soon became apparent that the immediate rural reality might not exactly match the critics' projections. Despite their hopes, the countryside did not immediately become a managed utopia efficiently supplementing the urban-industrial nation. Just as they had overestimated the prospects for the voluntary renovation of rural society, the critics overestimated the effectiveness of governmental action in achieving that end. It soon became apparent that the consequences of governmental activity were not always clear or predictable, and that social and economic patterns of long standing could not be immediately reversed. Thus the critics' optimism was soon balanced by a caution born of disturbing developments in the countryside. While the war advanced social and economic organization and efficiency and saw an expanded governmental role in the countryside, it paradoxically highlighted old rural maladies and exposed new ones, forcing Country Lifers to face unpleasant rural realities.

One continuing problem facing the critics was that of food production, and though yields advanced, demand increased even faster.[60] The unnatural economic situation caused by the war had several effects on farmers and their urban customers. First, it gave farmers three years of average income higher than that of those in other comparable occupations. With a higher income, farmers not only reinvested in land, stock, and machinery, they also began to achieve a twentieth century standard of living.[61] But rural material progress seemed proportional to urban economic distress, as retail food prices jumped 70 percent between 1916 and 1920.[62] Much of the increase was accountable to sharply higher costs of distribution and to the unnaturally high world demand for food, but consumers usually chose to attack the farmer as an inefficient, self-interested profiteer.[63] Spiraling food costs for urban consumers led the government to redouble its long-range efforts to increase food production and lower the cost of living.[64]

The government recognized that increasing rural economic efficiency was contingent on accelerating wartime organization. Hence, when the war ended farm bureaus were encouraged to expand their memberships and functions and counties were urged to retain agents. In unorganized areas agents were advised to use councils of defense and public safety as bases for farm bureau organization.[65] But the government soon discovered that even retaining the existing degree of organization would be difficult, and that expanding it would be virtually impossible. One basic problem was that many farmers and their wives had seen farm and home bureau work and county agents as wartime exigencies, and when the war ended so did their interest in extension. As one Indiana agent noted of extension work, "many people . . . believe it to have been a war measure and now that the war is over . . . the County Agent is no more deemed so essential by some, especially in the cause of economic production."[66] Many in Congress apparently shared this view, because emergency extension funding was not renewed in 1919. Moreover, the agents faced most of the same problems of suspicion and resistance they had always faced, and their loss of wartime social, economic, and political powers gave farmers less reason to cooperate with them. Consequently, the memberships of many local farm and home bureaus melted and agents, particularly those forced in under the emergency statutes, were dropped. From 1918 to 1919 the number of counties with farm agents dropped from 2,435 to 2,246, and the number with home agents declined from 1,715 to 1,053.[67]

Another fact that became apparent as the war ended was that the organization of farmers did not necessarily lead to the same ends for which the Country Life Movement hoped. Much to their discomfort, urban observers discovered that rural organizations could just as well promote political and economic radicalism as economic and social efficiency. Spurred by rising expectations and wartime sacrifices, farmers were increasingly anxious to assure the self-direction of postwar agriculture. As Grange official Edward E. Chapman warned in 1917, "the time has come for the Government to recognize not only the cooperation of the farmer, not only his productivity, not only his self-sacrifice, but the necessity of giving him some say in determining the rules under which he himself is compelled to work."[68] Increasingly, Granges, Farmers' Unions, and more radical groups like the Nonpartisan League sponsored measures aimed immediately at eliminating middlemen and local merchants completely and ultimately at production control. Such radical self-directive actions repelled conservative critics and brought opposition from the county agents and their conservative, government-sponsored farm bureaus.[69] By 1919 rural ferment had reached the stage where one perplexed observer was forced to admit, "It has been all but impossible to awaken rural people and next to impossible to control them when once aroused."[70]

In the postwar period of social anxiety and ferment, there were those who continued to believe that the farmer was the nation's primary conservative and its basic defender against urban radicalism. But more and more observers concluded that some farmers were becoming dangerous radicals, a conclusion that was not without some justification.[71] The wartime renaissance of rural radicalism tended to fragment rural communities and to create serious problems for the farm bureaus. The bureaus and the extension system had always opposed rural conservatism as reflected in resistance to scientific innovation, social regeneration, or governmental activism, but they had seldom questioned the rights and prerogatives of local or national businessmen and usually embraced most urban analyses of agriculture's problems. Indeed, if one thing united most of the farmers, businessmen, and bankers who comprised the membership of these organizations, it was the basic and deeply conservative assumption that the roots of agriculture's problems lay in the rural community itself. At best the farm bureaus merely asked for the right to share with other organized economic groups and with the government in making agricultural policy. Most bureau members "were not ragged and underprivileged people, but rugged and determined business men . . . [who] deeply believed that they could, by their own efforts, do much to make country life as attractive as they knew it could be made through further technological progress and improved incomes."[72] And, as longtime extension worker Russell Lord notes, the early farm bureaus were "officered and led, from the first, by the squire type in the South and East and by the equivalent owner or banker-farmer type in the Midland."[73] Rooted in the most politically conservative elements of the rural community, convinced that the source of rural economic ills lay in the countryside and not in the cities, often involved in local wartime campaigns against radicals, and allied with a federal government engaged in a campaign to destroy the left, the farm bureaus quickly became the primary bulwarks against rural insurgency, thus dashing the hopes of some idealistic agents and farmers.[74] "The Farm Bureaus in cooperation with our Extension Department represent a strong, patriotic, conservative force in agriculture," noted ex-Assistant Secretary of Agriculture R. A. Pearson in a revealing letter to the Iowa State Board of Education, "and this is one of the best agencies in the state for combating evil and harmful movements which have become so prevalent in other states and which show themselves here occasionally."[75] The farm bureaus' reaction to the left was consistent with their social position, but the rise of agrarian radicalism remained a factor which disturbed urban critics and which at least partially foiled their postwar plans for rural America.

Another problem revealed by the war, and one which critics associated with rural radicalism, was that of the unassimilated immigrant. The massive, forcible involvement of government in the rural community during the war had helped the nation win the conflict and had advanced the industrialization of agriculture, but it had also revealed substantial groups of people, sometimes third- or fourth-generation Americans, who were foreigners to all intents and purposes. "There are foreign provinces in the agricultural sections of the country," noted one shocked observer in 1919. "Such provinces have become self-sufficient; they have their own towns, their own schools, churches, industries, stores, select local public officials of their own nationality, speak their own tongue, and live according to the traditions and spirit of their home country."[76] Such survivals, of course, were made possible by the same self-sufficiency, isolation, local control, and absence of means of compulsion that operated nearly everywhere in rural America to thwart the aims of renovators. But un-Americanized immigrants were potentially even more dangerous than uncontrolled natives because they threatened the social and political basis of the countryside and, by extension, the nation. In addition to native radicals and uncontrolled farmers, then, the critics feared "the 5,000,000 foreign born in rural communities, among whom there are as many 'reds' as among any group in urban centers."[77]

The discovery of unassimilated aliens and unpatriotic natives in the countryside reemphasized the pivotal position of the rural school, which was expected to inculcate future citizens with the modern virtues of discipline, obedience, conformity, and deference to expert authority. This emphasis did not disturb educators since their pedagogical ideas had always stressed the same measures of control. Many Country Lifers, in fact, saw the war as a grand opportunity to press their idea that education should be a broadly practical training for a life of efficiency, cooperation, self-sacrifice, and social interdependence because the exigencies of the conflict would put a premium on these virtues. "The first duty of the public schools . . . is to train young people for citizenship," noted Paul Vogt in 1917, "that term meaning not merely ability to vote . . . but also ability to understand the principles of social ethics so that, as they grow up, they will have the proper attitude toward their fellows and will be reliable, trustworthy, efficient factors in community life, supporting themselves and their families and doing their part in maintaining the necessary social coördinations."[78] Of course, the critics noted once again that an expanded education responsible for "strengthening character, . . . teaching the rights of fellow men, loyalty to the state, . . . fear of God, . . . [and] practical training for bread winning" was far beyond the capabilities of "all but the *exceptional* one-teacher schools."[79] There were indications that the war would rapidly advance both consolidation and practical education. In the first place, there was a serious shortage of rural teachers as local instructors enlisted in the army or availed themselves of wartime opportunities offered by urban systems. At least some states used the teacher shortage as a pretext to force unwilling districts to consolidate.[80] Consolidation was also portrayed as a patriotic exercise which would lead to increased productive efficiency, and the war enlivened the attack on the one-room school as a symbol of narrow rural selfishness and lack of concern for others. "The truth is becoming universally diffused that the district must give up its traditional grip upon the school;" noted one observer in 1918, "that education is the business of the nation and the state and of the county under the state."[81]

Instead of revolutionizing education, however, the war often had the effect of crippling existing rural school systems without substituting anything better for them. Rural opposition to practical education continued, and even some prewar gains were lost when the USDA recruited teachers skilled in agriculture or home economics to be county agents.[82] Rural districts remained averse to consolidation, so they attempted to meet the teacher shortage by raising salaries, lowering standards, or both. Some even successfully resisted consolidation on the grounds that it was an unpatriotic expenditure during wartime.[83] The labor shortage also hampered the cause of rural education, and even reformist educators defended temporary school closings, school credit for farm work, and relaxation of compulsory attendance laws.[84] Although educators had seen the war as an opportunity to force change on the rural school, then, the end of the conflict found the rural educational system either worse or unchanged in most cases.

To all of the other rural wartime and postwar problems was added chaos and disorganization. Much of this was caused by war work which sometimes split communities, alienated neighbor from neighbor, and stimulated social ferment. "I found our county rather disturbed after so much anxiety and war work," noted a Tennessee home demonstration agent whose county's reaction was typical of that of isolated areas massively impinged upon by outside forces.[85] But rural chaos was also reflected and further stimulated by the tremendous physical mobility of the war years. Not only did the war see thousands of farmers and farm boys enlist or get drafted, it also saw thousands of others flee the farms for the cities. Marginal agricultural people in particular, black and white laborers and tenants from the South and white laborers and tenants from the North, abandoned farming for high industrial wages and city life. Most observers expected that the war's end would repopulate the countryside, but such was not the case. Farm boys who had served the flag found country living boring and primitive when they returned. It was true that high prices had improved the material condition of the countryside, but money and the luxuries it bought were poor substitutes for the social excitements many rural boys had learned to crave in the army.[86] Even less interested in returning were the rural refugees in the cities, who found wage rates, excitements, and sometimes freedoms country living could not duplicate.[87] Not only did those who had gone fail to return, but the rural exodus continued after the armistice. Ironically, the very improvements in farm living and communications brought by the war seemed to highlight the remaining gap between urban and rural standards of living and to disillusion country people regarding the desirability of their life-style, much as urban agrarians had feared they might. Thus the exodus continued unabated, filling the cities with farmers, heightening discontent in some rural districts, and leaving others virtually depopulated.[88] The war had the effect of artificially accelerating the pace of migration from farm to city, and had thus contributed to rural discontent and, many believed, to high farm prices. These manifestations in turn heightened urban concern about the state of the countryside and rural people.

III

The frustrations and concerns of the Country Lifers, their hopes for the future, and their enthusiam for the manipulative and compulsive potentials of the activist state revealed by the war were all reflected in the Land Settlement Movement. Indeed, in some ways land settlement can be seen as the logical culmination of twenty years of development of the Country Life Movement. Put simply, the Land Settlement Movement strove to place farmers in highly organized communities which would be run by government experts and would be forced to conform to industrial standards of efficiency. The state of California actually established one colony in 1917 and another in 1919, and for a season half of the states and substantial segments of the federal government seriously considered colonization schemes. There had been private colonization efforts before by various immigrant organizations, religious groups, land companies, and railroads, but it took the war for colonization to emerge as a highly organized, compulsive, and government-sponsored enterprise.

The Land Settlement Movement gained popularity during the war as a means of solving the anticipated postwar problems caused by the discharge of millions of soldiers and sailors. Secretary of the Interior Franklin K. Lane was its primary enthusiast in the federal government, and he was joined by liberal congressmen who saw land settlement as a means of rewarding war veterans and by western congressmen who saw it as a means of peopling the empty acres in their states. But despite the many motivations of its public advocates, land settlement was seen primarily as a means of social control. The prospect of millions of young men who had been trained to fight and who had possibly been infected with bolshevism in Europe being dumped into cities without jobs or job possibilities was disquieting to those planning for the postwar period. "The great danger is that there won't be enough jobs to go around;"

warned a worried commentator as the war drew to an end, "that unemployment will come with attendant misery and social unrest at a time when anarchistic tendencies are contagious."[89] Farm colonies were attractive because they would immediately provide employment and keep soldiers isolated from the volatile cities.[90] Just as social workers sometimes saw rural America as a dumping ground for undesirable immigrants, criminals, and degenerates, then, some supporters of land settlement conceived it as a place to isolate potentially dangerous veterans. In both cases, the countryside was nothing more than a means to the end of protecting the cities. But in addition to isolating them, the settlement of ex-soldiers would also help counter the flight of rural people to the cities, and a widened base of land ownership would protect the nation's social and political future and make soldiers conservative. As Franklin K. Lane wrote in 1918, "When a sense of property goes, it becomes more and more apparent to me, that all other conserving and conservative tendencies go, and the man who has something is the man who will save this country."[91]

Despite the verbal tributes they paid to the social control and philanthropic motives of their supporters, those who had conceived the land settlement idea were not primarily interested in the returned soldiers. Indeed, the land settlement idea predated the war, but its advocates were as willing as others with new ideas to use the conflict to advance their theories. The principal motivation of Elwood Mead, the University of California agricultural scientist who fathered the modern land settlement idea, and of his colleagues, was nothing less than the complete remaking of rural social and economic life.[92] The voluntary industrialization of the countryside had failed, but the war held out the possibility that organized governmental activity might force its success. "We are already learning the value of having the government as an active partner with the people in everyday affairs," noted Mead in 1918. "Nowhere is this more clearly shown than in changes and improvements in agriculture and in the social conditions of rural life foreshadowed by our efforts to secure an unprecedented increase in production."[93] The war showed the benefits of organized governmental activity, and colonization of new settlers on abandoned or previously uncultivated lands would give this activity maximum impact. By undertaking colonization, the government and the technocrats who ran the colonies freed themselves from the stays of rural tradition, localism, individualism, and institutional resistance. Colonization allowed a fresh start in which settlers could be handpicked and such things as scientific farming and stock breeding, economic cooperation, school reform, and social organization could be laid down as mandatory conditions. "In our century strenuous efforts have been made . . . for the betterment of rural conditions," recounted one commentator. "Now is the time to give these manifold, maturing plans a rapid realization through the creation of the Soldier Settlements on the best lines known, starting them *de novo,* without the fearful drag of hardened habits."[94]

Certainly, at the Durham Colony and later at the Delhi Colony in California the technocrats left little to chance. The California State Land Settlement Board, which oversaw the projects, kept a tight rein on the economic and social activities of its subjects. The Board and its field experts oversaw cultivation, building, property maintenance, animal breeding, and cooperative marketing, and settlers who failed to paint fences or use prescribed animal breeds or cooperate could be thrown out of the colony. Settlers also had to join stock breeders' and cooperative marketing associations, and to erect an agricultural training farm, and had to build and use a social hall.[95] The sponsors expected great benefits to accrue from such tight control. Economically, the controls would foster the scientific agriculture which would eventually solve the food crisis and would serve as a motivating example to traditional farmers.[96] In the social realm the sponsors believed that land settlement would bring satisfaction to country living, halt the flow of desirable farmers and workers from the land, tie farmers to the government, and, again, influence other farmers by force of example.[97]

To those few remaining nostalgics who believed that individualism was one of the more desirable rural characteristics and that rural people should change voluntarily, the degree of state control at Durham and Delhi was disconcerting. But those oriented toward land settlement noted that in a modern industrial society "a moral life is a socialized life," and that a tightly organized society was what rural people really needed, whether they knew it or not.[98] As the representative of an interdependent society, the state was duty-bound to counter selfish individualism. Elwood Mead embraced the increasingly popular idea that farming was "a trust involving obligations to the state," and another commentator added that "we must move boldly forward for the solution, through state activity, of those great problems of our social order which state power alone can meet."[99] A few settlement sponsors tried to cling to the fiction that colonization would promote individualism, but most frankly agreed that it included large elements of necessary, and even desirable, paternalism.

Despite a tremendous amount of enthusiasm over land settlement both as a solution for soldiers' problems and as a means of making agriculture over, in the end the California colonies and a few minor endeavors undertaken in other states were the only projects started.[100] There were several reasons for the failure of land settlement. For one thing, most returning soldiers were disinclined to become farmers, and when it became clear that most veterans were going to be conservative rather than radical politically, plans favoring their dispersion lost steam.[101] Also, states found it prohibitively expensive to offer settlers tillable land on attractive terms, and the fall in agricultural prices in 1920 and 1921 punctured the cheap food motivations. National plans were scrapped when the USDA and the farmers also fought land settlement; the latter because they feared increased competition and the former ostensibly for the same reason but probably also because of bureaucratic resentment of the Interior Department and the Bureau of Reclamation, both of which favored settlement and would have controlled it.[102] It is probably also true, as a student of land settlement, Bill G. Reid, contends, that the postwar reaction against social engineering and planning prevented widespread implementation.[103] Perhaps most important, however, land settlement was not widely undertaken because it failed at Durham and Delhi where farms were too small and conditions were too restrictive.[104] In the end, many early enthusiasts were forced to agree with Albert Shaw: "The reconstruction of rural life is a problem at once so fundamental in principle and so complicated in practice that its achievement is not a matter of a season or of a decade, but of a generation or a half-century."[105]

Land settlement proved a failure, but its inception and its progress was an interesting commentary on the position of the critics of agriculture during World War I. The land settlement scheme reflected the frustration of renovators with farmers and their declining faith in voluntarism. But even more important, it indicated their acceptance of, and even enthusiasm for, the sorts of compulsory and manipulative governmental devices used in the countryside during the emergency, and their belief that the activist state was the most efficient means to the industrialization of agriculture.

IV

As was the case in much of the rest of American society, World War I was a confused experience for the countryside. On the one hand, the war was marked by an increase in organization, efficiency, and social control in rural America. But it also spurred discontent, uncovered serious problems, and contributed to social and institutional disintegration. Consequently, Country Lifers and farmers alike emerged from the experience with no clear understanding of what the future would bring or what the recent past meant. Both had reasons for optimism and both had reasons for pessimism. The farmer emerged from the war with a better standard of living and a heightened political consciousness, but he also faced the disintegration of local society and some loss of self-direction. The critics of agriculture glimpsed the promise of the organized and efficient future, but they also recognized that the war had made no lasting beneficial changes in the characters of most rural people. Once again, the Country Lifers contemplated the return to step one as they recognized that 1920 would see the same basic rural America 1900 had seen. As rural social worker E. Fred Eastman wearily noted upon his return from the first meeting of the new National (American) Country Life Association, "some of the oldtimers who listened to the papers read at the Baltimore conference were at a loss to discover in what respect they differed from the papers read at similar conferences many years ago. The same problems were under discussion, and the same advice was being offered."[106]

Neither the Country Lifers nor the farmers realized it, but the war had wrought tremendous changes on American agriculture. Only in the twenties did it become clear that the war had changed the way some farmers carried on their business and the way many looked at their lives; that it altered the prejudices and commitments of many rural people regarding government, the role of government, the neighborhood, and neighborhood institutions. And only in the twenties, if ever, would farmers and their critics begin to understand that the changes brought by the war or accelerated by it were the main factors contributing to the industrialization of agriculture.

6

THE FIRST INDUSTRIAL DECADE

As the third decade of the twentieth century began, farmers and their critics in the Country Life Movement found agriculture in a confusing state. Progress in industrialization had been made during World War I, but developments in rural life exposed by the war made the future unclear. It was accepted by all concerned that the countryside was changing, but there was virtually no agreement on the direction of the change. "The present movement in the rural world is essentially transitional," concluded one bewildered rural sociologist in 1920. "We are perplexed by its maladjustments, its instability, its restlessness, its change, and decay."[1]

To social ferment was added economic collapse, as farm prices plummeted in 1920 and 1921. Some prices rose in some years later during the decade, but the Golden Age of Agriculture never returned and the state of the countryside came to be defined in terms of relative economic hardship and social retrenchment while the nation's urban-industrial sector enjoyed its most prosperous decade ever. The reasons for the depression were many. Increased productive efficiency in agriculture on a larger cropping area played a part, as did altered national eating habits and fashions and a declining export market. Although experts disagreed on the causes of depression, they agreed on the results. During the good times, farmers' standards of living had improved and their definition of material necessities had expanded. Optimistic about the future of agriculture, farmers had taken loans to buy more land, to purchase machinery, or to obtain purebred livestock. And farmers had increased their taxes in order to maintain or upgrade services in the inflationary period of the war. The farmers' fixed costs of living and doing business were higher than ever before, and to meet these expenses when prices collapsed farmers pursued the dual strategy of retrenchment and maximization of production.[2]

In combination with continuing rural resistance to urban-inspired change, the agricultural depression caused some Country Lifers to reassess their assumptions about rural people, their goals for agriculture, and their means of achieving those goals. Self-examination was undertaken particularly by critics whose primary interest was in rural society rather than agricultural economics. The rural sociologists, welfare workers, educators, and ministers who comprised the core of the new American Country Life Association were especially given to introspection and reassessment during the twenties. On the other hand, those Country Lifers who had always been concerned overwhelmingly with cheap food showed little interest in agriculture when that end was achieved. The twenties, then, was a decade of reassessment for some critics and disinterest for others. And yet, ironically, developments in American agriculture during the decade served to advance rapidly the goals enunciated by the early Country Life Movement.

I

The hopes forged on the anvil of war for the social regneration of the countryside remained largely unfulfilled in 1920. Despite its efforts, the Country Life Movement saw a countryside in which the quality of life and of institutions remained primitive. Individualistic, proud, and locally oriented, farmers continued to resist both the means and the ends of industrialization. To be sure, some changes had taken place during the long years of effort, agitation, persuasion, and compulsion. In rural education, for example, state compulsion and increased competition from urban systems for trained personnel had forced improved physical standards, expanded curriculum offerings, and higher teacher wages, and had lengthened school terms and raised attendance. This was particularly true in the South, where tremendous efforts were made to defeat illiteracy and bring schools up to modern standards. Also, the Smith-Hughes Act and numerous state measures had forced the introduction of vocational training into some schools, and a combination of force and persuasion had advanced school consolidation a great deal in many areas. And yet the accomplishment seemed minor when compared with the task remaining. Vocational training was still offered only in a handful of schools by poorly trained teachers, and in hard times practical courses were the first to be dropped. By 1920 perhaps 50,000 one-room schools had been absorbed into 10,500 consolidated schools, but 212,000 one-room facilities still functioned.[3] Where means of compulsion did not exist almost no consolidations took place, and even where it was popular consolidation took years to accomplish. Just as the quality of rural institutions lagged, so too did the quality of rural life. Despite high disease rates, for example, only 307 of 2,850 rural counties had full-time public health services in 1926, and these were confined mostly to the South.[4] Despite the great material progress farmers had made during the teens, the 1920 census showed that of 6,201,261 farmers, only ten percent had water in the house and but seven percent had gas or electric light.[5] Thus the minimal comforts that the urban working class rightly considered necessities by 1920 were still unattained luxuries for the vast majority of farm families.

Rural resistance remained the chief obstacle to Country Lifers' attempts to regenerate the countryside. Because they lacked power and their ideas lacked relevance in the countryside, critics' attempts to overcome rural individualism, localism, and conservatism usually failed. Changes came slowly, and what looked like progress was often reversed by hard times or aroused opposition. Even where institutional changes were made renovators faced stiff fights merely to hold their ground.[6] Farmer resistance to social modification had long been a function of rural defensiveness, pride, and conservatism. But in the twenties resistance was increasingly fueled by rural resentment of an urban America which encroached upon the countryside economically, socially, politically, physically, and psychologically, and by a heightened distrust of social engineering. "Farmers nowadays are not frightened by the idea of science in wheat-raising, potato-raising, cotton-production [or] hog-production," contended USDA sociologist Charles Josiah Galpin. "But many of these same farmers just naturally scout the idea of a science of human relationships."[7]

On their parts, many critics of rural society continued to cling to the ends of social and economic efficiency and organization through the means of institutional modification.[8] When confronted with rural resistance they continued to attack farmers as ignorant, reactionary degenerates and to plead for means of compulsion.[9] They had a few new tools of manipulation, like the radio and motion pictures, but their analysis of the situation and their ideas for its modification were not qualitatively different from what they had always been.[10] And yet, by the twenties more critics were openly questioning the old assumptions, the old means, and the old ends of industrialization.

One of the first assumptions to undergo reanalysis was that social reconstruction could and should be carried out without direct reference to economic conditions. Although some continued to believe that social factors constituted the main problems of rural America, the collapse of prices brought home to most critics the fact that institutional modification demanded a sound economic base. "While there is much to commend in the work of those seeking to imp[ro]ve social conditions in rural life . . . ," noted one commentator, "[they] would do well to remember that neither 'sky nor sea is capable of lifting the thoughts or widening the minds' of a people whose year's labor are sold for a price that subjects them to a bare living and harassing debts."[11] This conclusion reflected some Country Lifers' dawning realization of the costs of innovation in a poor and sparsely settled countryside. A few within the Country Life Movement had always believed that money was the prime prerequisite for rural social change, and the few changes which had taken place had forced rural taxes higher and thus contributed to the hardships of the agricultural depression.[12] But until the agricultural collapse confronted them with the financial facts of rural life social scientists had tended to gloss over the monetary cost of social renovation. The agricultural depression convinced them that money was a necessary, if not a sufficient, precondition for change. Because there was little money in the countryside, socially oriented Country Lifers in the twenties began to emphasize that the cities should lend financial aid to the cause of rural renovation. Occasionally, the appeal was made to urban altruism or to the urban sense of social interdependence. More often, Country Lifers appealed to urban fear as they noted that many rural children would live their adult lives in cities. If they grew up ignorant, immoral, degenerate, and unsocialized, the cities would eventually pay the price.[13] It was an index of urbanization, urban-rural conflict, and long-standing antagonism between Country Lifers and farmers that by the twenties the farmer would more often be perceived as a danger to the Republic than he would be seen as its safe foundation.

More important to the reassessment of Country Life ideas was some healthy, basic questioning, particularly among rural sociologists, of the validity, the efficacy, and even the morality of social engineering. This questioning was nurtured by the general postwar reaction to social engineering, but its genesis lay in continuing rural resistance to change and in the general failure of country life reform after a twenty-year campaign.[14] One of the problems the critics saw was the difficulty social engineers had translating theories into actions. As rural sociologist E. C. Lindeman admitted in 1922, "either the principles of rural sociology are hot-house products, too frail to stand transplanting to the rugged soil of an actual rural community, or the rural sociologists have failed to develop means of rendering their principles intelligible and usable."[15] This was, to some extent, true, and it was also true that the critics had expected too much of rural people and had understood too little. Viewing it from an urban perspective, critics saw the countryside as an unsocialized, disorganized, and socially inefficient wilderness, shot through with social and political anarchy and lacking the barest necessities of civilization. And yet by the twenties critics were beginning to see the social complexity of the countryside and the difficulty involved in arbitrarily attempting to make it over. Not only were many proposed changes irrelevant from the rural perspective, they also attacked social practices and groupings firmly anchored in tradition without regard for the desires of country people.[16] For the first time, then, some social scientists looked with disfavor upon the social manipulation of the countryside for the greater national good, particularly when that manipulation was based on incomplete or erroneous information.

In addition to reassessing social engineering, some critics began to wonder if the modifications they proposed would really improve rural life. As the evidence accumulated, it became apparent that institutional change often resulted in products the critics had not expected. This was due in part to the difficulty involved in putting theory into practice. In the field of rural education, for example, country life leaders were hard to find among teachers, vocational courses had a way of becoming irrelevant time fillers for inferior students, and consolidation often produced schools that retained most of the faults and none of the virtues of the one-room facilities they absorbed. Even when the theorists' ideal was approximated the expected ends were seldom realized. Vocational instruction in agriculture and home economics did not serve to keep young people on the farms, and students in consolidated schools did not learn more or learn it better than their counterparts in the ungraded one-room schools.[17] Although they were primarily concerned with rural education, the critics were also aware of their failures in other areas. They recognized, for example, that lessened isolation and an enhanced material standard of living did not necessarily keep people on farms, and in fact tended to whet some rural appetites for city life. They also discovered that the consolidated churches for which they had worked so hard were weaker than the denominational churches they replaced and were more likely to disintegrate or lose membership.

The failure of social engineers to achieve the desired ends through the prescribed means, particularly in education, led them to re-examine those means. Inevitably, this became a part of the larger critique of the morality of social engineering itself. In American society as a whole, reaction to the social engineering of the Progressive period took the form of the "return to normalcy" mentality and a conscious avoidance of reform issues. In the intellectual circles in which many of the social critics of agriculture traveled, the morality of social engineering was seriously debated when it became clear that it had been used during the war to manipulate people in ways, and for ends, which the critics did not approve in retrospect. Moreover, the social sciences were undergoing maturation and thoughtful self-examination in the twenties. Social scientists were increasingly accepting the notion that their role was to describe rather than prescribe, and as they did, social engineering came to seem less legitimate.

In the field of rural education, one of the first canons of social engineering that fell was that the school should prepare the country youth for his future role as a farmer. This idea declined in part, admittedly, because crop surpluses shifted critics to the view that there were too many, rather than too few, farmers. Thus, social engineering in itself was questioned less than was social engineering for one dubious purpose. But it also declined because of a growing perception that attempting to freeze a child into one role or another was immoral.[18] Educators began to ask other questions as well. Most of their doubts had been raised before, particularly by nostalgics like Liberty Hyde Bailey, but in the introspective climate of the twenties skepticism gained enhanced legitimacy. The morality of laws penalizing one-room school districts was questioned by those who said that since rural people wanted one-room schools they should be aided rather than harassed.[19] Some progressive educators began to contend that the one-room school was superior to the consolidated school in educating the individual, and others asked whether consolidation substituted efficiency for warm personal relationships among students and teachers found in ungraded schools.[20] Many Country Lifers remained true to their old beliefs, of course, but the twenties did see a greatly increased degree of sympathy and understanding for farmers among those who had spent the previous two decades attempting to make them over.

Ironically, this decade which saw increased understanding and sympathy for rural people among some critics saw also an accelerated realization of some of the long-term goals of the Country Life Movement. In the case of the rural school, consolidation was greatly advanced when migration from rural areas and a falling rural birthrate conspired against the maintenance of the tiny one-room schools. "Forty years ago . . . I taught a country school of sixty students," noted one commentator on the subject of rural population change. "This district is now combined with six others and has an enrollment of 65 students."[21] Even though the one-room schools got smaller, rural patrons continued to cling to them tenaciously. It was still true, as farm editor E. R. Eastman noted in 1927, that "any move to consolidate . . . schools is met with great opposition on the part of the people even though they have been nearly taxed off of the farms by the local school taxes," but rising costs and falling farm prices made the retention of one-room schools difficult.[22] Moreover, improvements in transportation allayed some rural fears of consolidated schools, and the depression led many farmers to conclude that their children should not, and probably could not, enter agriculture, and thus inclined them to schools which seemed to offer young people more options.[23]

The realization of the Country Lifers' goals for rural education was also facilitated by the accelerating disintegration of the rural neighborhood. Neighborhood unity had been declining for a long time due to both social and economic changes. But the war accelerated old disintegrative forces and introduced new ones. Not only did the war sever neighbor from neighbor politically and socially, it also removed a great many people from the countryside. By furthering mechanization the war lessened neighborhood economic activities and temporarily high price levels spurred the sort of selfish materialism that alienated rural individuals from one another. All of these factors continued to operate unabated in the new decade.[24]

The automobile both symbolized and contributed to the disintegration of rural society. It is difficult for Americans today to understand the rural fascination with the automobile and the car-buying fever that swept the countryside. Already in 1920 30.7 percent of farmers owned automobiles, and despite economic depression the number of cars on farms nearly doubled between 1920 and 1930. More than any other material convenience of the industrial age, the automobile caught the countryman's imagination. In 1930 the farmer was nearly twice as likely to own a car as a phone, four times as likely to have one as to have water in his house, and five times as likely to have a car as to have electric light. It was clear in the twenties that the automobile, which Sidney Glazer contends "influenced rural people more than any other tangible factor," had come to the country to stay.[25]

Country Lifers had long sensed some of the possible implications of the introduction of automobiles in rural society, and they had hoped automobiles would facilitate institutional consolidation and the building of large, centralized communities, while at the same time stimulating economic efficiency. And the automobile, along with the other advances in communication and transportation, also made it easier for urban critics to attempt to shape the countryside. Ease of penetration did not lead automatically to change, but as Samuel P. Hays notes, "The new forms of transportation and communication permitted the forces of modernization to reach into every nook and cranny of American life, to carry the ideals and values of a secular, technical urban society to every segment of the social order."[26]

For rural Americans, the fruits of the automobile age were not all sweet. In the first place, automobile ownership put a tremendous financial burden on rural people in a period of low prices. Cars were probably more efficient and were certainly faster than the horses and mules upon which farmers had depended before, but horses and mules could be bred and fed on the farm while automobiles could not. However, because the automobile rapidly became a necessity for them, farmers were willing to pay the increased costs its ownership entailed. "In 1920, the money invested in automobiles in Lee County was practically four times as much as the capital stock of our banks," complained three University of South Carolina investigators in 1925. "That same year, over one-third of our cotton crop was spent in meeting automobile expenses."[27] Expenditures of this magnitude, coming in a period of economic collapse, undoubtedly impeded rural captial accumulation and further crippled impoverished rural social institutions.

The farmer bore the economic burden of the automobile because it freed him spatially, making accessible towns and cities heretofore unreachable with horses and wagons.[28] And yet this too was a mixed blessing, for it led farm people to reject the neighborhood and also the home as they ranged far and wide for business and pleasure. The rural automobile fever reflected a growing ferment in the countryside and an increasing discontent with being farmers in an urban nation. The enthusiasm among farmers for this century's premier convenience of escape, the automobile, was far greater than their attraction to conveniences of accommodation and even to necessities. As Arthur F. Raper noted of two Georgia counties, though the farm tenant "needs food, clothing, education, medical service; he wants release . . . and for him the automobile provides it."[29] And though the case of farm tenants was perhaps an extreme one, farmers throughout the country made remarkable sacrifices to get and keep automobiles. This fact brought home to observers the likelihood that rural people were much less satisfied with rural life than the Country Lifers thought they should be.

By freeing rural people from the neighborhood, the automobile further damaged local institutions that were already in trouble. The country church, for example, was already suffering from depopulation and increasing secularism and materialism when the automobile struck. But the automobile sped the death of weak churches and started the decline of strong ones by encouraging farmers to joyride on Sundays or attend town services. By the mid-twenties many critics agreed that the country church was effectively doomed. Likewise, the automobile hastened the death of small local trade centers and country stores as farmers availed themselves of new opportunities to buy elsewhere.[30]

The automobile attacked rural isolation and localism, but many rural people also worried about its effect on morals. The mobility afforded by the car opened great opportunities and great dangers, and in the twenties there was more concern about the latter than the former as the farmer's children neglected their duties for the amusements the cities had to offer or used the automobile to escape the restrictive confines of family and neighborhood.[31] Social commentators complained that, whether because of increased communication with outside influences or the natural course of social change, rural morals were undergoing rapid modification. "We have an appalling breaking down of the fine moral stamina in the country districts," complained one educator, and for the first time rural people themselves publicly complained of neighborhood immorality.[32] Moreover, just as improved communications allowed farmers to reach the bad things of the cities, they also allowed the urban evils to reach them. Consequently, the twenties saw a rising concern with the victimization of countrymen by urban thieves, bootleggers, and other newly mobile criminal elements.

Country Lifers interested in rural social life faced the decline of the rural neighborhood and the rural family with some ambivalence. Their prescriptions for country life had always attacked neighborhood localism and, implicitly, the role of the rural family. Consequently, there were those who believed that social disintegration held the seeds of a new and broader social organization and efficiency.[33] And yet, there were indications that more would be lost than gained from social disintegration, and that what existed to take the place of old forms was of dubious value. Remarkably, many Country Lifers began to fear the destruction of the very social institutions and practices they had fought for so long. Rural isolation, individualism, localism, and familiocentrism had long hampered the realization of the ends of the Country Life Movement, yet they also provided a stability that nostalgic critics in particular believed was beneficial to the larger society. In a very real sense, nostalgics like Liberty Hyde Bailey were as doomed as most of the farmers they hoped to change. They had attempted to save the past with the tools of the future, and this was impossible. When rural society finally did change, then, the direction of the change saddened and dismayed them. Consequently, critics interested in the social aspects of rural life began worrying about the demise of the neighborhood, the decline of the family, and what would replace that which was lost.[34]

All of this is not to say that the social institutions and practices of rural society all came crashing down between 1920 and 1930. Indeed, rural people still tried to cling to familiar institutions and ways and were in many cases successful. But the twenties saw no slackening of the war-accelerated actions of social solvents like population changes, materialism, and improved communications and transportation. The old forms of neighborhood life held on, but they lost effective meaning and local people became less reticent about letting them go. For better or worse, the countryside was being integrated socially into the urban nation. In its institutions and practices rural America was becoming a part of the larger social whole. Rural people resisted the social and psychological encroachment of urban America in the twenties in ways that seemed irrational to city people, but with the half-compliance of the countryside itself, the social absorption of rural by urban America continued unabated.[35]

II

Despite continuing social concerns, the agricultural depression over-shadowed virtually every aspect of rural life in the twenties. In the urban centers material prosperity and self-indulgence reigned to the point that the twenties became synonymous with wealth, comfort, security, tranquility, and hedonism. But on America's forgotten farms the twenties meant poverty, loss, struggle, and little else. While most urbanites enjoyed a glamorous decade in glittering cities, farmers battled to hold what little they had in the face of low relative incomes, high taxes, declining values, and oppressive debts.

In order to save themselves from continuing hardship and potential disaster, farmers cast about for solutions to their plight. Potential solutions seldom went beyond attempts to preserve the status quo, namely, to keep farmers on the farms. Debt adjustment plans, loan programs, and even indirect subsidy schemes like McNary-Haugenism were merely attempts to arrest the erosion of the farmer's economic position. But because country-born solutions smacked of class interest, economic unorthodoxy, and federal support, farmers found themselves with few urban allies in the politically conservative twenties.

Of course, there were urbanites who sympathized with the farmer's financial plight, and some even believed that, since the government had helped manipulate the farmer into his unfortunate overproductive position, the government had obligations to him.[36] Others offered sympathy, but little else, worrying that federal aid would diminish rural independence and subsidize the unproductive. "Time alone . . . ," pontificated retired Agriculture Secretary David Houston, "could bring the necessary relief."[37] Still others, much less sympathetic, blamed the farmer for his own problems and accused him of being "a profiteer, an ingrate, a follower after false political gods, [and] a potential Bolshevik."[38] Most striking, however, was the lack of interest in rural economic problems shown by many who had spent the previous two decades attempting to renovate the countryside economically. The twenties saw the reversal of the twenty-year spiral of staple food and fiber prices. Between 1919 and 1929 the price of a bushel of wheat dropped from $2.19 to $1.05, a bushel of potatoes dropped from $2.20 to $1.29; and a bale of cotton costing $176.46 in 1919 cost $85.68 ten years later.[39] More than any other factor, the realization of their cheap food aims led businessmen and bankers in particular to lose interest in agriculture.

To be sure, the farmer appeared to be in a better economic position after the war than he had been before. Between 1910–1915 and 1920–1925 food costs rose 64.7 percent and the total amount farmers received for food rose 41.7 percent. But the total payments the farmer made for the means of production leaped 87.0 percent in the same period and the price he paid for consumer goods sped ahead as well. Consequently, while real income on the farm struggled ahead a mere .8 percent, real wages among factory workers advanced 13.6 percent, giving the latter relatively cheap food and enhancing opportunities to enjoy the material fruits of an advanced industrial society.[40]

Despite the slackening of interest in the economic aspects of agriculture, some Country Lifers in the twenties searched for solutions to the farmer's problems that fell short of direct or indirect federal subsidization. As was the case earlier, urban critics tended to blame agriculture for its own problems and to look to further industrialization as the only acceptable solution. The USDA was particularly active in the twenties, defending its early emphasis on efficiency and contending that only more of the same would save the farmer. It was true that there were ways in which further modification of methods might aid the farmers as a group. If, for example, farmers could emulate industry's attempts to match production to demand, the gains of marketing efficiency might cancel the losses of productive efficiency. But matching production to demand usually meant reducing acreage, a solution that offended cheap-food enthusiasts and struck many of those sympathetic to the farmer's plight as immoral. Perhaps most important, however, bringing production into line with demand contemplated an unprecedented, and nearly impossible, degree of organization and cooperation among the nation's 6,000,000 farmers.

A possible solution to the agricultural depression that was at once more acceptable to Country Lifers and more practical for farmers was cooperative marketing. Hence, the early twenties saw an increased espousal of cooperation by those who continued to see agricultural inefficiency as the root of farm problems.[41] Of course, there continued to be those nostalgic critics who feared that cooperation would fuel class consciousness, undermine rural individualism, and destroy the rural village. But they were answered by those who saw cooperation as a means of controlling farmers politically, stabilizing the agricultural sector economically, and generally insuring "a prosperous and contented agricultural population."[42] The Country Lifers were particularly enthusiastic about cooperation because they believed it would advance the cause of efficiency by promoting crop standardization and advancing the rational distribution of foodstuffs. "The enormous losses and wastes due to unsystematic and unscientific marketing of farm products . . . ," noted Chicago meat-packer Thomas Wilson in a speech calling for cooperative marketing, "affects adversely both the producer and the consumer."[43] Cooperation might aid the farmer, but the critics found it unacceptable if it did not aid urban consumers as well. "The success of cooperation can not rest upon the establishment of artificial control of prices," concluded the prestigious Joint Commission of Agricultural Inquiry in 1922. "It must rely rather upon the association's ability to perform the necessary service more efficiently and with greater advantage both to the producer and the general public than the service is now performed by existing agencies."[44] Hence, urban critics embraced agricultural cooperation in part because it would aid the farmers, but primarily because it would help the urban consumer by furthering agricultural efficiency.

Cooperation was also attractive because farmers were generally familiar with some aspects of it and many of them believed it could be agriculture's salvation. Official sanction and rural inclination thus combined in the early twenties to foster a tremendous expansion in the numbers and membership of cooperative marketing associations. Almost immediately, however, it became apparent that cooperation would not lead automatically to rural prosperity. In the first place, it continued to be difficult to get individualistic farmers to join cooperatives or to stay in once they joined.[45] Organizational problems were exacerbated when conservative pressure forced the USDA to prohibit county agents from directly sponsoring or managing cooperative marketing associations.[46] Moreover, cooperatives often turned out to be expensive and competent management was hard for farmers to find. Most important, members of cooperatives often found that membership did not benefit them financially, and that in some cases the existence of cooperatives aided nonmembers more than members. Cooperative membership was often expensive and overhead was high relative to the savings achieved, and nonmembers were quick to profit by local cooperative crop-holding or market-shifting operations.[47] Successful cooperatives were those which dealt with minor crops in limited geographic areas, and by 1925 it was clear that cooperation would not solve the problems most farmers faced. Between 1924 and 1929 the percentage of farmers selling through cooperatives dropped from 13.9 to 11.0.[48] Cooperatives, if well managed, could achieve some economies, but they could seldom address the farmer's basic problem of overproduction with any degree of effectiveness. By 1926 even the USDA was forced to conclude that "cooperative marketing, despite its demonstrated advantages, has not been sufficient to overcome the unfavorable conditions that have existed since 1920."[49]

Unable to cure the ills of productive efficiency with the prescriptions of distributive efficiency and unwilling to question the general idea of progress, most critics had little to offer farmers in the twenties. Ultimately, all that they could suggest was more efficient production, management, and marketing. That was fine for the man whose farm was primarily a business, who had the intelligence and capital to take advantage of what was offered. But such suggestions were useless to farmers with no special expertise, who saw farming as a way of living first and as a way of making a living only second. There was no place in industrialized agriculture for the average man of no special talents who in an earlier age had found success in the countryside.

There were those farmers who profited during the agricultural depression, particularly the most efficient and scientifically oriented who used economies of scale and method to make money. But the increased efficiency and productivity of the few injured the many, and the survival of most of the parts was no longer insured by the inefficiency of the whole. Some observers even began to admit that increased agricultural productivity had not presented farmers with the benefits some myopic renovators had anticipated. "Increased efficiency in an industry does not necessarily mean increased general prosperity to the people engaged in it. In the case of agriculture it leads to overbalanced production and depression."[50] Farmers readily agreed with this analysis, and many blamed the depression on the federal government, which had monopolized the credit for production increases. This was in a sense ironic, for just as the USDA was undeserving of all the credit it took for increased production so too was it undeserving of all the blame for the collapse. It was as much for the sin of pride as for actual instrumental activities that the

USDA paid in the twenties. Without question, however, it was true that throughout agriculture's "Golden Age" the programs of the USDA had mainly benefited urban people and had aimed at making agriculture an efficient supplement to the industrial nation, the goals and opinions of farmers notwithstanding. As the director of the Ohio Experiment Station admitted, some farmers "have gone so far as to hold the experiment stations responsible *for* the present situation, stating that were it not for the experiment station and the agricultural extension service there would be no agricultural situation, of the present sort at least. This is very likely true."[51] The practical effect of rural hostility was not to turn back the clock, but further to alienate farmers from county agents and their supporters in the local farm bureaus. Many agents attempted to shift their emphasis from production to management or marketing, but their training in production and the federal edict banning cooperative activity by agents usually deflected their good intentions. Their past practices and their continuing emphasis on production eroded the agents' positions among most farmers and hastened their transformation into servants of the county farm bureaus.[52] But the county farm bureaus, because of their close connections with the agents, usually were forced to share with them the onus for agricultural conditions. The legacy of economic collapse, in addition to Farm Bureau Federation cooperative marketing failures, alienated farmers from the organization and led to declining membership. From a high of 466,421 in 1921, membership in the Farm Bureau Federation had dropped to 163,246 by 1933.[53]

Ironically, despite the overproduction of major farm products and the rural realization that overproduction was the principal cause of the agricultural depression, production remained high in the twenties.[54] The farmer recognized that his own productivity was his worst enemy, but since there was no way to limit the output of the agricultural sector as a whole he was reluctant to gamble on limiting his own output. Before the war many farmers could face profitless years and emerge relatively unscathed. But the farmer was much less self-sufficient in the twenties than he had been in the teens. Taxes were higher and more farms were mortgaged, and these fixed payments had somehow to be met. The Census Bureau reported that in 1929 the average farmer paid taxes of $110 per year, and between 1920 and 1930 the percentage of owner-operated farms under mortgage rose from 37.2 to 42.0.[55] Moreover, for the means of producing anything at all the farmer was increasingly dependent upon the expensive accoutrements of modern agriculture which his farm could not supply.[56] Finally, numerous items, like automobiles, that had been luxuries in the teens had become necessities by the twenties, and these had to be paid for and serviced with some kind of income. Thus the farmer's financial situation was rendered particularly acute because prosperous times had altered his material standards and expectations. Many farmers had become captives of their material desires, less able to weather economic adversity than their relatively independent fathers had been. They "demanded the same material comforts which magazines advertised for residents of Indianapolis and Chicago. Their standard of living had increased. Their 'belt' no longer would cinch up as tightly as had [their] parents'."[57]

This increased need for money by decreasingly self-sufficient farmers fueled further production at the very time when disastrous surpluses already plagued agriculture. The logical solution to the problem would have been cooperation and production restriction, but in the face of 6,000,000 highly independent producers the logical answer was not a possible one. Hence, farmers found themselves producing more and more—and thus exacerbating their basic problem—in order to stay in the same relative economic position. Rural sociologists Edward O. Moe and Carl C. Taylor noted the effect of this desperate, depression-born expediency on one Iowa county: "Every effort was made to keep the farms. Every acre had to be cropped intensively. . . . More and more was taken out of the soil, less and less put back. Many farmers believed they were ruining their farms, but thought only about making them produce in order to save them. They argued that it was better to have a run-down farm than none at all."[58] Such scenes were repeated throughout the nation as farmers struggled to survive.

The emphasis on production in the twenties pushed agricultural efficiency forward as narrow profit margins increased the importance of lowering unit costs of production and achieving economies of scale. One popular means of increasing efficiency was through mechanization, and the use of the farm tractor, the most familiar symbol of the agricultural revolution, became widespread. Critics of agriculture had been interested in the tractor and had promoted its use since before World War I, but the imperfections of the machine, its high price, and general rural conservatism had retarded its adoption by farmers. By the early twenties tractors had been improved and prices had been lowered, encouraging progressive farmers to buy them. The tractor gained enhanced importance during the highly competitive decade of the twenties because it allowed farmers to crop more land and to eliminate horses, mules, and hired hands.[59] Between 1920 and 1930, therefore, the number of tractors on American farms jumped from 246,083 to 920,021, most of which were on Northern acres.[60]

The tractor, like the automobile, was not an unmixed blessing for American agriculture, and it represented still another way in which the farm had lost self-sufficiency. The tractor was just one more item which had to be bought with farm profits and which could be supported no other way. The use of tractors by some, moreover, put increased pressure on those who did not have them. Nor could all efficiently use them. The USDA estimated in 1918 that tractors could not be used profitably on farms of less than 130 acres, and yet in 1920 nearly three in five farms were under 100 acres.[61] Smaller and cheaper tractors were developed in the twenties, but many farmers remained unable to utilize them efficiently. The tractor helped increase productivity and heighten competition in the twenties, and though it probably raised the position of some who had it, the economic pressure on those who did not intensified. Those who were not mechanized often made strenuous efforts to mechanize because their economic survival seemed to hinge on it. But the agricultural depression, exacerbated by the mechanization of some, made the mechanization of others particularly difficult. As the editor of the *American Agriculturalist,* E. R. Eastman, put it, "Many a farmer today finds himself in the vicious circle of not having the money with which to purchase new equipment, and by not having the new equipment he is not able to make a profit on his business which will enable him to purchase the equipment."[62] Thus the possession of advanced machinery immediately put one ahead of his fellows, and gave him the potential to leap far ahead. Certainly it allowed and sometimes compelled him to use more land, widening the gap between rural social classes. Between 1925 and 1930 the size of the average farm went from 145.1 acres to 156.9 acres, and some feared that this was only the beginning of farm consolidation and the decline of the small operator.[63] Already in the late twenties the thoroughly mechanized corporate farm of thousands of acres seemed to be the wave of the future as agriculture trod the path of industry.[64]

Not surprisingly, economic depression and tight competition drove thousands from the land. The first to go were the single young people, who were both attracted by the prosperous cities and repelled by agriculture's stark economic future. But the twenties also saw the flight of many families as owners and tenants in their twenties and thirties hurried to get out before they were too old to build new futures. It was a sad truth that farming was rapidly becoming an occupation for the old. Already in 1920 48.1 percent of farmers were forty-five years of age or over, and by 1930 the percentage of farmers in this age group had risen to 52.6.[65] The migration fluctuated but was continuous. The 1930 Census showed that farm population declined in seven of the nine census divisions and that there were nearly 160,000 fewer farms and 1,200,000 fewer people in rural America than there had been in 1920.[66] Half-forced from the only life they knew, rural people poured into the burgeoning cities. Unskilled and ill-trained, the rural migrants often became the new urban mudsills as they vied with immigrants for unskilled positions in the mines, mills, and factories of the industrial nation.

The rural migration had its effect on the countryside as well as on the cities. As young people with children left, the neighborhood institutions of the Golden Age suffocated. One-room schools became harder to justify and maintain, churches dwindled, and the vitality of rural society trickled away. The countryside began to take on the appearance of a place with a past but no future. Not only were the migrants disproportionately young, they were also disproportionately members of the rural middle class. The subsistence farmers weathered the agricultural depression because they did not need the market, and the economies allowed by size preserved the large commercial farmers. It was the farmer who was large enough to need the market but who was too small to produce efficiently who felt the most pressure. Between 1920 and 1930 the number of farms in the United States declined by 159,695. The number of farms between 100 and 174 acres declined by 106,703, while the number between 50 and 174 acres dropped by 206,483. But the number of very small and very large farms increased sharply, indicating that the rural middle class, so dear to the hearts of urban agrarians, was dying.[67] The class structure of rural society was coming to resemble that of industrial society, raising fears that heightened class conflict and diminished rural conservatism would follow.

While the agricultural depression forced some to leave, it brought grinding economic hardship to many who stayed. Low financial returns dictated retrenchment, and the standard of living of many farmers declined. In an effort to hold their farms many men took second jobs, but farm bankruptcy still stalked the countryside. In spite of all their efforts, tens of thousands of producers lost their farms and still tried to cling to the land by becoming tenants. Tenancy rose rapidly throughout the land, illustrating the development of widely separated social classes that accompanied industrialization. Between 1920 and 1930 the percentage of farm operators under tenancy jumped from 38.1 to 42.4.[68] Tenancy, once regarded by many as a temporary rung on the ladder of upward agricultural social mobility, came to be seen in the twenties as a mark of rural failure. The nature of tenancy was often misunderstood, but a 1924 study showing that one of nine tenants had once been an owner supported those who tied the phenomenon to the agricultural depression.[69] Rural women and children joined the men in paying the high price holding the land demanded. Not only did they pay indirectly through retrenchment which affected the quality of rural lives and institutions, they also paid directly because their labor was increasingly demanded in the fields.[70] By 1930 child labor had become almost exclusively a rural problem, with over 70 percent of the employed children in the nation engaged in agriculture.[71] Perhaps no other fact so well illustrates the relative deprivation and desperation of agriculture in the twenties. And yet, whether through fear, hope, sentiment, or semirational choice, millions stayed on the land. Increasing agricultural efficiency, as reflected by high productivity, mechanization, and enlarged individual holdings, threatened the small family farmer and doomed his way of life, yet he clung to the land, praying for the best but fearing the worst.

In the twenties, many urban critics who had earlier lavished much attention on the shortcomings of agriculture showed little interest in the farmer's plight. "There is in American life today a distressing indifference, if not disregard, as to what becomes of our rural civilization," noted rural sociologist Wilson Gee, who added that once agriculture became an efficient economic "subsidiary to the functioning of an urban civilization" outside concern with it receded.[72] Indeed, the economic hardships suffered by farmers indicated to many renovators that the long-term efforts of the Country Life Movement were finally bearing fruit.[73] Moreover, efficiency multiplied itself as intensified competition stimulated even further progress. "The . . . national spasm for standardization, modernization, and efficiency . . . is driving the old-time, bucolic, turkey-in-the-straw style of farmer from the . . . countryside," noted one popular writer in 1926. Instead of a self-sufficient yeoman, the farmer was becoming "a business man, a capitalist, an executive; . . . a cog in a machine well oiled with efficiency."[74] The apparent demise of the independent farmer brought few tears to most economically oriented Country Lifers' eyes, and was indeed seen as inevitable. "The traditional 'independence' of the farmer, in so far as that independence permits him to work without ample capital, without competent direction, without suitable equipment, will be surrendered," claimed farm editor Wheeler McMillan. "That is what has happened in every other industry."[75] And E. R. Eastman added coldly: "We have begun to see the working of the law of survival of the fittest. This law will continue to operate until there will be few left on the farms except those who know how to run a farm in the way it must be managed under modern conditions."[76]

Similarly, few critics of rural economic practice retained their early concerns regarding rural depopulation. There was some concern that those who were leaving might be the best farmers, but the fact of cheap food erased the compulsion to keep people on the land.[77] Now that productive quantity was being achieved, human quantity was no longer necessary. "Our future need is going to be not for an increased proportion of farmers to the rest of the population," concluded Secretary of Agriculture William Jardine in 1927, "but for farmers with greater ability to apply the results of research in the natural sciences of invention, and of economic and sociological analysis, to agriculture and rural life."[78] The American Country Life Association and other socially oriented groups sympathized with the unwilling victims of the agricultural revolution. But many observers of rural economic problems encouraged marginal farmers to leave the countryside for the cities, arguing that this would lessen agricultural competition while helping meet the industrial labor shortage many anticipated would come with immigration restriction.[79] Consequently, USDA policy on the national and local levels shifted from attempting to keep most farmers on the land to encouraging the least efficient to leave.[80] Increased efficiency had made it possible, and even desirable, to remove economically marginal people from the countryside.

III

On the surface, rural life in 1930 looked much like it had in 1920. The social institutions of rural America remained, for the most part, small, local, isolated, and informal, and the material quality of life in the countryside continued to lie far below urban standards. Most farmers still distrusted government and still resisted the canons of economic organization and efficiency, impeding the progress of industrialization. Indeed, the early thirties brought many urban people as well to question the desirability of industrialization when the Great Depression seemed to indicate that the nation was already overindustrialized and overly efficient. Nor had the farmer's self-image changed significantly. He still saw himself as a self-sufficient yeoman, as an individualist in the best sense of the term, and as the firm foundation of the Republic.[81]

And yet the appearance of stasis masked the reality of change. By 1930 most observers perceived the practical irrelevance of the farmer's social and political forms and ideals and the inevitability that his ancient economic practices were doomed. The neighborhood social institutions of rural America dragged on, but materialism, population changes, and changes in communications and transportation rendered them irrelevant even to their own people, and by 1930 their decay was already well advanced. As more and more rural people became dependent upon increased efficiency for survival and as they came to need more of those things they could not obtain on their farms, the government also grew in importance. McNary-Haugenism was just one early indication that, despite their disclaimers, farmers increasingly needed the government. As rural needs increased, moreover, and as agricultural competition heightened, farmers found it increasingly difficult to survive using the old, traditional methods. Many of the Country Lifers had assumed that agriculture as a whole had to be made economically efficient, but the twenties proved them wrong. If even a small minority of farmers became scientific agriculturalists, it put economic pressure on the rest while lowering food costs. Moreover, efficiency became a dynamic process in which innovation fathered competition which fathered further innovation and so on. Agriculture had passed the crucial stage by 1930. Enough development had taken place that the complete ultimate industrialization of agriculture was no longer in doubt. It would be a long process, detoured by shifting government policy and the continuing resistance of many farmers, but the revolution in agriculture was well under way by 1930. Agriculture, and the people who practiced it, would never be the same again.

7

THE PRICE OF PROGRESS

By 1930 the industrialization of agriculture was assured. The twenties saw a continuation of the social and economic trends accelerated by World War I, and a consolidation of the economic gains made during the war. The road to an organized and efficient agricultural sector was marked by turns and detours which reflected the difficulties involved in social and economic modification. A major detour came during the New Deal, when the need to keep farmers out of the depression-ridden cities fostered federal initiatives designed to slow, but not reverse, the course of economic change in agriculture. But the basic commitment among policymakers to an organized and efficient agriculture never changed, and when peacetime urban prosperity returned after World War II the agricultural revolution again intensified. Urban America has been able to enjoy the benefits of agricultural industrialization in the post–World War II years because the foundations of an organized and efficient agriculture were laid between 1900 and 1930.

The industrialization of agriculture resulted from both internal and external developments. Certainly, agriculture became more efficient in part because of internal factors. Surplus products had always been needed to pay for land, equipment, and taxes, so the farmer had always been at least part businessman. In addition, the twentieth century saw a tremendous expansion in the production of consumer goods and, for the first time, a systematic exploitation of the rural market. The result was an explosion of rural wants which rapidly became rural needs that had to

be filled by surplus production. Because of their organizational difficulties and because of the unique market situation presented by the
war, farmers came to believe that increased production was the only
practical way to increase profits. Increased production, in turn, demanded increased investment in the factors of production which had to be
paid for by further production increases. "Rising standards of rural living, increased use of power and mechanical equipment, and vastly more
abundant contact with urban affairs," noted William Jardine in 1929,
"all tend to require that farmers place more emphasis than ever before
upon cash income."[1] Thus, the relatively self-sufficient and independent
yeoman of 1900 had by 1930 become a businessman striving for efficiency, dependent upon suppliers and consumers to fill his needs and wants
and buy the surplus he had to sell to survive.

Developments in the countryside were important factors in the industrialization of agriculture, but they were not the only factors. Partially responsible for industrialization was outside pressure from a larger
society that demanded an organized and efficient agricultural sector to
supplement the emergent industrial nation. The story of American
agriculture in the first thirty years of this century is the story of an urban
attack on rural isolation, individualism, and self-sufficiency which aimed
to make agriculture a socially and economically organized and efficient
part of an increasingly interdependent nation. Though they were
fascinated by the developments of the urban-industrial nation and attracted by the material fruits it produced, rural people resisted the
pressures for industrialization because it was socially and politically irrelevant and economically threatening to them. The ambivalence of rural
people regarding social and economic change reflected their ambivalence
about rural society. The farmer was proud of his independence and his
self-sufficiency, but his life was one of relative social isolation and
economic deprivation. He recognized the tangible advantages change
might bring, but he also perceived that it potentially endangered his way
of life. "The misgiving aroused in the minds of many farmers by the
decline of self-sufficiency and the spread of commercialization and urban
ways . . . amounted to a perception of the social and economic malad-
justment that the modern world was bringing to the countryside," noted
Paul H. Johnstone of the USDA in 1940. "The farmer himself, pushed
one way by the impact of the new and pulled the other by the persistence
of the old, sensed the cultural conflict that was frequently ignored by
professional experts, who were for the most part one-sided enthusiasts."[2]

Due to rural resistance, the attempts of the Country Life Movement
to industrialize agriculture met with little success until World War I.
Then, because of an unnatural market situation and rural patriotism,
many farmers became more receptive to increasing production by expanding acreage and by becoming more efficient. When the farmers were
ready to produce more, the farsighted missionaries of the New
Agriculture were there to help them. Also, the relative scarcity of the

means of production and the expansion of federal power gave the USDA tools with which to command the respect and attention of farmers and with which to forward both the short- and long-term goals of industrialization. Not only did the war see an increase in production, it also enhanced the opportunity of the government to identify and organize those farmers most efficient and most likely to see the advantages of industrialization. Even after the war, when the American Farm Bureau Federation became a semiprivate pressure group, the government retained close ties with it because it was the farm organization most likely to agree with the urban critics that agricultural problems derived from rural inefficiency and demanded industrial solutions. The Farm Bureau Federation gave those farmers most likely to embrace the modern ideals of organization and efficiency a say in the future of agricultural policy, but it also gave urban pressure groups and the federal government a means of dealing with agriculture.[3] The war, then, was the pivotal occurrence in the industrialization of agriculture. It unnaturally speeded the attainment of agricultural efficiency to the point where depression resulted, which in turn decreed that the gains of the war would not be lost. Not only did the depression assure the cities of the cheap food that had been their primary goal all along, it also stimulated the sort of sharp competition in agriculture which assured that it would become still more productive. And finally, the war accelerated those trends which were breaking down rural social institutions, leading to increased realization of Country Lifers' social goals.

The way in which public policy was directed toward the industrialization of agriculture presents an interesting case study of decision making in an industrial society. Seldom in the first thirty years of this century was agricultural change made an issue amenable to decision by the representative branches of government. Industrialization was a bureaucratic exercise undertaken by state and federal agencies with the support of powerful private urban interests. Representative bodies never had the opportunity to draw the broad outlines of agricultural policy. They were allowed, as in the Smith-Lever Act, to have some say regarding the vehicles through which the policy would be carried out, but the policy was made by the bureaucracy. And even in the cases where legislation was needed, that legislation was implemented not by the legislators, but by the bureaucrats who had shaped the policy. The extraordinary power of the professional bureaucracy in modern society should not surprise us. Because it can plan, because it has continuity of personnel, and because it is little affected by the vicissitudes of public opinion, the professional bureaucracy assumes an increasingly important role in an industrial society, where planning and continuity are both possible and necessary. In Robert Wiebe's terms, the bureaucracy can provide order in a society which desires it. Most historians who have studied agriculture in the early part of this century have been concerned primarily with agrarian unrest and the legislative response to that unrest. And yet the most significant decisions in agricultural policy came not from legislators and executives concerned with transitory problems, but from bureaucrats, primarily in the USDA, who never lost sight of their goals of rural social and economic efficiency and organization. Elected officials, and the farmers they represented, sometimes pestered the bureaucracy or put it on the defensive, but they were never able significantly to alter its policies.

The crucial role of the bureaucracy in the agricultural revolution conveys the impression that change resulted from the machinations of a manipulative and undemocratic elite. In a discussion of the development of the organizational society in the twentieth century, Samuel P. Hays touches on this manipulation by noting that "while the agents of science and technology have professed to themselves and to the world at large that they were neutral instruments rather than goal-makers, they, in fact were deeply preoccupied with shaping and ordering the lives of other men. They claimed to speak for, to embody, the values of society as a whole."[4] This characterization fits many in the Country Life Movement, including most of the crucial people in the USDA. But it is also true that the Country Lifers did speak for important segments of the larger society, and that their values were values on the ascendancy in that society. The Country Lifers in and out of the bureaucracy embraced the modern, amoral, industrial values of organization and efficiency, values which were coming to replace the Christian and republican values which had traditionally defined the good man and the good society for Americans in the preindustrial age. In enunciating the new values and attempting to put them into practice, the bureaucracy believed it was expressing the goals of the larger society, and it did enjoy the support of important segments of society. Their belief that they represented society and advanced its goals allowed the bureaucrats to resolve the tension between technocracy and democracy, but their virtue was never as clear as they pretended. Certainly, the bureaucracy did not represent the interests of most farmers, and many of its activities were manipulative of and detrimental to those farmers. In short, the activities of the bureaucracy were aimed at aiding one segment of society and expressing its values without regard to the consequences for another segment. It was, in Hays's terms, representing some men by "shaping and ordering the lives of other men." It is an important normative question whether such behavior by government, even if it does express the will of a majority or has the best interests of that majority at heart, is justifiable in a free society.

So in the industrialization of agriculture the bureaucracy played a key role, acting as an equal and perhaps even as a superior branch of government. In their actions the professional bureaucrats were neither impartial brokers nor inert tools. Indeed, they acted as technocrats would be expected to act. They saw more clearly than most of their contemporaries the long-range trends in the United States, and they pursued policies which would make agriculture conform to those trends. Once on their course they did not waver, and even after World War I when most Country Lifers lost interest in agriculture the bureaucrats retained their fidelity to the means and ends of industrialization without questioning the morality of either.

Of course, Country Lifers in and out of the bureaucracy always contended that their innovations would aid farmers, but despite their pronouncements the industrialization of agriculture had never been promoted primarily for the benefit of agriculture. It had been aimed at helping the cities and the nation by making agriculture an efficient supplement to industry which would supply it with cheap food. For the Country Life Movement as a whole the farmer's primary importance was always as a means to urban ends. Of course, there were farmers who accepted the ascendant values of urban society, farmers who benefited from increased efficiency and organization. But, as Paul H. Johnstone noted in 1940, "the deliberate attempts to improve agriculture and rural life . . . have for the most part concentrated their benefits upon the more prosperous element of the farm population. For only the more prosperous ones have been able to take full advantage of modern technology and commercialism."[5] Indeed, the twenties made it abundantly clear that the main beneficiaries of rural progress would be the cities and the efficient farmers, while the majority of rural people would suffer. The developments of the twenties did, however, force some of the critics of agriculture to finally begin seriously to question the effect of rural change on the farmer and the nation.

One of the first facts to become apparent was that as a business proposition farming was made much more difficult as increasing efficiency was demanded. Often beginning his career as an average man with few special talents, the farmer was increasingly "forced to make adjustments to the demands of the new industrial order, involving progressive mechanization, scientific technique, adequate capital, available credit, and dependable markets."[6] Moreover, even if the farmer did improve his techniques he was not assured of greater profits, for his competitors were improving too and he was producing the sorts of inelastic goods which did not sell proportionally better when supplies went up and prices went down. Perhaps most important, the increasing business demands of successful farming effectively closed it as an occupation readily open to the average man. When the century opened farming was the only major occupation in which the citizen without special skills or large capital could achieve the status of an independent businessman. By 1930 farming had been industrialized to the point where the man entering it without expertise or capital faced a marginal existence at best.

Even more important than the effect of industrialization on farming as a business was its effect on the farm as a home. The American farm had always been a home first and a business second. And yet rural change was moving inevitably in the direction of making the farm a business primarily and a home only secondarily, for economic success was unrelated to the emphasis placed on the home or the breadth of its function. Indeed, economic success even seemed to hasten the decline of familial cohesion and to limit the function of the home as a social and educational institution.[7]

Of equal concern was the effect of industrialization on the individual. Rural individualism had long impeded the drive for efficiency and organization, but some commentators began to ask whether it was not preferable to the sort of interdependence in which the farmer was merely a subsidiary adjunct to an industrial society. For years most Country Lifers had assumed a conjunction between efficiency and morality, yet the question was increasingly asked whether these two things were necessarily related. "There is a flood of literature urging the industrialization of agriculture," noted New York pomologist Ulysses P. Hedrick. "From it one would glean that the object of life is to attain efficiency. Some of the happiest, most worthy, and most influential farmers in the State are dreadfully inefficient. A self-respecting freeman is a more desirable citizen than a slave to industry."[8] And Garet Garrett added that, in all its "emphasis on production," the USDA had completely forgotten that the primary value of agriculture came in "spiritual satisfaction, as a manner of living."[9]

Concern over the effect of industrialization on the farmer was inextricably bound to anxiety regarding its effect on the nation as a whole. Declining rural population and rapid urban growth was particularly disturbing to those who feared for the future of the Republic. Urban agrarians had earlier embraced social and economic efficiency as the best means of holding the farmer on the land, but when the twenties proved that efficiency actually sped the demise of the family farm, it was re-examined. "People tell us that the workman at his bench succumbed to the mechanized shop . . . so the small farmer must succumb to the great farming corporation which will operate on a large scale," lamented one commentator. "When we shall have one millionaire farmer driving a thousand people to produce one crop instead of a thousand families producing a thousand crops, then we shall have suffered an irretrievable loss in our national human assets."[10] The farmer would lose, but the nation would be the main loser. Not surprisingly, some critics contended that the nation would suffer because the cities would no longer be assured of a steady stream of moral people; but others steeped in the agrarian myth began to question the very future of liberty and democracy in a nation of few farmers.[11] The survival of republicanism in a nation where more and more people were dependent upon others and upon the government was uncertain. Liberty and democracy had been erected on an agrarian base composed of independent, self-sufficient people. Some believed that as the ancient base disintegrated, danger to the structure it supported increased.[12]

Questions arose, then, particularly during the Great Depression when the basic desirability of industrialism came under some doubt. But it was generally true that, as always, few Americans were anxious to probe what was defined as "progress." In the first years of this century urban America had delineated an agricultural problem. The problem was that an economically and socially inefficient and disorganized agriculture threatened the development, and perhaps even the survival, of a nation increasingly dominated by industry. Unlike other agricultural problems, this one was not perceived as a problem by farmers but only by those among whom urban-industrial concerns were paramount. Thus, the urban-based Country Life Movement was concerned with the social and economic difficulties an unindustrialized agriculture created for urban-industrial society, identifying them as rural problems despite the fact that farmers did not see them as such. What ensued was the classic urban-rural confrontation, in which the countryside resisted urban-born changes which were largely irrelevant to rural people and which attacked traditional practices and institutions. The process of revolutionizing agriculture was an arduous one, and one which continues even today. And yet a combination of factors rising both from within and without rural society had by 1930 given the nation a highly productive agriculture which could only become more efficient. Throughout the period, remarkably few people outside the farm community questioned the means or ends of industrialization. Agricultural renovation was necessary for national economic and social progress and was therefore good. Thus, though the critics' means changed from persuasion to manipulation and compulsion, they were seldom questioned. Nor was their end of an organized and efficient agriculture examined. Seldom did they ask, until it was too late, what the effect of industrialization might be on the farm family. To the social engineers the farmer was first a producer whose virtue was exactly proportional to his productivity. Only secondarily, if at all, was the farmer a human being with hopes and dreams and ideas of his own. Thus, like so many others in the increasingly dehumanized industrial society, the farmer was a means but not an end. Never did his detractors consider shaping the industrial future to him, but only shaping him to the industrial future. Nor were they willing to probe the effect of change on a rural society that, though inefficient in their eyes, had imparted definition and consistency to people's lives for generations. To the critics, rural institutions were merely anachronisms to be modified in the interest of progress, never traditional structures which might be appropriate and valuable. Likewise, the Country Lifers were unwilling to explore the effect of agricultural industrialization on the nation. They were interested in securing an agricultural population at once socially and economically organized and efficient. But the critics failed to wonder if this end would benefit the nation in any but the material sense. Cheap food might be in the national interest, but was it in the national interest effectively to eliminate the primary path to economic independence and proprietorship open to the average American? And once the self-suffi-

cient agrarian base out of which the nation's political principles had
grown and upon which its political institutions were erected was altered
or diminished, might not the principles and institutions resting thereon
face alteration as well? But these doubts were seldom expressed, and
were never expressed before the agricultural revolution was well under
way. The nation as a whole and the people who wished to renovate
agriculture remained unwilling to consider the possible price of progress.

NOTES

CHAPTER 1

1. Department of Commerce and Labor, Bureau of the Census, *Thirteenth Census of the United States Taken in the Year 1910, Abstract* (Washington: USGPO, 1913), p. 55.
2. Bureau of the Census, *Abstract of the Twelfth Census of the United States, 1900* (Washington: USGPO, 1904), p. 24.
3. United States Department of Commerce, *Abstract of the Fifteenth Census of the United States* (Washington: USGPO, 1933), p. 546; *Twelfth Census,* p. 24.
4. *Twelfth Census,* p. 217.
5. *Fifteenth Census,* p. 501.
6. Ibid.
7. *A Son of the Middle Border* (New York: Grosset and Dunlap, 1917), p. 155.
8. *Ranch on the Laramie* (Boston: Little, Brown, 1973), pp. 26–27.
9. *My Antonia* (Boston: Houghton Mifflin, 1918), p. 365. "We had one neighbor who even went so far as to say that every boy born into a farm family was worth a thousand dollars," N. C. Hagen, *Vikings of the Prairie* (New York: Exposition Press, 1958), p. 106.
10. Charles Josiah Galpin, *Rural Life* (New York: Century, 1918), p. 119.
11. "Letter to the Editor," *Everybody's Magazine* 21, no. 2 (Aug. 1909):288.
12. Garland, *Middle Border,* p. 88.
13. Ruth McIntire, National Child Labor Committee, "Children in Agriculture" (New York: National Child Labor Committee, Pamphlet 284, Feb. 1918), p. 12.
14. Dean Albertson, *Roosevelt's Farmer: Claude R. Wickard in the New Deal* (New York: Columbia University Press, 1961), p. 11.
15. Galpin, *Rural Life,* p. 120.
16. The average farm was worth $3,563 in 1900, and by 1910 its value had risen to $6,444. *Fifteenth Census,* p. 501.
17. "The Farmer's Income," *USDA Farmers' Bulletin 746* (Washington: USGPO, 1916), pp. 5, 7.
18. Dr. Samuel W. Abbott, "The Relation of Agriculture to the Public Health," *Annual Report of the Secretary of the Massachusetts State Board of Agriculture* (Boston: Wright and Potter Printing, 1901), pp. 261–279; Edith Ellicott, "Rural Conditions in Pennsylvania," "Virginia Rural Life Conference," *Alumni Bulletin* (University of Virginia) 4, no. 4 (Aug. 1911):451–454; Isaac Williams Brewer, *Rural Hygiene* (New York: Macmillan, 1911); Thomas D. Wood, "Child Welfare and Rural Schools," *School and Society* 2, no. 43 (Oct. 23, 1915):590–591.
19. Elizabeth Moore, "Maternity and Infant Care in a Rural County in Kansas," United States Department of Labor, Children's Bureau, *Bureau Publication no. 26* (Washington: USGPO, 1917). The Florida farmer is quoted in "Educational Needs of Farm Women," *USDA, Report no. 105,* 1915, p. 41.
20. Carl W. Thompson and G. P. Warber, *Social and Economic Survey of a Rural Township in Southern Minnesota* (Minneapolis: University of Minnesota, 1913), p. 13. See also H. F. Harris, *Health on the Farm* (New York: Sturgis and Walton, 1911).
21. Liberty Hyde Bailey, *The Training of Farmers* (New York: Century, 1909), p. 50.
22. Harvey B. Bashore, *Overcrowding and Defective Housing in the Rural Districts* (New York: John Wiley, 1915), p. 55, and the remarks of Mamie Bunch, *Proceedings of the Twentieth Annual Meeting of the American Association of Farmers' Institute Workers* (East Lansing, Mich.: 1915), p. 85.
23. Allen W. Freeman, "Sanitation on Farms," *Annual Report of the Board of Regents of the Smithsonian Institution Showing the Operations, Expenditures and Condition of the Institution for the Year Ending June 30, 1910* (Washington: USGPO, 1911); Edith E.

Powers, "Rural Health Conditions in Pennsylvania," *Proceedings of the National Conference of Charities and Correction* (Fort Wayne, Ind.: Fort Wayne Printing, 1911), p. 422.

24. L. L. Lumsden, "Rural Sanitation," United States Public Health Service, *Public Health Bulletin no. 94* (Washington: USGPO, 1918), pp. 40–41.

25. M. Taylor Matthews, *Experience-Worlds of Mountain People* (New York: Teachers College, Columbia University, 1937), p. 159.

26. See, for example, James Mickel Williams, *Our Rural Heritage* (New York: Knopf, 1925), who notes: "Neighbors were generous in time of need but, otherwise, each family was centred on its own affairs, and there was more or less rivalry, jealousy, and suspicion between families. This family centredness restrained free relaxation in the social gathering." P. 202.

27. O. Latham Hatcher, *Rural Girls in the City for Work* (Richmond: Garrett and Massie, 1930), p. 51.

28. J. A. Dickey and E. C. Branson, *How Farm Tenants Live, University of North Carolina Extension Bulletin* (Chapel Hill: University of North Carolina Press, 1922), p. 35.

29. Adolph Schock, *In Quest of Free Land* (Assen, Neth.: Royal Vangorcum, 1964), p. 142.

30. Glenn Steele, "Maternity and Infant Care in a Mountain County in Georgia," U.S. Department of Labor Children's Bureau *Publication no. 120* (Washington: USGPO, 1923), p. 7.

31. *Rural Sociology* (New York: Macmillan, 1922), p. 538.

32. Horace Boies Hawthorn, *The Sociology of Rural Life* (New York: Century, 1926), p. 42.

33. Liberty Hyde Bailey, "Moon-Farming," *Independent* 67, no. 3177 (Oct. 21, 1909):909.

34. Ibid. See also Lewis Edwin Theiss, "The Moon and the High Cost of Living," *Outlook* 113 (Aug. 16, 1916):924–928.

35. Department of Church and Country Life of the Board of Home Missions of the Presbyterian Church in the U.S.A., *A Rural Survey in Pennsylvania* (New York: Department of Church and Country Life of the Board of Home Missions of the Presbyterian Church in the U.S.A., n.d.), p. 5.

36. *The Search for Order, 1877–1920* (New York: Hill and Wang, 1967).

37. E. R. Eastman, *These Changing Times: A Story of Farm Progress during the First Quarter of the Twentieth Century* (New York: Macmillan, 1927), p. 8.

38. "The Social Anatomy of an Agricultural Community," *Agricultural Experiment Station of the University of Wisconsin Research Bulletin 34* (May 1915), p. 15; Dwight Sanderson and Warren S. Thompson, "The Social Areas of Otsego County," *Cornell University Agricultural Experiment Station Bulletin 422* (July 1923), p. 11; "Rural Primary Groups: A Study of Agricultural Neighborhoods," *University of Wisconsin Agricultural Experiment Station Research Bulletin 51* (Dec. 1921), p. 16.

39. Albert H. Leake, *The Means and Methods of Agricultural Education* (Boston: Houghton Mifflin, 1915), p. 34.

40. George S. May, "The Rural School Problem," *Palimpsest* 37, no. 1 (Jan. 1956):6; A. C. Monahan, "The Status of Rural Education in the United States," *United States Bureau of Education Bulletin,* no. 515 (1913), pp. 27–30.

41. May, "Rural School Problem," p. 9.

42. Monahan, "Status of Rural Education," p. 9; Fletcher B. Dressler, "Rural Schoolhouses and Grounds," *United States Bureau of Education Bulletin,* no. 585 (1914).

43. *Boy Life on the Prairie* (Boston: Allyn and Bacon, 1926), p. 21.

44. *Ranch on the Laramie,* p. 44.

45. Monahan, "Status of Rural Education," pp. 23, 13.

46. Charles King, "The Rural Church," *Forty-Fifth Annual Report of the Missouri State Board of Agriculture* (Jefferson City: Hugh Stevens Printing, 1913), p. 289.

47. Matthew B. McNutt, "The Vitalizing of the Rural Religious Forces," "Virginia Rural Life Conference," p. 489.

48. Department of Church and Country Life of the Board of Home Missions of the Presbyterian Church in the U.S.A., *A Rural Survey in Indiana* (New York: Department of Church and Country Life of the Board of Home Missions of the Presbyterian Church in the U.S.A., 1912), p. 10; Paul L. Vogt, "A Rural Life Survey of Greene and Clermont Counties, Ohio," *Miami University Bulletin* series 12, no. 11 (July 1914):63–64; Fred C. Ayer and Herman N. Morse, *A Rural Survey of Lane County, Oregon* (Eugene: University of Oregon Extension Division, 1916), p. 40.

49. Kenyon L. Butterfield, *Chapter in Rural Progress* (Chicago: University of Chicago Press, 1908), p. 38.
50. Presbyterian Church in the U.S.A., *A Rural Survey in Pennsylvania,* p. 11.
51. Department of Church and Country Life of the Board of Home Missions of the Presbyterian Church in the U.S.A., *A Rural Survey in Missouri* (New York: Department of Church and Country Life of the Board of Home Missions of the Presbyterian Church in the U.S.A., 1912). These investigators found: "One township has not had a constable for seven years. The constable of another township is 86 years old." P. 21.
52. *Rural Municipalities* (New York: Century, 1930), p. 120.
53. Frank DeWitt Alexander makes this point in *Owners and Tenants of Small Farms in the Life of a Selected Community* (Nashville: Vanderbilt University, 1938), pp. 77-78.
54. William T. Cross, "Rural Social Work," *Proceedings of the National Conference of Social Work at the Forty-Fourth Annual Session held in Pittsburgh, Pennsylvania, June 6-13, 1917* (Chicago: National Conference of Social Work, 1917), p. 641.
55. *Proceedings of the Ninth Conference for Education in the South* (Chattanooga: Executive Committee of the Conference, 1906), p. 114.
56. Hatcher, *Rural Girls,* pp. 28-31; the Department of Church and Country Life of the Board of Home Missions of the Presbyterian Church in the U.S.A., *A Rural Survey in Tennessee* (New York: Department of Church and Country Life of the Board of Home Missions of the Presbyterian Church in the U.S.A., n.d.), p. 18.
57. "Up the Coulee," *Main-Travelled Roads* (New York: New American Library, 1962), p. 89.
58. Remarks of W. S. Chamberlain, *Fifty-Sixth Annual Report of the Ohio State Board of Agriculture* (Cincinnati: C. J. Krehbiel, 1902), p. 508; George S. Reeves, *A Man from South Dakota* (New York: E. P. Dutton, 1950), p. 52.
59. "Neighbour Rosicky," *Obscure Destinies* (New York: Knopf, 1932), p. 59.
60. Remarks of Ernest Hitchcock, *Twenty-Sixth Annual Vermont Agricultural Report* (Burlington: Free Press, 1906), p. 49.
61. Address, *Journal of Proceedings of the Forty-Second Annual Session of the National Grange of the Patrons of Husbandry Washington, D.C. 1908* (Concord, N.H.: Rumford Printing, 1908), p. 11.
62. *One of Ours* (New York: Knopf, 1922), p. 101.
63. T. J. Miller, "Does the Farmer Boy Need a College Education," *Fifty-Sixth Annual Report of the Ohio State Board of Agriculture,* p. 524.
64. Remarks of E. Trumbo, *Fifty-Sixth Annual Report of the Ohio State Board of Agriculture,* p. 502; Charles Simon Barrett, *The Mission, History and Times of the Farmers' Union* (Nashville: Marshall and Bruce, 1909), p. 53.
65. *Industrial Relations: Final Report and Testimony Submitted to Congress by the Commission on Industrial Relations* (Washington: USGPO, 1916), p. 9126.

CHAPTER 2

1. E. Benjamin Andrews, *The Call of the Land* (New York: Orange Judd, 1913), p. 29.
2. "The Country Life Situation," in the *Seventeenth Annual Report of the Pennsylvania Department of Agriculture* (Harrisburg: Harrisburg Publishing, State Printers, 1912), p. 237.
3. Liberty Hyde Bailey, *The Holy Earth* (New York: Scribner's, 1915), p. 131.
4. Kenyon Butterfield, *Chapters in Rural Progress* (Chicago: University of Chicago Press, 1908), p. 69.
5. William R. Lighton, "The Riches of a Rural State," *World's Work* 1, no. 1 (Nov. 1900):99.
6. See, for example, Walter E. Fernald, "The Massachusetts Farm Colony for the Feeble-Minded," *Proceedings of the National Conference of Charities and Corrections* (Boston: George H. Ellis, 1902), p. 489; William Hemstreet, "Agrarian Revival," *Arena* 29, no. 2 (Feb. 1903):142-151; Robert A. Woods, "The All-Summer Boys Camp," *Survey* 27, no. 1 (Oct. 7, 1911):926-927.
7. *Rural Progress,* p. 5.
8. Clarence H. Poe, "Farmer Children Need Farmer Studies," *World's Work* 6, no. 4 (Aug. 1903):3762.

9. John D. Quakenbos, "The New Hampshire Farmer's Opportunity," State of New Hampshire, *Report of the Board of Agriculture* (Manchester: Arthur E. Clarke, 1900), p. 62.

10. *Call of the Land,* p. 232.

11. George M. Twitchell, "Outlook for New England Agriculture," *Fifty-First Annual Report of the Secretary of the Massachusetts State Board of Agriculture* (Boston: Wright and Potter, 1904), p. 86.

12. O. B. Stevens, State of Louisiana, *Annual Report of the Commissioner of Agriculture* (Baton Rouge: Truth Book and Job Office, 1901), p. 47.

13. Seaman A. Knapp, "Causes of Southern Rural Conditions and the Small Farm as an Important Remedy," *Yearbook, USDA, 1908,* p. 318.

14. See, for example, a 1903 article by Thomas Nixon Carver, "Life in the Corn Belt," reprinted in John Phelan, ed., *Readings in Rural Sociology* (New York: Macmillan, 1920), pp. 43-44.

15. George Walter Fiske, *The Challenge of the Country* (New York: Association Press, 1912), p. xi.

16. Robert H. Wiebe, *The Search for Order, 1877-1920* (New York: Hill and Wang, 1967), pp. 111-132.

17. For two good examples see F. W. Blackmar, "Social Degeneration in Towns and Rural Districts," *Proceedings of the National Conference of Charities and Corrections* (Boston: George H. Ellis, 1901), p. 116; Charles Richmond Henderson, "Social Duties in Rural Communities," *Biblical World* 30, no. 3 (Sept. 1907):181-184.

18. Charles Roads, *Rural Christendom, or the Problems of Christianizing Country Communities* (Philadelphia: American Sunday-School Union, 1909), pp. 124, 34.

19. See, for example, Fiske, *Challenge of the Country,* p. 118, and Butterfield, *Rural Progress,* pp. 17-22.

20. Walter G. Beach, "Moral and Social Deficiencies of the Community," in Joseph K. Hart, ed., *Educational Resources of Village and Rural Communities* (New York: Macmillan, 1913), pp. 167-171; Edward J. Ward, *The Social Center* (New York: Appleton, 1913), p. 306.

21. C. W. Larmon, "Putting Men on Farms in New York State," *Charities and the Commons* 20, no. 1 (Apr. 4, 1908):57-60; editorial, "Foreign Farm Communities in Kansas," *Harper's Weekly* 46, no. 2365 (Apr. 19, 1902):513.

22. Lajos Steiner, "Our Recent Immigrants as Farmers," *Review of Reviews* 49, no. 3 (Mar. 1914):342-345. Some American farmers even believed that immigrants were superior agriculturalists. See, for example, E. E. Rockwood, "Renters. Foreigners. Wet Weather," *Hoard's Dairyman* 44, no. 8 (Sept. 20, 1912):206.

23. "The Influence of Immigration on Agricultural Development," in Emory R. Johnson, ed., *Annals of the American Academy of Political and Social Science* (Philadelphia: America Academy of Political and Social Science, Mar. 1909), p. 150.

24. "Country Versus City," *Papers and Proceedings of the Eleventh Annual Meeting of the American Sociological Society* (Chicago: University of Chicago Press, 1917), p. 12.

25. "Immigrant Rural Communities," in Emory R. Johnson, ed., *Annals of the American Academy of Political and Social Science* (Philadelphia: American Academy of Political and Social Science, Mar. 1912), pp. 75, 74.

26. *Principles of Rural Economics* (Boston: Ginn, 1911), pp. 27-28.

27. C. C. Carstens, in "The Rural Community and Prostitution," *Proceedings of the National Conference of Charities and Correction at the Forty-Second Annual Session Held in Baltimore, Maryland May 12-19, 1915* (Chicago: Hildmann Printing, 1915), pp. 267-272.

28. "The Problem of the Rural Community, with Special Reference to the Rural Church," *American Journal of Sociology* 8, no. 6 (May 1903):816.

29. "Folk Depletion as a Cause of Rural Decline," in Newell Leroy Sims, ed., *The Rural Community* (New York: Scribner's, 1920), p. 543.

30. Department of Commerce and Labor, Bureau of the Census, *Thirteenth Census of the United States Taken in the Year 1910, Agriculture,* vol. 5 (Washington: USGPO, 1913), pp. 105, 115. See also Homer C. Price, "Farm Tenancy a Problem in American Agriculture," *Popular Science Monthly* 72, no. 1 (Jan. 1908):40-45; Benjamin H. Hibbard, "Tenancy in the North Central States," *Quarterly Journal of Economics* 25, no. 4 (Aug. 1911):710-729.

31. Walter J. Stein, *California and the Dust Bowl Migration* (Westport, Conn.: Greenwood,

1973), for example, notes that most of the large California growers are technically tenants; and Joseph D. Reid, Jr., "Sharecropping in History and Theory," *Agricultural History* 49, no. 2 (Apr. 1975):426-440, notes that sharecropping status in the South did not necessarily indicate poverty, inefficiency, or transience.

32. Theodore Roosevelt, "The Man Who Works with His Hands," *USDA, Circular no. 24, 1907,* p. 6.

33. "A Campaign for Rural Progress," *Fifty-Third Annual Report of the Secretary of the Massachusetts State Board of Agriculture* (Boston: Wright and Potter, 1906), pp. 140-141.

34. Butterfield, *Rural Progress,* p. 201.

35. *The State and the Farmer* (New York: Macmillan, 1908), p. 61.

36. Ibid., p. 15.

37. Roy Hinman Holmes, "The Passing of the Farmer," *Atlantic Monthly* 110, no. 4 (Oct. 1912):517-523; Walter A. Dyer, "The Case of Kelly and Hannah Belden: Why Our Country Communities Need More Play," *Craftsman* 26, no. 4 (July 1914): 399-405.

38. "The Church and the Rural Community," *American Journal of Sociology* 16, no. 5 (Mar. 1911):677.

39. Nesmith, *Rural Church,* p. 814.

40. William T. Cross, "Rural Social Work," *Proceedings of the National Conference of Social Work at the Forty-Fourth Annual Session Held in Pittsburgh, Pennsylvania June 6-13, 1917* (Chicago: National Conference of Social Work, 1917), pp. 640-641; Ernest R. Groves, *Using the Resources of the Country Church* (New York: Association Press, 1917), p. 28.

41. John M. Gillette, *Constructive Rural Sociology* (New York: Sturgis and Walton, 1916), pp. 365-367; Dell C. Vandercook, "Rural Delinquency," *Rural Manhood* 4, no. 5 (May 1913):151.

42. Butterfield was one of those who realized this early. See Kenyon L. Butterfield, "The Study of Rural Life," *Chautauquan* 32, no. 1 (Oct. 1900):27-28.

43. See, for example, Bailey, *Outlook to Nature,* p. 63.

44. Harold Barger and Hans H. Landsberg, *American Agriculture, 1899-1939: A Study of Output, Employment and Productivity* (New York: National Bureau of Economic Research, 1942), p. 279.

45. *Yearbook, USDA, 1931,* pp. 583, 615, 672-673.

46. Samuel Haber, *Efficiency and Uplift: Scientific Management in the Progressive Era* (Chicago: University of Chicago Press, 1964), p. 51.

47. U.S., Congress, Senate, *Report of the Select Committee on Wages and Prices of Commodities,* 61st Cong., 2d sess., 1910, S. Rept. 912, p. 12.

48. A. P. Austin, "Imports and Exports of Agricultural Produce," in Liberty Hyde Bailey, ed., *Cyclopedia of American Agriculture* (New York: Macmillan, 1910), vol. 4, 18-19.

49. *Yearbook, USDA, 1901,* pp. 798, 804; *Yearbook, USDA, 1911,* pp. 667, 677.

50. *The Work of the Rural School* (New York: Harper, 1913), pp. 2-3.

51. George Herbert Betts and Otis E. Hall, *Better Rural Schools* (Indianapolis: Bobbs-Merrill, 1914), p. 29.

52. Probably the best account of the vague and shadowy, Back-to-the-Land Movement is in Paul K. Conkin, *Tomorrow a New World: The New Deal Community Program* (Ithaca: American Historical Association, 1959).

53. Two good examples of Back-to-the-Landism for the rich are William Henry Bishop, "The Abandoned Farm Found or the Country Home," *Century Magazine* 62, no. 6 (Oct. 1901); and Thomas Dixon, Jr., "From the Horrors of City Life," *World's Work* 4, no. 6 (Oct. 1902):2603-2611.

54. Editorial, "Why 'Back to the Farm'?" *Craftsman* 19, no. 5 (Feb. 1911):523; and Isaac Phillips Roberts, *The Farmstead* (New York: Macmillan, 1911).

55. (New York: Macmillan, 1907), p. 4.

56. Olga Brennecke, "One Acre and Happiness, as Demonstrated by the Littlelanders of San Ysidro Valley," *Craftsman* 22, no. 5 (Aug. 1912):556-558. Editors, "Ford's Plan of Small Farms near Detroit," *Survey* 32, no. 17 (July 25, 1914):425.

57. Edgar J. Hollister, "Getting Back to Our Base of Supplies: What the Revival of Small Farming Would Mean to This Country," *Craftsman* 14, no. 3 (June 1908):267-274; "Can Intensive Farming Be Made Practical and Profitable for the Inexperienced Man from the City," *Craftsman* 14, no. 4 (July 1908):397-403.

58. Lyman Beecher Stowe, "Training City Boys for Country Life," *Outlook* 102 (Nov. 9,

1912):537–541; John Smith, "Back to the Farm," *Collier's* 46, no. 23 (Feb. 25, 1911):34; C. L., "Go Slow," *World's Work* 23, no. 6 (Apr. 1912):716–717.

59. Walter A. Dyer, "Eighty Acres and 'Bondage': A Spiritual Investment," *Craftsman* 23, no. 5 (Feb. 1913):535. The USDA also rushed to pour cold water on overheated Back-to-the-Landers; see W. J. Spillman, "Farming As an Occupation for City-Bred Men," *Yearbook, USDA, 1909,* pp. 239–248.

60. This was the Malthusian version of race suicide, Garland Armor Bricker, "Agriculture in the Public Schools," *Educational Review* 41, no. 4 (Apr. 1911):395–403; see also Eugene Davenport, *Education for Efficiency* (Boston: Heath, 1909), p. 152.

61. For example, Scott Nearing, *Reducing the Cost of Living* (Philadelphia: Jacobs, 1914); see also Frank A. Fetter," A Study of Our Food and Population Problem," *Farmer* 32, no. 18 (May 9, 1914):727–728, 733.

62. *Highways of Progress* (Garden City: Doubleday, Page, 1912), p. 202.

63. J. A. Warren, "Small Farms in the Corn Belt," *USDA Farmers' Bulletin 325, 1908.*

64. Cyril G. Hopkins, "Soil Fertility—the Greatest Necessity and the Best Investment," *Proceedings of the Fortieth Annual Convention of the American Bankers Association Held at Richmond, Virginia, October 12–16, 1914* (New York: American Bankers Association, 1914), pp. 199–210; Paul L. Vogt, "A Rural Survey in Southwestern Ohio," *Miami University Bulletin,* series XI, no. 8 (Apr. 1913):14.

65. "The Agricultural Outlook," *North Dakota Farmer* 10, no. 9 (Mar. 15, 1909):9.

66. C. P. Hartley, "Corn Growing," *USDA Farmers' Bulletin 199, 1904.*

67. L. R. Taft, ed., *Proceedings of the Twentieth Annual Meeting of the American Association of Farmers' Institute Workers* (East Lansing, Mich., 1914), p. 125.

68. Editorial, "Modern Farming," *Hoard's Dairyman* 44, no. 10 (Oct. 4, 1912):266.

69. M. M. Schayer, "Irrigation and the High Cost of Living," *Moody's Magazine* 17, no. 4 (Apr. 1914):195.

70. Grant McConnell, *The Decline of Agrarian Democracy* (Berkeley: University of California Press, 1953), pp. 30–34, 32. For the agricultural extension activities of one railroad see Richard C. Overton, *Burlington West: A Colonization History of the Burlington Railroad* (Cambridge: Harvard University Press, 1941), pp. 486–487.

71. Editorial, "One Billion Bushels," *Financier* 103, no. 1555 (May 16, 1914):1472. For an analysis of the effect of high food prices on business, see U.S. Congress, Senate, *Select Committee on Wages and Prices of Commodities.*

72. "Agricultural Leadership," *Fourteenth Biennial Report of the Kansas State Board of Agriculture* (Topeka: Kansas Department of Agriculture, 1905), p. 5.

73. *Annual Reports, USDA, 1906,* pp. 567–568.

74. *Annual Reports, USDA, 1913,* pp. 20–21.

75. Howard W. Ottoson, Eleanor M. Birch, Philip A. Henderson, and A. H. Anderson, *Land and People in the Northern Great Plains Transition Area* (Lincoln: University of Nebraska Press, 1966), p. 48.

76. "The American Farmer of To-Day," in Robert Marion LaFollette, ed., *The Making of America: Agriculture* (Chicago: De Bower, Chapline, 1907), vol. 5, p. 16.

77. Earley Vernon Wilcox, *Tama Jim* (Boston: Stratford, 1930), p. 33.

78. *Annual Reports, USDA, 1914,* p. 6.

79. *Proceedings of the Twenty-Eighth Annual Convention of the Association of American Agricultural Colleges and Experiment Stations Held at Washington, D.C., November 11–13, 1914* (Montpelier, Vt.: Capital City Press, 1915), p. 22. For Woodrow Wilson's attitude see his Nov. 14, 1916, speech, "Bigger Crops Needed," to the Grange in Ray Stannard Baker and William E. Dodd, eds., *The New Democracy: Presidential Messages, Addresses, and Other Papers of Woodrow Wilson (1913–1917)* (New York: Harper, 1926), vol. 2, pp. 396–399.

80. "Intensive Farming," in LaFollette, ed., *Agriculture,* p. 332.

81. "Fourth Annual Message to Congress," in *The Works of Theodore Roosevelt, State Papers as Governor and President* (New York: Scribner's, 1925), vol. 17, p. 270.

82. Ibid., pp. 270–271.

83. *Proceedings of the Twenty-Fifth Annual Convention of the Association of American Agricultural Colleges and Experiment Stations Held at Columbus, Ohio, November 15–17, 1911* (Montpelier, Vt.: Capital City Press, 1912), p. 88.

84. Woodrow Wilson, "Want to Do for the Farmer," Baker and Dodds, *New Democracy*, p. 369.

85. James Wilson, "The Education of the American Farmer," *Journal of Proceedings and Addresses of the Forty-First Annual Meeting of the National Educational Association Held at Minneapolis, Minnesota, July 7–11, 1902* (Chicago: National Educational Association, 1902), p. 94.

86. See, for example, Theodore Roosevelt, "Conservation the Great Problem," *North Dakota Farmer* 12, no. 5 (Nov. 15, 1910):6–8.

87. U.S., Congress, Senate, Special Message from President Roosevelt, *Report of the United States Country Life Commission*, 1909, S. Doc. 705, pp. 6, 20.

88. Ibid., p. 21.

89. Ibid., pp. 21–22; 30–36; 37–51.

90. Ibid., pp. 15–16; 53–56; 60–63.

91. Ibid., pp. 63–65; 50.

92. Ibid., p. 4.

93. John Chamberlain, *Farewell to Reform: The Rise, Life and Decay of the Progressive Mind in America* (New York: John Day, 1932); Richard Hofstadter, *The Age of Reform, from Bryan to F.D.R.* (New York: Knopf, 1955).

94. William L. Bowers, *The Country Life Movement in America, 1900–1920* (Port Washington, N.Y.: Kennikat, 1974).

95. *The Triumph of Conservatism: A Reinterpretation of American History, 1900–1916* (New York: Free Press, 1963); *The Corporate Ideal in the Liberal State: 1900–1918* (Boston: Beacon, 1968).

96. *Conservation and the Gospel of Efficiency: The Progressive Conservation Movement 1890–1920* (Cambridge: Harvard University Press, 1959); *Businessmen and Reform: A Study of the Progressive Movement* (Cambridge: Harvard University Press, 1962); also Wiebe, *Search for Order*.

97. James Bale Morman, *The Principles of Social Progress* (Rochester, N.Y.: E. Darrow, 1901); Algie M. Simmons, *The American Farmer* (Chicago: Kerr, 1902), p. 157.

98. T. D. Harmon, "What's the Matter with the Pennsylvania Farmer," *Seventeenth Annual Report of the Pennsylvania Department of Agriculture* (Harrisburg: Harrisburg Publishing, State Printers, 1912), p. 234.

99. *The Training of Farmers* (New York: Century, 1909), p. 234.

100. John W. Cook, "The Need of a New Individualism," *Journal of Proceedings and Addresses of the Forty-Third Annual Meeting of the National Educational Association Held at St. Louis in Connection with the Louisiana Purchase Exposition, June 27–July 1, 1904* (Chicago: National Educational Association, 1904), p. 68.

101. Ernest Burnham, *Two Types of Rural Schools* (New York: Teachers College, Columbia University, 1912), p. 121.

102. Cook, "The Need of a New Individualism," p. 68.

103. *Better Rural Schools*, p. 16.

104. George M. Twitchell, "Outlook for New England Agriculture," *Fifty-Third Annual Report . . . Massachusetts State Board of Agriculture*, pp. 97–98; remarks of Bruce R. Payne, "Rural Life Conference," *Alumni Bulletin* (University of Virginia) 4, no. 4 (Aug. 1911):331.

105. Remarks of David Houston, *Annual Reports, USDA, 1913*, p. 21.

106. *Efficiency and Uplift*, p. ix.

107. Skeptics included Bailey, *The State and the Farmer*, pp. 31–32; and Josiah Strong, *The Challenge of the City* (New York: Young People's Missionary Movement, 1907), p. 33, who shrewdly believed that if farmers doubled production there would soon be half as many farmers. See also Ewing Galloway and R. H. Moulton, "The Agricultural Revolution," *Collier's* 51, no. 19 (July 26, 1913):19.

108. Editorial, "The Problems of Country Life," *World's Work* 17, no. 4 (Feb. 1909):11196.

109. "The Social Problems of American Farmers," *American Journal of Sociology* 10, no. 5 (Mar. 1905):613; "The Morrill Act Institutions and the New Epoch," *Proceedings of the Thirty-First Annual Convention of the Association of American Agricultural Colleges and Experiment Stations Held at Washington, D. C., November 14–16, 1917* (Burlington, Vt.: Free Press, 1918), p. 47.

110. Charles McCarthy, "Standardization of Farm Products," *Sixty-Third Annual Report of the Secretary of the Massachusetts State Board of Agriculture* (Boston: Wright and Potter, 1916), p. 39.

111. Warren H. Wilson, *The Church of the Open Country* (New York: Missionary Education Movement of the United States and Canada, 1911), p. 39.

112. Joseph B. Ross, "Agrarian Changes in the Middle West," *Political Science Quarterly* 25, no. 4 (Dec. 1910):625-637.

113. Garland Armor Bricker, ed., *Solving the Country Church Problem* (Cincinnati: Jennings and Graham, 1913), p. 19.

114. Bailey, *The State and the Farmer,* p. 120.

115. Remarks of David Houston, *Annual Reports, USDA, 1914,* p. 46.

116. Butterfield, "The Social Problems of American Farmers," p. 611.

CHAPTER 3

1. Sir Horace Plunkett, *The Rural Life Problem of the United States* (New York: Macmillan, 1910), p. 86.

2. Kenyon L. Butterfield, *The Country Church and the Rural Problem* (Chicago: University of Chicago Press, 1911), p. 35.

3. Remarks of J. M. Hamilton, *Proceedings of the Twenty-Seventh Annual Convention of the Association of American Agricultural Colleges and Experiment Stations* (Montpelier, Vt.: Capital City Press, 1914), p. 170.

4. "Agricultural Schools," *Agriculture of Vermont: Second Annual Report of the Commissioner of Agriculture* (Montpelier, Vt.: Capital City Press, 1910), p. 169.

5. George Herbert Betts and Otis E. Hall, *Better Rural Schools* (Indianapolis: Bobbs-Merrill, 1914), p. 9; Frederick K. Noyes, abstracter, "Current Educational Topics," *United States Bureau of Education Bulletin* 16, no. 487 (1912):18.

6. A. C. Monahan, "The Status of Rural Education in the United States," *United States Bureau of Education Bulletin,* no. 515 (1913), p. 9.

7. Ibid., p. 53. For a typical set of complaints from county superintendents regarding the difficulties of the job see the *Seventh Report of the Superintendent of Public Instruction of the State of Utah for the Biennial Period Ending June 30, 1908* (Salt Lake City: State of Utah, 1908), pp. 297-394; see also the remarks of State Superintendent Henry C. Morrison in the *Report of the Superintendent of Public Instruction Being the Fifty-Eighth Report upon the Public Schools of New Hampshire* (Concord: Ira C. Evans, 1914), p. 134; Harold Waldstein Foght, "The Country School," *Annals of the American Academy of Political and Social Science* (Philadelphia: American Academy of Political and Social Science, Mar. 1912), p. 153.

8. Plunkett, *Rural Life Problem,* p. 132; remarks of William Carter Stubbs, *Report of the United States Industrial Commission on Agriculture,* 1901, p. 779; Liberty Hyde Bailey, *The State and the Farmer* (New York: Macmillan, 1908), p. 138; Liberty Hyde Bailey, *The Training of Farmers* (New York: Century, 1909), p. 138; G. W. Conn, "A Federation of Rural Forces," *Charities and the Commons* 17, no. 5 (Nov. 3, 1906):248.

9. J. B. Sears, "The Problem for the Rural Schools," *Popular Science Monthly* 86, no. 8 (Feb. 1915):177-178.

10. Irving King, *Education for Social Efficiency* (New York: Appleton, 1913), p. 32; A. F. Woods, "Agricultural Education and Its Relation to Rural Sociology," *Papers and Proceedings of the Sixth Annual Meeting of the American Sociological Society* (Chicago: University of Chicago Press, Aug. 1912), p. 82.

11. George Herbert Betts, *New Ideals in Rural Schools* (Boston: Houghton Mifflin, 1913), p. 2.

12. Kenyon L. Butterfield, *Chapters in Rural Progress* (Chicago: University of Chicago, 1908), p. 122; see also Eugene Davenport, "The Next Step in Agricultural Education; or, the Place of Agriculture in Our American System of Education," (Urbana, Ill.: Oct. 31, 1907 address at Illinois College at Jacksonville, published by Missouri University at Columbia, Jan. 9, 1908). In "The Common School and the Ideal Citizen: Iowa, 1876-1921" (Ph.D. diss., University of Iowa, 1969), Carroll Lee Engelhardt delineates the manipulative, social control aims of new, "progressive" courses and methods of instruction.

13. A. C. True, "Some Problems of the Rural Common School," *Yearbook, USDA, 1901,* pp. 134–135; J. D. Eggleston, "Educating the Producer," *Proceedings of the Fortieth Annual Convention of the American Bankers Association Held at Richmond, Virginia October 12 to 16, 1914,* p. 210.

14. Foght, "The Country School," *American Academy of Political and Social Science,* p. 157; Ellwood P. Cubberley, *Rural Life and Education* (Boston: Houghton Mifflin, 1914), pp. 105–106.

15. See, for example, the remarks of Cornell Professor George Warren in the *Journal of Proceedings and Addresses of the Forty-Eighth Annual Meeting of the National Education Association of the United States Held at Boston, Massachusetts, July 2–8, 1910* (Chicago: National Education Association, 1910), p. 1097.

16. Liberty Hyde Bailey, *The Nature-Study Idea* (New York: Doubleday, Page, 1904); Alfred Charles True, *A History of Agricultural Education in the United States, 1785-1925* (Washington: USGPO, 1929), p. 275.

17. Butterfield, *Chapters in Rural Progress,* p. 124; remarks of Liberty Hyde Bailey in the *Fourteenth Annual Report of the Cornell University Agricultural Experiment Station* (Albany: J. B. Lyon, State Printers, 1902), p. 221; Sidney Morse, "The Boy on the Farm: and Life as He Sees It," *Craftsman* 16, no. 2 (May 1909):195–200.

18. S. A. Hoover, "Nature Study in the Public Schools," *Thirty-Fourth Annual Report of the Missouri State Board of Agriculture* (Jefferson City: Tribune Printing, 1902), pp. 244–245; Liberty Hyde Bailey, *The Outlook to Nature* (New York: Macmillan, 1911), p. 133.

19. For example, Eugene Davenport, *Education for Efficiency* (Boston: Heath, 1909).

20. Frederick T. Gates, "The Country School of To-Morrow," *World's Work* 24, no. 4 (Aug. 1912):464; Gates was the chairman of the General Education Board, a Rockefeller creation at the forefront of country life reform; see also the *Annual Report of the State Board of Education and of the Commissioner of Education of New Jersey for the School Year Ending June 30, 1913* (Paterson: New Printing, State Printers, 1913), p. 168.

21. Remarks of Secretary Wilson, *Annual Reports, USDA, 1904,* p. xcviii.

22. Remarks of State Superintendent E. D. Cameron in the *Third Biennial Report, Department of Public Instruction of Oklahoma 1908-1910* (Guthrie: Leader Print, 1910), pp. 31–32; John M. Gillette, *Constructive Rural Sociology* (New York: Sturgis and Walton, 1916), p. 335.

23. Editorial, "Agriculture in the Common Schools," *Independent* 63, no. 3081 (Dec. 19, 1907):1508–1509; Davenport, "The Next Step in Agricultural Education," p. 1.

24. T. A. Erickson with Anna North Coit, *My Sixty Years with Rural Youth* (Minneapolis: University of Minnesota Press, 1956), pp. 87–89, 156–157; O. B. Martin, "Boys' and Girls' Club Work," and Susie V. Powell, "Industrial Clubs and the Rural School," *Alumni Bulletin* (University of Virginia) 9, no. 4 (Aug. 1911):394, 475–478.

25. Remarks of Nebraska State Superintendent William K. Fowler, *Journal of Proceedings and Addresses of the Forty-Second Annual Meeting of the National Educational Association Held at Boston, Massachusetts, July 6–10, 1903* (Chicago: National Educational Association, 1903), p. 922; remarks of State Superintendent C. G. Schultz, *Sixteenth Biennial Report of the Superintendent of Public Instruction for the School Years 1909 and 1910 in the State of Minnesota* (Minneapolis: Syndicate Printing, 1910), p. 10.

26. J. C. Brockert, "Consolidated Country School," *Second Wisconsin Country Life Conference* (Madison: College of Agriculture, Feb. 1912); Fred C. Ayer and Herman N. Morse, *A Rural Survey of Lane County, Oregon* (Eugene: University of Oregon Extension Division, 1916), p. 82; Frank Nelson, "The Consolidation of Country Schools: The Plan and Its Merits," *Review of Reviews* 26, no. 6 (Dec. 1902):705.

27. Lawrence S. Hill, "Physical Education in the Rural Schools," in John Phelan, ed., *Readings in Rural Sociology* (New York: Macmillan, 1920), pp. 229–233; Betts and Hall, *Better Rural Schools,* p. 429; and Gillette, *Constructive Rural Sociology,* p. 337.

28. Laura H. Wild, "Efficiency and the Rural School," *Survey* 30, no. 16 (July 19, 1913):527–528; Eggleston and Bruère, *Rural School,* pp. 176–177.

29. Herbert Quick, "The Awakening in the Rural Districts," *LaFollette's Weekly Magazine* 3, no. 46 (Nov. 18, 1911):7.

30. Mason S. Stone, "Educational Readjustment of Country Life," in Henry Israel, ed., *The Country Church and Community Cooperation* (New York: Association Press, 1913), p. 54. Many people were interested in making the rural schools instruments of strict social

control. A few examples are Taliaferro Clark, "The School as a Factor in the Mental Hygiene of Rural Communities," *Proceedings of the National Conference of Charities and Correction at the Forty-Third Annual Session Held in Indianapolis, Indiana May 10-17, 1916* (Chicago: Hildmann Printing, 1916), p. 223; A. E. Pickard, *Rural Education* (St. Paul: Webb, 1915), p. 22; editorial, "Regenerating the Country School," *Nation* 88, no. 2281 (Mar. 18, 1909), 271-272.

31. Harold Waldstein Foght, *The American Rural School* (New York: Macmillan, 1910), p. 240. See also Joseph Woodbury Strout, "The Rural Opportunity and the Country School," *Popular Science Monthly* 86, no. 8 (Feb. 1914), 176-183; Mabel Carney, *Country Life and the Country School* (Chicago: Row, Peterson, 1912), p. 206.

32. Booker T. Washington, "Educational Engineers," *Outlook* 95 (June 4, 1910):267; remarks of Minnesota State Superintendent J. W. Olsen, *Journal of Proceedings and Addresses of the Forty-Fifth Annual Meeting of the National Education Association Held at Los Angeles, California, July 8-12, 1907* (Chicago: National Education Association, 1907), p. 267; see also Kenyon L. Butterfield, "The Leadership of the Agricultural College," *Independent* 65, no. 3115 (Aug. 13, 1908):368-370.

33. C. H. Forbes-Lindsey, "The Rural Settlement: Its Social, Economic, and Aesthetic Advantages," *Craftsman* 14, no. 4 (July 1908):413; and the *Twenty-Third Biennial Report of the State Superintendent of Public Instruction of the State of Indiana for the School Years Ending July 31, 1905 and July 31, 1906* (Indianapolis: William B. Burford, State Printer, 1906) are good examples of the critics' optimism. See also Kenyon L. Butterfield, "Neighborhood Coöperation in School Life—the 'Hesperia Movement,'" *Review of Reviews* 23, no. 4 (Apr. 1901):443-446.

34. Charles Otis Gill and Gifford Pinchot, *The Country Church* (New York: Macmillan, 1913), p. vii; R. O. Brandt, "The Clergyman and Community Progress," *Second Wisconsin Country Life Conference,* p. 28; introductory remarks of Bruce R. Payne, "Rural Life Conference," *Alumni Bulletin* (University of Virginia) 4, no. 4 (Aug. 1911):332; U.S., Congress, Senate, *Report of United States Country Life Commission,* pp. 8, 60.

35. Charles Otis Gill, "The Ohio Country Church Survey," *Fifty-First Annual Report of the Missouri State Board of Agriculture* (Jefferson City: Missouri State Board of Agriculture, 1919), p. 122.

36. George Walter Fiske, *The Challenge of the Country* (New York: Association Press, 1912), p. 14.

37. Charles King, "The Rural Church," *Forty-Fifth Annual Report of the Missouri State Board of Agriculture* (Jefferson City: Hugh Stevens Printing, 1913), p. 290; see also Charles Roads, *Rural Christendom, or the Problems of Christianizing Country Communities* (Philadelphia: American Sunday-School Union, 1909), p. 41.

38. Bailey, *The State and the Farmer,* p. 132; see also Department of Church and Country Life of the Board of Home Missions of the Presbyterian Church in the U.S.A., *A Rural Survey in Indiana* (New York: Department of Church and Country Life of the Board of Home Missions of the Presbyterian Church in the U.S.A., 1912), pp. 12-16; William A. McKeever, *Farm Boys and Girls* (New York: Macmillan, 1912), p. 94. Joseph Woodbury Strout, "The Rural Problem and the Country Minister," *Atlantic Monthly* 110, no. 3 (Sept. 1912):359; Paul L. Vogt, "A Rural Life Survey of Greene and Clermont Counties, Ohio," *Miami University Bulletin,* series 12, no. 11 (July 1914):72.

39. Gill and Pinchot, *Country Church,* pp. 42-43.

40. Washington Gladden, "Empty Pews in the Country Church—Why?" *Everybody's Magazine* 34, no. 5 (May 1916):614-615.

41. D.C.C.L.B.H.M. Presbyterian Church U.S.A., *A Rural Survey in Indiana,* p. 63.

42. Fiske, *The Challenge of the Country,* p. 124.

43. Martha Bensley Bruère and Robert U. Bruère, "A New Day for the Country Church," *Outlook* 110 (June 23, 1915):465; Harry Deiman, "The Institutional Church for the Rural Community," *Survey* 30, no. 8 (May 24, 1913):281. Woodrow Wilson also favored a greatly expanded role for the rural church. See his "A New Kind of Church Life," an address before the Federal Council of Churches at Columbus, Ohio, on Dec. 10, 1915, quoted in Ray Stannard Baker and William E. Dodd, eds., *The New Democracy: Presidential Messages, Addresses, and Other Papers of Woodrow Wilson, 1913-1917* (New York: Harper, 1926), 1:429-438.

44. J. O. Ashenhurst, *The Day of the Country Church* (New York: Funk and Wagnalls,

1910), p. 51; see also D.C.C.L.B.H.M. Presbyterian Church U.S.A., *A Rural Survey in Pennsylvania,* p. 25.

45. Joseph Heyde, "The Country Church and Community Life," *Second Wisconsin Country Life Conference,* p. 26; Warren H. Wilson, *The Evolution of the Country Community* (Boston: Pilgrim Press, 1912), pp. xiii, 189–193; Butterfield, *The Country Church and the Rural Problem,* pp. 84–85.

46. Warren H. Wilson, *The Church of the Open Country* (New York: Missionary Education Movement of the United States and Canada, 1911), pp. 91, 194; U.S., Congress, Senate, *United States Country Life Commission Report,* pp. 60–62.

47. Warren H. Wilson, "The Church and the Rural Community," *Papers and Proceedings of the Fifth Annual Meeting of the American Sociological Society* (Chicago: University of Chicago Press, Aug. 1911), p. 174; Otis Moore, "The Spiritual Evangelization of the Rural Community through Its Church," in Garland Armor Bricker, *Solving the Country Church Problem* (Cincinnati: Jennings and Graham, 1913), p. 183; Thomas Nixon Carver, *Principles of Rural Economics* (Boston: Ginn, 1911), pp. 345–46; Cubberley, *Rural Life and Education,* pp. 80–81.

48. G. Walter Fiske, "Rural Interest in the Bible," *Biblical World* 45, no. 5 (May 1915):282–288; editorial, "The Commission and Rural Religion," *Independent* 66, no. 3151 (Apr. 22, 1909):871–872; Wilson, *The Evolution of the Country Community,* pp. 53–54; D.C.C.L.B.H.M. Presbyterian Church U.S.A., *A Rural Survey in Pennsylvania,* p. 33. One enthusiast even recommended that rural ministers push the idea that "Experiment Station Bulletins are one of the modern forms of inspiration; revelations of the Divine Will in Nature." Editorial, "The Country Life Commission and the Church," *Independent* 67, no. 3169 (Aug. 26, 1909):490.

49. Henry C. Adams, "Higher Education and the People," in "Social Problems of the Farmer," *Publications of the Michigan Political Science Association* (Ann Arbor: Michigan Political Science Association, July 1902) 4, no. 6:22.

50. Butterfield, *Chapters in Rural Progress,* p. 177; see also Adams, "Higher Education," p. 22.

51. Edwin L. Earp, "A Suggested Home Missions Policy," *Rural Manhood* 5, no. 2 (Feb. 1914):49–50; John R. Boardman, "The Association and the Country Community," *Rural Manhood* 1, no. 1 (Jan. 1910):23; Henry Israel, "A Coordinating Factor," in *The Country Church and Community Cooperation,* p. 50; B. R. Ryall, "The Work of the Country Y.M.C.A. in Building Rural Manhood," in Bricker, *Solving the Country Church Problem,* p. 266.

52. Henry S. Curtis, "The Rural Church as a Social Center," *Education,* 34, no. 2 (Oct. 1913):115; Edmund deSchweinitz Brunner, *The New Country Church Building* (New York: Missionary Education Movement of the United States and Canada, 1917).

53. Cubberley, *Rural Life and Education,* p. 120; Wilson, *The Evolution of the Country Community,* p. 205. For neighborhood beautification, improvement, and pageant movements see Renée B. Stern, *Neighborhood Entertainments* (New York: Sturgis and Walton, 1911), and Charles Shepherd Phelps, *Rural Life in Litchfield County* (Norfolk, Conn.: Litchfield County University Club, 1917), p. 121. Support for the library movement can be seen in J. C. Metcalf, "A Plea for a State Library Commission," "Virginia Rural Life Conference," pp. 426–433. For rural recreation see Myron T. Scudder, "Rural Recreation, a Socializing Factor," *Annals of the American Academy of Political and Social Science* (Philadelphia: American Academy of Political and Social Science, Mar. 1912); Henry S. Curtis, *Play and Recreation for the Open Country* (Boston: Ginn, 1914), pp. 130–131; Myron T. Scudder, "Play Days for Country Schools," *Outlook* 92 (Aug. 28, 1909):1031–1038; Anna B. Taft, *Community Study for Country Districts* (New York: Missionary Education Movement of the United States and Canada, 1912), p. 69. For the rural drama movement see Alfred G. Arvold, "Drama for Rural Communities," *Review of Reviews* 54, no. 3 (Sept. 1916):309; George Creel, "The Little Country Theatre," *Collier's* 53, no. 7 (May 2, 1914):22.

54. Editorial, "The Farmer and the Future," *World's Work* 15, no. 4 (Feb. 1908): 9847; Clarence H. Matson, "Improved Conditions in the American Farmer's Life," *Review of Reviews* 26, no. 3, (Sept. 1902):329; Fiske, *The Challenge of the Country,* p. 24; Albert H. Leake, *The Means and Methods of Agricultural Education* (Boston, Houghton Mifflin, 1915), p. 23.

55. Editorial, "The Country Home to Woman," *Independent* 54, (May 22, 1902):2790;

Sylvester Baxter, "The Renascence of the Country Home," *Outlook* 85, no. 10 (Mar. 9, 1907):551-556; Gillette, *Constructive Rural Sociology*, p. 257.

56. Author Unknown, "Domestic Needs of Farm Women," *USDA, Report no. 104, 1915*, pp. 9-15; W. C. Funk, "Farm Household Accounts, *USDA, Farmers' Bulletin 964, 1918;* Helen Dodd, *The Healthful Farmhouse* (Boston: Whitcomb and Barrows, 1906); C. H. Hanson, "A Successful Rural Cooperative Laundry," *Yearbook, USDA, 1915*, pp. 189-194.

57. Marie T. Harvey, "Woman's Relation to the Farm Problem," "Virginia Rural Life Conference," p. 469; Martha Foote Crow, *The American Country Girl* (New York: Frederick A. Stokes, 1915).

58. Editorial, "Evolution in Country Life," *Independent* 52, no. 2693 (July 12, 1900):1688-1689; editorial, "The Farmer and the Telephone," *Independent* 54, no. 2780 (Mar. 31, 1902):648-649; Hugh S. Fullerton, "Bringing the Market Nearer," *Collier's* 43, no. 4 (Apr. 17, 1909):20; Reynold M. Wik, *Henry Ford and Grass-roots America* (Ann Arbor: University of Michigan Press, 1972), p. 24; F. L. Mulford, "Beautifying the Farmstead," *USDA Farmers' Bulletin 1087*.

59. Roy Hinman Holmes, "The Passing of the Farmer," *Atlantic Monthly* 110, no. 4 (Oct. 1912):523; editorial, "Country Life Problems," *Nation* 89, no. 2316 (Nov. 18, 1909), 479-480.

60. Remarks of Henry Wallace, *Tenth Annual Iowa Yearbook of Agriculture* (Des Moines: Iowa Department of Agriculture, 1909), p. 110; Author Unknown, "Better Days Coming," *Iron Trade Review* 54, no. 15 (Apr. 9, 1914):650; Plunkett, *Rural Problems*, p. 126; remarks of Commissioner W. C. Gilbreath, *Biennial Report of the Commissioner of Agriculture and Labor of North Dakota* (Bismarck: Tribune, State Printers, 1906), p. 5; Edward J. Ward, *The Social Center* (New York: Appleton, 1913), p. 306; Kenyon L. Butterfield, "Social Problems of American Farmers," *American Journal of Sociology* 10, no. 5 (Mar. 1905):610.

61. Henderson, "Social Duties in Rural Communities," p. 184; Charles S. Phelps, *Rural Life in Litchfield County*, p. 122; L. O. Howard, "How Insects Affect Health in Rural Districts," *USDA Farmers' Bulletin 155*, pp. 5-6; editorial, "Health in Country Life," *Independent* 68, no. 3208 (May 26, 1910):1146-1148.

62. Allen W. Freeman, "Sanitation on Farms," *Annual Report of the Board of Regents of the Smithsonian Institution Showing the Operations, Expenditures, and Condition of the Institution for the Year Ending June 30, 1910* (Washington: USGPO, 1911), p. 652.

63. Remarks of Secretary Houston, *Annual Reports, USDA, 1918*, p. 54; C. W. Stiles and L. L. Lumsden, "The Sanitary Privy," *USDA Farmers' Bulletin 463*.

64. Dell C. Vandercook, "Rural Delinquency," *Rural Manhood* 4, no. 5 (May 1913): 150-152; L. H. Weir, "A Probation Officer in Rural Communities," *Rural Manhood* 1, no. 7 (Aug. 1910):10-12; C. C. Carstens, "The Rural Community and Prostitution," *Proceedings of the National Conference of Charities and Correction at the Forty-Second Annual Session Held in Baltimore, Maryland May 12-19, 1915* (Chicago: Hildmann Printing, 1915), pp. 267-272; D.C.C.L.B.H.M. Presbyterian Church U.S.A., *A Rural Survey in Missouri*, p. 21; Gillette, *Constructive Rural Sociology*, p. 364; F. W. Blackmar, "Social Degeneration in Towns and Rural Districts," *Proceedings of the National Conference of Charities and Corrections* (Boston: Ellis, 1901), p. 116.

65. "The Social Anatomy of an Agricultural Community," *Agricultural Experiment Station of the University of Wisconsin Research Bulletin 34*, May 1915, p. 15; see also G. T. Nesmith, "The Problem of the Rural Community, with Special Reference to the Rural Church," *American Journal of Sociology* 8, no. 6 (May 1903):815; Paul L. Vogt, "A Rural Survey in Southwestern Ohio," *Miami University Bulletin*, series XI, no. 8 (Apr. 1913):29.

66. Liberty Hyde Bailey, *The Country-Life Movement in the United States* (New York: Macmillan, 1911), p. 108; *The Training of Farmers* (New York: Century, 1909), pp. 26, 65-68.

67. Bailey, *The State and the Farmer*, pp. 63-64; Matthew B. McNutt, "Modern Methods in the Country Church," "Virginia Rural Life Conference," p. 504.

68. H. L. Russell, "Some Factors That Make for Better Rural Living," *Rural Social Development: Being the Third Annual Report of the Wisconsin Country Life Conference, Bulletin of the University of Wisconsin*, serial no. 591, general series no. 413 (Madison: College of Agriculture, Jan. 1913), p. 14; Curtis, *Play and Recreation for the*

Open Country, p. xv; Warren H. Wilson, *The Evolution of the Country Community* (Boston: Pilgrim Press, 1912), p. 127; Walter A. Dyer, "The Case of Kelly and Hannah Belden: Why Our Communities Need More Play," *Craftsman* 26, no. 4 (July 1914):405.

69. Liberty Hyde Bailey, *Outlook to Nature* (New York: Macmillan, 1911), p. 72; *The Holy Earth* (New York: Scribner's, 1915), p. 54.

70. Russell Lord, *The Agrarian Revival* (New York: American Association for Adult Education, 1939), p. 46; Phelps, *Rural Life in Litchfield County,* pp. 119–120; Bailey, *Outlook to Nature,* pp. 88–89.

71. E. A. Rumeley, "The Passing of the Man with the Hoe," *World's Work* 20, no. 4 (Aug. 1910):13246–13258.

72. A few of those who noted possible consequences were Joseph B. Ross, "The Agrarian Revolution in the Middle West," *North American* 190, no. 646 (Sept. 1909):390; Don D. Lescohier, "Work Accidents and the Farm Hand," *Survey* 27, no. 1 (Oct. 7, 1911):946; E. H. Thomson and H. M. Dixon, "A Farm-Management Survey of Three Representative Areas in Indiana, Illinois, and Iowa," *USDA Bulletin 41,* p. 42.

73. Charles McCarthy, "The Cost of Living and the Remedy," *National Agricultural Organization Society Circular no. 7* (Madison, Wis.: National Agricultural Organization Society, 1916), p. 6.

74. Office of Public Roads, "Benefits of Improved Roads," *USDA Farmers' Bulletin 505,* p. 12; remarks of Secretary Houston, *Annual Reports, USDA, 1914,* p. 30; U.S., Congress, Senate, *United States Country Life Commission Report,* p. 38.

75. Lyman Beecher Stowe, "Training City Boys for Country Life," *Outlook* 102 (Nov. 9, 1912):588. See also A. W. Douglas, "The State University and the State Agricultural College," *Nation's Business* 2, no. 5 (May 15, 1914):11; Walter H. Main, "The Weak Point in Farming," *Collier's* 53, no. 13 (June 13, 1914):28; U.S., Congress, Senate, *United States Country Life Commission Report,* p. 58.

76. W. L. Nelson, "Hired Labor on the Farm and in the Home," *Second Wisconsin Country Life Conference,* p. 86; U.S., Congress, Senate, *United States Country Life Commission Report,* p. 42; Gillette, *Constructive Rural Sociology,* pp. 228–229.

77. Editorial, "Agricultural Colleges and Their Adjuncts," *Independent* 66, no. 3143 (Feb. 25, 1909):432; Peter McArthur, "The Stubborn Farmer," *Forum* 67, no. 3 (Mar. 1912):343.

78. The standard work on the night-riders is James O. Nall, *The Tobacco Night Riders of Kentucky and Tennessee: 1905–1909* (Louisville: Standard Press, 1939); see also editorial, "The Night-Rider Folly," *Independent* 65, no. 3123 (Oct. 8, 1908):850–851; Edward A. Jonas, "The Night-Riders: A Trust of Farmers," *World's Work* 17, no. 4 (Feb. 1909):11216; John G. Miller, *The Black Patch War* (Chapel Hill: University of North Carolina Press, 1936).

79. July 3, 1917, remarks by New York Senator James W. Wadsworth, Jr., U.S., Congress, Senate, *Congressional Record,* 65th Cong., 1917, 55, pt. 5:4618; "Organization and Conduct of a Market Service in the Department of Agriculture, Discussed at a Conference Held at the Department on April 29, 1913" (Washington: USGPO, 1913), pp. 6–7.

80. Charles Moreau Harger, "The New Life on the Farm," *Outlook* 94 (Apr. 16, 1910):841–844; Theodore Roosevelt, "The Welfare of the Farmer," *Outlook* 100, no. 16 (Apr. 20, 1912):855.

81. Truman S. Vance, "Why Young Men Leave the Farms," *Independent* 70, no. 3250 (Mar. 16, 1911):560.

82. Editorial, "Better Farming in North Dakota," *World's Work* 27, no. 6 (Apr. 1914):614.

83. The General Education Board was a strong advocate of this position. *The General Education Board: An Account of Its Activities, 1902–1914* (New York: General Education Board, 1915), p. 22.

84. Louis H. Douglas, ed., *Agrarianism in American History* (Lexington, Mass.: Heath, 1969), p. 112; see also David F. Houston, *Eight Years with Wilson's Cabinet* (Garden City: Doubleday, Page, 1926) vol. 1, pp. 200–201; Eugene Davenport, "Scientific Farming," *The Annals of the American Academy of Political and Social Science* (Philadelphia: American Academy of Political and Social Science, Mar. 1912), p. 49.

85. Ray Hinman Holmes, "The Passing of the Farmer," *Atlantic Monthly* 110, no. 4 (Oct. 1912):523; Hibbard, "The Decline in Rural Population," *Second Wisconsin Country Life Conference,* p. 122.

86. "The Country Banker's Awakening," *Independent* 75, no. 3380 (Sept. 11, 1913):611.

87. Vogt, "A Rural Survey in Greene and Clermont Counties, Ohio," p. 48; Liberty Hyde Bailey, "Moon-Farming," *Independent* 67, no. 3177 (Oct. 21, 1909):907-909; C. P. Hartley, "Corn Growing," *USDA Farmers' Bulletin 199, 1904*, p. 18; D.C.C.L.B.H.M. Presbyterian Church U.S.A., *A Rural Survey in Pennsylvania*, p. 5.

88. Remarks of A. C. True, *Annual Reports, USDA, 1902*, p. 244; Ernest Burnham, *Two Types of Rural Schools* (New York: Teachers College, Columbia University, 1912), p. 31; remarks of A. C. True, *Annual Report, USDA, 1900*, p. 176; Carl Vrooman, "Meeting the Farmer Halfway," *Yearbook, USDA, 1916*, pp. 67-68; Thomas Clark Atkeson and Mary Meek Atkeson, *Pioneering in Agriculture* (New York: Orange Judd, 1937), p. 153.

89. Carl W. Thompson and G. P. Warber, *Social and Economic Survey of a Rural Township in Southern Minnesota* (Minneapolis: University of Minnesota, 1913), p. 47.

90. Remarks of Secretary of Agriculture N. B. Critchfield, *Tenth Annual Report of the Pennsylvania Department of Agriculture* (Harrisburg: Harrisburg Publishing, State Printers, 1905), p. 8; John Hamilton, "Influences Exerted by Agricultural Fairs," *Annals of the American Academy of Political and Social Science*, Mar. 1912, p. 204; Bailey, *The Country-Life Movement*, p. 166.

91. Edward Wiest, *Agricultural Organization in the United States* (Lexington: University of Kentucky, 1923), pp. 63-64; Jason Sexton, "The County Chairman," *Tenth Annual Report of the Pennsylvania Department of Agriculture*, pp. 329-334. A good history of the institute movement in general can be found in Roy V. Scott, *The Reluctant Farmer* (Urbana: University of Illinois Press, 1970).

92. Author Unknown, "County Fairs," *USDA Weekly News Letter* 3, no. 5 (Sept. 8, 1915):2; William L. Wanless, *The United States Department of Agriculture: A Study in Administration* (Baltimore: Johns Hopkins Press, 1920), p. 37; Houston, *Eight Years with Wilson's Cabinet* 1:202-203.

93. Remarks of John Hamilton, *Journal of Proceedings of the National Grange of the Patrons of Husbandry Forty-Third Annual Session Des Moines, Iowa 1909* (Concord, N. H.: Rumford, 1909), p. 48.

94. Seaman A. Knapp, "The Mission of Cooperative Demonstration Work in the South," *USDA Circular no. 33, 1910;* the remarks of B. T. Galloway, *Annual Reports, USDA, 1912*, p. 442.

95. Author Unknown, "Education in the South," *United States Bureau of Education Bulletin*, no. 540 (1913):24.

96. Vogt, "A Rural Survey in Greene and Clermont Counties, Ohio," p. 42.

97. "The Farmers' Cooperative Demonstration Work," *Yearbook, USDA, 1909*, p. 159; Rosa Pendleton Chiles, "Making Good Farmers Out of Poor Ones," *Review of Reviews* 42, no. 5 (Nov. 1910):569.

98. The agricultural colleges and experiment stations were particularly reticent about federalizing the county agent movement. See W. H. Jordan, "Presidential Address," *Proceedings of the Twenty-Fifth Annual Convention of the Association of American Agricultural Colleges and Experiment Stations Held at Columbus, Ohio, November 15-17, 1911* (Montpelier, Vt.: Capital City Press, 1912), p. 41; remarks of R. J. Aley, *Proceedings of the Twenty-Seventh Annual Convention of the Association of American Agricultural Colleges and Experiment Stations Held at Washington, D.C., November 12-14, 1913* (Montpelier, Vt.: Capital City Press, 1914), p. 170.

99. Alfred Charles True, *A History of Agricultural Extension Work in the United States, 1785-1923, USDA Miscellaneous Publication no. 15*, p. 105; remarks of H. H. Gross, *Proceedings of the Association of American Agricultural Colleges and Experiment Stations, 1911*, pp. 204, 123; H. H. Gross, *Proceedings of the Twenty-Sixth Annual Convention of the Association of Agricultural Colleges and Experiment Stations Held at Atlanta, Georgia, November 13-15, 1912* (Burlington, Vt.: Free Press, 1913), p. 102.

100. John J. Lacey, *Farm Bureau in Illinois* (Bloomington, Ill.: Illinois Agricultural Association, 1965), pp. 14-15; Bert Ball, "Commercial Organizations and Agriculture," *Nation's Business* 2, no. 6 (June 18, 1914): 16; A. D. Welton, "The Banker-Farmer Movement," *Journal of the American Bankers Association* 8, no. 2 (Aug. 1915):103; L. A. Baker, "How Bankers Can Aid Agricultural Extension," *First Wisconsin Country Life Conference, Bulletin of the University of Wisconsin*, serial no. 472, general series no. 308 (Madison: College of Agriculture, Feb. 1911), p. 41.

101. L. L. Waters, *Steel Rails to Santa Fe* (Lawrence: University of Kansas Press, 1950), p. 353; Carlton J. Corliss, *Main Line of Mid-America: The Story of the Illinois Central*

(New York: Creative Age, 1950), pp. 415–418; Elisha Hollingsworth Talbot, "A New Agricultural Empire," *Moody's Magazine* 17, no. 12 (Dec. 1914):578; Richard C. Overton, *Burlington West: A Colonization History of the Burlington Railroad* (Cambridge: Harvard University Press, 1941), pp. 486–487; Erickson with Coit, *Rural Youth,* p. 45.

102. Forest Crissey, "Speeding Up the Farm—Business Men at Wheel Make Good," *Banker-Farmer* 1, no. 6 (May 1914):2; William Hirth, "Practical Suggestions for the Banker Who Wants to Help," *Banker-Farmer* 1, no. 10 (Sept. 1914):5; B. H. Gitchell, "Developing a Spirit of Co-operation in Rural Communities," "Virginia Rural Life Conference," pp. 347–355. Julius Rosenwald of Sears-Roebuck was directly financially involved in the stimulation of agricultural extension, as was the General Education Board. See M. R. Werner, *Julius Rosenwald: The Life of a Practical Humanitarian* (New York: Harper, 1939).

103. H. P. Miller, "The Future of the County Agent," *Ohio Farmer* 150, no. 20 (Nov. 11, 1922):503; U.S., Congress, Senate, 63d Cong., 2d sess., 1914, 51, pt. 3:3032.

104. Ibid., p. 2738, 2735.

105. U.S., Congress, House, *Congressional Record,* 63d Cong., 2d sess., 1914, 51, pt. 2:1938; ibid., pt. 17:76; ibid., pt. 2:1933.

106. See, for example, the remarks of Representative Gilbert Haugen, ibid., p. 1939; remarks of William S. Kenyon, U.S., Congress, Senate, *Congressional Record,* 63d Cong., 2d sess., 1914, 51, pt. 9:8889.

107. Remarks of Senator Porter J. McCumber, ibid., pt. 3:2513; remarks of Senator Harry Lane, ibid., pt. 2:1836–1837.

108. Remarks of Senator Porter J. McCumber, ibid., p. 1834.

109. Ibid., pt. 3:2741.

110. Remarks of Senator Joseph L. Bristow, ibid., pt. 2:1824; J. V., "Farm Demonstrators," *Twentieth-Century Farmer* 700 (May 9, 1914):14–15.

111. Woodrow Wilson, "Helping the Farmer," letter to Representative A. F. Lever, in Baker and Dodd, eds., *Presidential Messages,* 2:261, 263.

CHAPTER 4

1. Samuel Haber finds this same view of the role of the expert in democracy among the scientific managers he studies. See Haber, *Efficiency and Uplift: Scientific Management in the Progressive Era* (Chicago: University of Chicago Press, 1964), p. xi.

2. Kenyon Butterfield, "The Morrill Act Institutions and the New Epoch," *Proceedings of the Thirty-First Annual Convention of the Association of American Agricultural Colleges and Experiment Stations Held at Washington, D.C., November 14–16, 1917* (Burlington, Vt.: Free Press, 1918), p. 46.

3. Ibid., p. 55.

4. Ibid.

5. Remarks of L. D. Harvey, *Journal of Proceedings and Addresses of the Forty-First Annual Meeting of the National Educational Association Held at Minneapolis, Minnesota, July 7–11, 1902* (Chicago: National Educational Association, 1902), p. 222.

6. See Theodore Saloutos, *Farmer Movements in the South, 1865–1933* (Berkeley: University of California Press, 1960), pp. 208–210; Harriet Ann Crawford, *The Washington State Grange, 1889–1933* (Portland, Oreg.: Binfords and Mort, 1940), pp. 129–135.

7. Remarks of C. P. Cary, *Journal of Proceedings and Addresses of the Forty-Fifth Annual Meeting of the National Education Association Held at Los Angeles, California, July 8–12, 1907* (Chicago: National Education Association, 1907), p. 288.

8. Allen S. Woodward, "Vitalizing a Rural School Course," *Education* 37, no. 9 (May 1917):564; see also Raymond G. Fuller, "Recreation and Child Welfare," *Pamphlet no. 295* (New York: National Child Labor Committee, 1919), p. 43.

9. E. C. Bishop, "The Present Status of Agricultural Education in the Public Schools," *Journal of Proceedings and Addresses of the Forty-Seventh Annual Meeting of the National Education Association Held at Denver, Colorado, July 3–9, 1909* (Chicago: National Education Association, 1909), pp. 980–981.

10. Remarks of John F. Riggs, *Report of the Iowa Department of Public Instruction for the*

Biennial Period Beginning July 1, 1906 and Ending June 30, 1908 (Des Moines: Department of Public Instruction, 1908), p. 30; see also N. G. Thomas, "Report of Work of the McCormick County Agent—1917," *Extension Service Annual Reports: South Carolina, 1909-1944*, National Archives, Microcopy T-887, roll 2; Joseph A. Cocannouer, *Trampling Out the Vintage* (Norman, Okla.: University of Oklahoma Press, 1945), pp. 183-184.

11. H. N. Loomis, "State Normal Schools and the Rural-School Problem," *Educational Review* 39, no. 5 (May 1910):486; A. C. Monahan and Robert H. Wright, "Training Courses for Rural Teachers," *United States Bureau of Education Bulletin*, no. 509 (1913).

12. Author Unknown, "The Autobiography of a Country Schoolteacher," *World's Work* 20, no. 3 (July 1910):13160.

13. Arthur J. Todd, "Reconstruction of Existing Rural Agencies," *Proceedings of the National Conference of Social Work at the Forty-Fourth Annual Session Held in Pittsburgh, Pennsylvania June 6-13, 1917* (Chicago: National Conference of Social Work, 1917), p. 624.

14. Remarks of Grant County Superintendent R. J. Stromme, *State of Minnesota, Sixteenth Biennial Report of the Superintendent of Public Instruction for the School Years 1909 and 1910* (Minneapolis: Syndicate Printing, 1910), p. 117; Thomas Jackson Woofter, *Teaching in Rural Schools* (Boston: Houghton Mifflin, 1917), p. 277; Cocannouer, *Trampling Out the Vintage*, p. 64.

15. Remarks of Clayton F. Palmer, *Journal of Proceedings and Addresses of the Forty-Ninth Annual Meeting of the National Education Association Held at San Francisco, California, July 8-14, 1911* (Chicago: National Education Association, 1911), pp. 1118-1125; Charles A. Mahan, "Annual Report of County Agent Work in Randolph County, Indiana—1916," *Extension Service Annual Reports: Indiana, 1912-1944*, National Archives, Microcopy T-859, roll 2, p. 16; Ronald J. Slay, *The Development of the Teaching of Agriculture in Mississippi* (New York: Teachers College, Columbia University, 1928), p. 122.

16. Stevenson Whitcomb Fletcher, *Pennsylvania Agriculture and Country Life* (Harrisburg: Pennsylvania Historical and Museum Commission, 1955), pp. 478-479; Harold Waldstein Foght, *The American Rural School* (New York: Macmillan, 1910), p. 211.

17. Graduate School of Education, University of Nebraska, "The Rural Teacher of Nebraska," *United States Bureau of Education Bulletin*, no. 20 (1919), p. 64.

18. Remarks of New Jersey State Commissioner of Education Calvin N. Kendall, in A. C. Monahan, "Consolidation of Rural Schools and Transportation of Pupils at Public Expense," *United States Bureau of Education Bulletin*, no. 604 (1914), p. 23; remarks of State Superintendent Barksdale Hamlett in the *Biennial Report of the Superintendent of Public Instruction of Kentucky for the Two Years, Ending June 30, 1915* (Frankfort: State Journal, 1915), p. xxxi.

19. Remarks of Aiken County, South Carolina, Superintendent Cecil H. Seigler, *Forty-First Annual Report of the State Superintendent of Education of the State of South Carolina, 1909* (Columbia: Gonzales and Bryan, 1910); State Superintendent F. G. Blair, *Thirty-Second Biennial Report of the Superintendent of Public Instruction of State of Illinois, July 1, 1916-June 30, 1918* (Springfield: Illinois State Journal, 1919), p. 19; remarks of J. W. Jarnagin, "Proceedings of the First National Conference on Rural School Consolidation," *Bulletin of the Iowa State Teachers College* 20, no. 4, pt. 2 (June 1920):56.

20. Remarks of Jerauld County Superintendent A. V. Hall, *Seventh Biennial Report of the Superintendent of Public Instruction, State of South Dakota, 1903-1904* (Aberdeen: News Printing, 1904), p. 68.

21. Author Unknown, "Educational Needs of Farm Women," *USDA, Report no. 105, 1915*, p. 12; T. A. Erickson with Anna North Coit, *My Sixty Years with Rural Youth* (Minneapolis: University of Minnesota Press, 1956), pp. 61-62.

22. Author Unknown, "Educational Needs of Farm Women," p. 10; remarks of Maine State Superintendent Payson Smith in Monahan, "Consolidation and Transportation of Pupils," p. 20. See also J. Harold Williams, "Reorganizing a Country System of Rural Schools," *Bureau of Education Bulletin, no. 16* (1916) (Washington: USGPO, 1916).

23. Remarks of Pickens County Superintendent W. H. Storey, *Annual Report of the Department of Education of the State of Alabama for the Scholastic Year Ending September 30, 1909* (Montgomery: Brown Printing, 1909), p. 81; remarks of the Luna

County Superintendent in the *Nineteenth and Twentieth Annual Reports of the Territorial Superintendent of Public Instruction to the Governor of New Mexico* (Santa Fe: New Mexican Printing, 1911), pp. 66-67.

24. Remarks of C. P. Colegrove, "Proceedings of the First National Conference on Rural School Consolidation," p. 49; Lester Burton Rogers, *A Comparative Study of the Township, District, Consolidated, Town and City Schools of Indiana* (Menasha, Wis.: Lester Burton Rogers, 1915), p. 203; Albert H. Leake, *The Means and Methods of Agricultural Education* (Boston: Houghton Mifflin, 1915), pp. 92-94.

25. Rogers, *Comparative Study,* p. 206; see also John Franklin Babbitt, "The Efficiency of the Consolidated Rural School," *Elementary School Teacher* 12, no. 4 (Dec. 1911):173.

26. Fletcher, *Pennsylvania Agriculture,* p. 536; Fred Trump, *The Grange in Michigan* (Grand Rapids: Fred Trump, 1963), p. 103. There were some rural expressions of consolidation sentiment; see W. K., "Township School Consolidation," *Twentieth Century Farmer,* no. 688 (Feb. 14, 1914):13; Theodore Saloutos, "The Rise of the Nonpartisan League in North Dakota, 1915-1917," *Agricultural History* 20, no. 1 (Jan. 1946):58.

27. K. L. Hatch, "The Small-Scale Country School," *Rural Social Problems, Being the Fourth Annual Report of the Wisconsin Country Life Conference, Bulletin of the University of Wisconsin,* serial no. 711, general series no. 515 (Madison: College of Agriculture, n.d.), p. 15.

28. Remarks of L. J. Gilkeson and Lee Driver, "Proceedings of the First National Conference on Rural School Consolidation," pp. 26, 30; Betts and Hall, *Better Rural Schools,* p. 217. The best summary I found on the state of rural school consolidation laws and the trend toward compulsion is in Monahan, "Consolidation and Transportation of Pupils," pp. 34-43.

29. Ellwood P. Cubberley, *The Improvement of Rural Schools* (Boston: Houghton Mifflin, 1912), p. 12; see also A. E. Pickard, *Rural Education* (St. Paul, Minn.: Webb Publishing, 1915), p. 83; Laura H. Wild, "Efficiency and the Rural School," *Survey* 30, no. 16 (July 19, 1913):526-527.

30. Julius Bernard Arp, *Rural Education and the Consolidated School* (Yonkers-on-Hudson, N.Y.: World Book, 1918), p. 26; George S. May, "Overcoming Opposition," *Palimpsest* 37, no. 1 (Jan. 1956):36-45.

31. Frank M. Goodchild, "The Country Church," *Outlook* 110 (June 30, 1915):526.

32. Arthur E. Holt, "The Church in the Country," *Biblical World* 47, no. 6 (June 1916):391.

33. Paul L. Vogt, "A Rural Life Survey of Greene and Clermont Counties, Ohio," *Miami University Bulletin,* series XII, no. 11 (July 1914):53.

34. Department of Church and Country Life of the Board of Home Missions of the Presbyterian Church in the U.S.A., *A Rural Survey in Indiana* (New York: Board of Home Missions of the Presbyterian Church in the U.S.A., 1912), p. 27; Charles Otis Gill and Gifford Pinchot, *The Country Church* (New York: Macmillan, 1913), p. 51; Ilena M. Bailey and Melissa Farrell Snyder, "A Survey of Farm Homes," *Journal of Home Economics* 13, no. 8 (Aug. 1921):354.

35. The most complete and thoughtful treatment of the problems of the consolidated rural church is Elizabeth R. Hooker, *United Churches* (Garden City: Doubleday, Doran, 1928).

36. John Robert Hargreaves, "The Rural Community and Church Federation," *American Journal of Sociology* 20, no. 2 (Sept. 1914):258-260.

37. Leroy A. Ramsdell, "Rural Social Work," in Henry Israel and Benson Y. Landis, eds., *Handbook of Rural Social Resources* (Chicago: University of Chicago Press, 1926), p. 57.

38. E. C. Branson, "The Present Demand for Improvement in Rural Government and Needed Legislation," (American) National Country Life Association, *Proceedings of the First National Country Life Conference, Baltimore 1919* (Ithaca, N.Y.: National Country Life Association, 1919), p. 68.

39. See United States Public Health Service, "Transactions of the Twelfth Annual Conference of State and Territorial Health Officers with the United States Public Health Service," *Public Health Bulletin no. 67* (Washington: USGPO, 1915), pp. 42-60; H. F. Cassell, "Report of the Work of the Franklin County Agent: Calendar Year 1915," *Extension Service Annual Reports: Arkansas, 1909-1944,* National Archives, Microcopy T-848, roll 1, frame 47; H. E. Wheat, "Report of Work of the Harper County Agent—1918," *Extension Service Annual Reports: Oklahoma, 1909-1944,* Microcopy

T-881, roll 3, frame 47; editorial, "City Milk and the Farmer," *Farm Journal* 38, no. 9 (Sept. 1914):496.

40. Ballard Campbell, "The Good Roads Movement in Wisconsin, 1890–1911," *Wisconsin Magazine of History* 49, no. 4 (Summer 1966):280; George S. May, "Good Roads Organizations," *Palimpsest* 46, no. 2 (Feb. 1965):79; Sam Huston, "Good Roads Indifference," *American Agriculturalist* 75, no. 22 (June 3, 1905):12.

41. Author Unknown, "Economic Needs of Farm Women," *USDA, Report no. 106, 1915*, pp. 10, 13.

42. Remarks of Mary E. Sweeney, in L. R. Taft, ed., *Proceedings of the Twentieth Annual Meeting of the American Association of Farmers' Institute Workers* (East Lansing, Mich.: American Association of Farmers' Institute Workers, 1915), p. 94; Author Unknown, "Domestic Needs of Farm Women," *USDA, Report no. 104, 1915*, p. 22; Ida M. Shepler, "Are Farmers' Wives Neglected and Abused?" *Twentieth Century Farmer*, no. 696 (Apr. 11, 1914):p. 3.

43. Author Unknown, "Social and Labor Needs of Farm Women," *USDA, Report no. 103, 1915*, p. 20.

44. See editorial, "Will Farmers Help themselves?" *Independent* 66, no. 3146 (Mar. 18, 1909):595; "One of Them," "The Farmers' Side," *Outlook* 95, no. 1 (May 7, 1910):29–31; Author Unknown, "Farmers' Problems," *Farm Journal* 37, no. 1 (Jan. 1915):31.

45. *Journal of Proceedings of the Forty-Second Annual Session of the National Grange of the Patrons of Husbandry Washington D.C. 1908* (Concord, N.H.: Rumford Printing, 1908), p. 22.

46. Ila J. Marsh to David F. Houston, Dec. 16, 1918, National Archives, record group 16, "Correspondence of Secretaries of Agriculture," "Farm—Farmers— Farming—1918" file, p. 1.

47. *Farm Policies of the United States, 1790–1950* (New York: Twentieth Century Fund, 1953), p. 158.

48. Some examples of socially involved agents are L. E. Hall, "Report of Work of the Columbus County Negro Agent—1915," *Extension Service Annual Reports: North Carolina, 1909–1944*, National Archives, Microcopy T-878, roll 1, frames 27–28; Charles E. Smith, "Annual Report of the Las Animas County Agent—1916," *Extension Service Annual Reports: Colorado, 1913–1944*, National Archives, Microcopy T-850, roll 1, p. 12; J. E. Neil, "Annual Report of Redwood County Agent—1916," *Extension Service Annual Reports: Minnesota, 1914–1944*, National Archives, Microcopy T-868, roll 1, p. 16. Negro agents seemed to be particularly interested in social involvement and social control. See O. B. Martin, "A Decade of Negro Extension Work, 1914–1924," *USDA, Miscellaneous Circular no. 72, 1926*.

49. Rob R. Slocum, "The Poultry Club Work in the South," *Yearbook, USDA, 1915*, p. 195; see also E. C. Lindemann, "Boys' and Girls' Clubs as Community Builders," *Proceedings of the National Conference of Social Work, 1917*, p. 635.

50. James Luther McGinnis, "Annual Report of Northeastern District Agent—1916," *Extension Service Annual Reports: Nevada, 1915–1944*, National Archives, Microcopy T-873, roll 1, p. 3; Josiah Main, "Decline and Fall of a State System of Boys' and Girls' Agricultural Clubs," *School and Society* 3, no. 67 (Apr. 8, 1916):514–520.

51. Remarks of S. F. Morse, *Proceedings of the Twenty-Ninth Annual Convention of the Association of American Agricultural Colleges and Experiment Stations Held at Berkeley, California, August 11–13, 1915* (Montpelier, Vt.: Capital City Press, 1915), p. 227; see also J. W. Rigney, "First Annual Report of the County Agriculturalist for Chaves County, New Mexico—1915," *Extension Service Annual Reports: New Mexico, 1914–1944*, National Archives, Microcopy T-876, roll 1, p. 1; Sallie Mai Hudson, "Annual Report of Home Demonstration Work for Women and Girls Calendar Year 1919," *Extension Service Annual Reports: Arkansas, 1909–1944*, National Archives, Microcopy T-848, roll 3, frame 4.

52. M. C. Burritt, *The County Agent and the Farm Bureau* (New York: Harcourt, Brace, 1922), p. 39; Joseph Cannon Bailey, *Seaman A. Knapp: Schoolmaster of American Agriculture* (New York: Columbia University Press, 1945), p. 156.

53. Dean Albertson, *Roosevelt's Farmer: Claude R. Wickard in the New Deal* (New York: Columbia University Press, 1961), p. 16.

54. H. C. M., "Kind of Help Farmers Need," *Twentieth Century Farmer*, no. 691 (Mar. 7,

1917):22; see also the remarks of county agent E. C. Palmore of Monroe County in the State of Kentucky, *Twenty-First Biennial Report of the Bureau of Agriculture Labor and Statistics* (Frankfort: Kentucky State Journal Publishing, 1916), p. 407; remarks of Kansas Senator Joseph L. Bristow, U.S., Congress, Senate, *Congressional Record,* 63d Cong., 2d. sess., 51, pt. 2:1824–1825.

55. R. I. Moore, "The Farm Journal Forum," *Farm Journal* 40, no. 4 (Apr. 1916):264; see also Author Unknown, "Social and Labor Needs of Farm Women," *USDA, Report no. 103, 1915,* p. 24; W. F. McSparren to David F. Houston, July 28, 1913, National Archives, record group 16, "Correspondence of Secretaries of Agriculture," "Rural Organization Service, 1912–1913" file, pp. 3–4.

56. "Educational Needs of Farm Women," *USDA, Report 105, 1915,* p. 39; report of Jane Kane Foulke, *Twentieth Annual Report of the Pennsylvania Department of Agriculture* (Harrisburg: William Stanley Ray, State Printer, 1915), p. 245; Kate Adele Hill, *Home Demonstration Work in Texas* (San Antonio: Naylor, 1958), p. 7.

57. M. S. Shrock, "Annual Report of Yamhill County Agent—1916," *Extension Service Annual Reports: Oregon, 1914–1944,* National Archives, Microcopy T-882, roll 1, p. 5; see also M. H. Fedderson, "Annual Report of Washington County Agent," *Extension Service Annual Reports: Iowa, 1912–1944,* National Archives, Microcopy T-860, roll 4, p. 14.

58. "Social and Labor Needs of Farm Women," *USDA, Report 103, 1915,* p. 55.

59. *Proceedings of the Twenty-Seventh Annual Convention of the Association of American Agricultural Colleges and Experiment Stations* (Montpelier, Vt.: Capital City Press, 1914), p. 64; see also Bradford Knapp, "Report of Farmers' Cooperative Demonstration Work to the General Education Board," National Archives, record group 16, "Correspondence of Secretaries of Agriculture," "Demonstration—1912–1913" tray 74.

60. Gifford Pinchot, "The Farmers' Part in Winning the War," *Pacific Rural Press* 96, no. 22 (Nov. 30, 1918):592.

61. William H. Groninger to David F. Houston, October 8, 1913, National Archives, record group 16, "Correspondence of Secretaries of Agriculture," "Cost of Living—1913" file; *Journal of Proceedings of the National Grange of the Patrons of Husbandry Fiftieth Annual Session Washington, D.C. 1916* (Concord, N.H.: Rumford, 1916), p. 210; *Journal of the Proceedings of the Fortieth Annual Session of the California State Grange Patrons of Husbandry Held in Masonic Hall, Sebastopol October 15 to 19, 1912* (California State Grange, 1912), p. 57; remarks of Washington State Master C. B. Kegley in the *Journal of the Proceedings of the National Grange, 1916,* pp. 100–101.

62. Samuel Morgan, "Report of Work of the Laurel County Agent—1917," *Extension Service Annual Reports: Kentucky, 1912–1944,* National Archives, Microcopy T-862, roll 2, frame 4; Author Unknown, "County Agent Hits Short Crop Fallacy," *Banker-Farmer* 1, no. 6 (May 1914):14.

63. J. A. Evans, *Recollections of Extension History* (Athens, Ga.: Georgia Agricultural Extension Service Circular no. 224, Aug. 1938), p. 18; Burritt, *County Agent,* p. 104.

64. *USDA, Yearbook, 1931,* pp. 615, 583.

65. D. H. Doane, "Annual Report of State Leader of County Agricultural Agents—1915," *Extension Service Annual Reports: Missouri, 1910–1944,* National Archives, Microcopy T-870, roll 1, p. 31; Maurice E. Miller, "Report of the Work of the Franklin County Agent: Calendar Year 1917," *Extension Service Annual Reports: Mississippi, 1909–1944,* National Archives, Microcopy T-869, roll 2, frame 57; O. S. Fletcher, "Annual Narrative Reports, 1919: Latah County," *Extension Service Annual Reports: Idaho, 1913–1944,* National Archives, Microcopy T-857, roll 3, frame 1; Seaman A. Knapp, "Demonstration Work in Cooperation with Southern Farmers," *USDA, Farmers' Bulletin 319, 1908,* p. 9; Author Unknown, "When Badger Blood Gets Up," *Banker-Farmer* 2, no. 2 (Jan. 1915):13; Author Unknown, "Work of the A.B.A. Agricultural Commission," *Journal of the American Bankers Association* 2, no. 2 (Aug. 1918), 84.

66. R. W. Persons, "Bell County Agent's Annual Report—1917," *Extension Service Annual Reports: Texas, 1909–1944,* National Archives, Microcopy T-890, roll 2, p. 1; Roy V. Scott, *The Reluctant Farmer* (Urbana: University of Illinois Press, 1970), p. 214.

67. For an Extension plea for banker aid see Stanley F. Morse, "The Arizona Banker and Agricultural Development," *Extension Service Annual Reports: Arizona, 1915–1944,* National Archives, Microcopy T-847, roll 1, p. 8. Examples of agents who apparently believed that their job was to organize businessmen's organizations are H. B. Derr,

"Report of Accomplishments of the Scott County Agent: Calendar Year 1914," *Extension Service Annual Reports: Missouri, 1914-1944,* National Archives, Microcopy T-870, roll 1, frames 6-8; W. H. Garner, "Narrative Report of County Agent, Paulding County, Georgia," *Extension Service Annual Reports: Georgia, 1909-1944,* National Archives, Microcopy T-855, roll 21, frame 3.

68. S. B. Stowe, "First Annual Report of Clermont County Agricultural Agent—1916," *Extension Service Annual Reports: Ohio, 1915-1944,* National Archives, Microcopy T-880, roll 1, p. 6; N. D. Guerry, "Report of Work of the Chickasaw County Agent: Calendar Year 1917," *Extension Service Annual Reports: Mississippi, 1909-1944,* National Archives, Microcopy T-869, roll 2, frames 51-63; H. C. Carr, "The Banker and the Farmer," *Coast Banker* 20, no. 6 (June 10, 1918):54.

69. Ernest A. Riggs, "Narrative Report for 1916 of Washington County Agricultural Agent," *Extension Service Annual Reports: Ohio, 1915-1944,* National Archives, Microcopy T-880, roll 1, p. 3; Glenn A. Ellis, "Report of the County Agent of Johnson County, Indiana," *Extension Service Annual Report: Indiana, 1912-1944,* National Archives, Microcopy T-859, roll 2, p. 4.

70. "Report of the Agricultural Commission of the American Bankers Association and the Banker-Farmer," *Proceedings of the Fortieth Annual Convention of the American Bankers Association Held at Richmond, Virginia October 12 to 16, 1914* (New York: American Bankers Association, 1914), p. 180; H. L. Eichling, "Report of Page County Farm Bureau—1918," *Extension Service Annual Reports: Iowa, 1912-1944,* National Archives, Microcopy T-860, roll 4, p. 2.

71. David F. Houston to Wallace Buttrick, Oct. 20, 1913, National Archives, record group 16, "Correspondence of Secretaries of Agriculture," "Rural Organization Service, July-December 1913" file, p. 1; Walter Hines Page, "A Rural Organization Service," National Archives, record group 16, Correspondence of Secretaries of Agriculture," "Rural Organization Service, July-December 1913" file, p. 1; C. W. Thompson, "How the Department of Agriculture Promotes Organization in Rural Life," *USDA, Yearbook, 1915,* pp. 272a-p.

72. R. A. Kolb, "Annual Report of Taylor County Agent—1921," *Extension Service Annual Reports: Wisconsin, 1913-1914,* National Archives, Microcopy T-896, roll 4, p. 1; see also James A. Armstrong, "Semi-Annual Report of the San Diego County Agent from January 1, 1914, to June 30, 1914," *Extension Service Annual Reports: California, 1913-1944,* National Archives, Microcopy T-849, roll 1, p. 5; J. E. Readnimer, "Semi-Annual Report of Kane County Agent: Due June 30, 1915," *Extension Service Annual Reports: Illinois, 1914-1944,* National Archives, Microcopy T-858, roll 1, p. 8.

73. T. A. Coleman, "Summary Report of the Supervision of the County Agent Work of Indiana for the Year Beginning January 1, and Ending November 30, 1916," *Extension Service Annual Reports: Indiana, 1912-1944,* National Archives, Microcopy T-859, roll 1, frame 2; R. J. Evans, "Annual Report of County Agent Work in State of Utah—1916," *Extension Service Annual Reports: Utah, 1914-1944,* National Archives, Microcopy T-891, roll 1, p. 4.

74. "The Work of Rural Organization," *Journal of Political Economy* 22, no. 9 (Nov. 1914):838.

75. M. G. Lewis, "Report of Work of the Scott County Agent—1919," *Extension Service Annual Reports: Virginia, 1908-1944,* National Archives, Microcopy T-893, roll 4, frame 54; Paul L. Vogt, "A Rural Life Survey in Southwestern Ohio," *Miami University Bulletin,* series XI, no. 8 (Apr. 1913):38; E. E. Miller, "The American Farmer as a Coöperator," *Forum* 52, no. 4 (Oct. 1914):592-602.

76. David Elder, "Annual Report of County Agricultural Agent for Providence and Bristol Counties—1916," *Extension Service Annual Reports: Rhode Island, 1914-1944,* National Archives, Microcopy T-885, roll 1, pp. 2-3; W. L. Stallings, "Report of Work of the Harris County Agent—1917," *Extension Service Annual Reports: Texas, 1909-1944,* National Archives, Microcopy T-890, roll 3, frame 5; Pearl Polk, "Annual Report of Home Demonstration Work for Women and Girls Calendar Year 1919," *Extension Service Annual Reports: Alabama, 1909-1944,* National Archives, Microcopy T-845, roll 4, pp. 16-17; E. H. Walworth, "Annual Report of Farm Adviser of Clark County Farm Bureau—1919," *Extension Service Annual Reports: Illinois, 1914-1944,* National Archives, Microcopy T-858, roll 4, p. 3.

77. Burritt, *County Agent,* pp. 80-81.

78. W. A. Lloyd, "What Should Be the Relationship of the County Agent to the Farm Bureaus," *Proceedings of the Thirty-Third Annual Convention of the Association of American Agricultural Colleges and Experiment Stations Held at Chicago, Illinois, November 12-14, 1919* (Burlington, Vt.: Free Press, 1919), p. 296.

79. Burritt, *County Agent,* p. 81.

80. L. Cantrell, "Report of Work of the Putnam County Agent: Calendar Year 1916," *Extension Service Annual Reports: Florida, 1909-1944,* National Archives, Microcopy T-854, roll 1, frame 60; Fred Steward, "Report of the Work of the Limestone County Agent Calendar Year 1919," *Extension Service Annual Reports: Alabama, 1909-1944,* National Archives, Microcopy T-845, roll 4, frame 8; Fred J. Blackburn, "Annual Narrative Report of Farm Adviser of Marion County Farm Bureau—1919," *Extension Service Annual Reports: Illinois, 1914-1944,* National Archives, Microcopy T-858, roll 4, p. 7.

81. See Charles J. Jones, "Lawrence County's Annual Report—1916," *Extension Service Annual Reports: Indiana, 1912-1944,* National Archives, Microcopy T-859, roll 2, p. 2; Nelson G. Malin, "Narrative Report—Dubuque County—1918," *Extension Service Annual Reports: Iowa, 1912-1944,* National Archives, Microcopy T-860, roll 3, p. 7.

82. C. L. McNelly, *The County Agent Story: The Impact of Extension Work on Farming and Country Life, Minnesota* (Berryville, Ark.: Braswell Printing, 1960), p. 40.

83. Harold G. Halcrow, *Agricultural Policy of the United States,* (Englewood Cliffs, N.J.: Prentice-Hall, 1953), pp. 169-171.

84. Editorial, "County Agents Repudiated," *Farmer* 32, no. 13 (Apr. 4, 1914):538.

85. B. D. Gilbert, "Semi-Annual Report of Lackawanna County Agent—June 30, 1915," *Extension Service Annual Reports: Pennsylvania, 1914-1944,* National Archives, Microcopy T-883, roll 1, p. 8; Ernest J. Riggs, "Semi-Annual Report of Washington County Agent—June 30, 1915," *Extension Service Annual Reports: Ohio, 1915-1944,* National Archives, Microcopy T-880, roll 1, frame 9.

86. Dwight Sanderson, "Community Organization for Extension Service," *Proceedings of the Thirty-Second Annual Convention of the Association of American Agricultural Colleges and Experiment Stations Held at Baltimore, Maryland, January 8-10, 1919* (Burlington, Vt.: Free Press, 1919), p. 251.

87. H. C. Hochbaum, *Proceedings, Association of American Agricultural Colleges and Experiment Stations, January, 1919,* p. 261.

88. S. G. Baxter, "Annual Monroe County Agent Report—1918," *Extension Service Annual Reports: Iowa, 1912-1944,* National Archives, Microcopy T-860, roll 3, p. 6; James E. Price, "Narrative Report—Yakima County Agent—1920," *Extension Service Annual Reports: Washington, 1913-1944,* National Archives, Microcopy T-894, roll 5, p. 5.

89. M. C. Burritt, "What Should Be the Relation of the County Agent to the Farm Bureau and of the College to a State Farm Bureau Federation?" *Proceedings of the Thirty-Third Annual Convention of the Association of American Agricultural Colleges and Experiment Stations Held at Chicago, Illinois, November 12-14, 1919* (Burlington, Vt.: Free Press, 1919), p. 280.

90. Memorandum for the secretary from Bradford Knapp, December 20, 1916, National Archives, record group 16, "Correspondence of Secretaries of Agriculture," "Cost of Living—1916" file; W. A. Taylor, "Memorandum for Mr. Harrison," Dec. 23, 1917, National Archives, record group 16, "Correspondence of Secretaries of Agriculture," "Farms—Farmers—Farming—1916" file, p. 2.

91. Irving King, *Education for Social Efficiency* (New York: Appleton, 1913), p. 32.

92. Peter McArthur, "The Stubborn Farmer," *Forum* 47, no. 3 (Mar. 1912):337. For an example of a model renovated community see A. J. Dadisman, "French Creek as a Rural Community," *Agricultural Experiment Station, College of Agriculture, West Virginia University Bulletin 176* (Morgantown: Agricultural Experiment Station, College of Agriculture, West Virginia University, June 1921).

93. John M. Gillette, *Constructive Rural Sociology* (New York: Sturgis and Walton, 1916), p. 286; Frederick A. Conrad, "Agrarian Discontent: A Study of Class Conflict Based on Farmer Movements in the United States, 1860-1930" (Ph.D. diss., Stanford, 1932), p. 80.

94. "Countryside and Nation," *Papers and Proceedings of the Eleventh Annual Meeting of the American Sociological Society* (Chicago: University of Chicago Press, 1917), p. 3.

CHAPTER 5

1. A few good examples are the remarks of Thomas D. Wood, *Journal of Proceedings and Addresses of the Fifty-Third Annual Meeting and International Congress on Education Held at Oakland, California, August 16–27, 1915* (Chicago: National Education Association, 1915); editorial, "Surveying the Health of Hoosier Farmers," *Survey* 37, no. 15 (Jan. 13, 1917):436; L. L. Bernard, "A Theory of Rural Attitudes," *American Journal of Sociology* 22, no. 5 (Mar. 1917):630–649; Paul L. Vogt, *Introduction to Rural Sociology* (New York: Appleton, 1917), p. 217; Kate Holladay Claghorn, "Juvenile Delinquency in Rural New York," U.S. Department of Labor *Children's Bureau Publication no. 32* (Washington: USGPO, 1918); Ernest R. Groves, *Rural Problems of Today* (New York: Association Press, 1918).

2. *USDA, Yearbook, 1931*, pp. 583, 615, 768; E. G. Nourse, "The War and the Back-to-the-Land Movement," *North American Review* 203, no. 2 (Feb. 1916):246–255; editorial, "Are Americans Poor Farmers?" *North American Review* 204, no. 6 (Dec. 1916):822–824.

3. "The Farmer, the Cornerstone of Civilization," *North Dakota Farmer* 19, no. 4 (Oct. 15, 1917):3.

4. *Introduction to Rural Sociology,* p. 9.

5. Warren H. Wilson, "Farm Co-operation for Better Business Schools [*sic*] and Churches," *Survey* 36, no. 2 (Apr. 8, 1916):53; see also William B. Aspinwall, "The New Conception of the Rural School Problem," *Education* 37, no. 9 (May 1917): 541–544.

6. "Countryside and Nation," *Papers and Proceedings of the Eleventh Annual Meeting of the American Sociological Society* (Chicago: University of Chicago Press, 1917), p. 4.

7. Remarks of David Houston, *Proceedings of the Thirty-First Annual Convention of the Association of American Agricultural Colleges and Experiment Stations Held at Washington, D.C., November 14–16, 1917* (Burlington, Vt.: Free Press, 1918), p. 31.

8. Ben W. Rieke, "Narrative Statement of Sibley County Annual Report—1918," *Extension Service Annual Reports: Minnesota, 1914–1944,* National Archives, Microcopy T-868, roll 4; C. L. McNelly, *The County Agent Story: The Impact of Extension Work on Farming and Country Life, Minnesota* (Berryville, Ark.: Braswell Printing, 1960), notes that by 1916, 16 of 26 Minnesota counties had dropped the agent program. Some agents were saved by personal appeals to county governments by Houston. See copy of a telegram from David F. Houston to the Cody, Wyoming, Board of Commissioners, Dec. 17, 1917, National Archives, record group 16, "Correspondence of Secretaries of Agriculture," "Extension—1917" drawer 384.

9. *Annual Reports, USDA, 1918*, pp. 335–336, 353, 355, 359.

10. Seward W. Livermore, *Politics Is Adjourned: Woodrow Wilson and the War Congress, 1916–1918* (Middletown, Conn.: Wesleyan University Press, 1966), p. 138; for a local example see E. M. Hunter, "Report of Work of the Loudoun County Agent—1917," *Extension Service Annual Reports: Virginia, 1908–1944,* National Archives, Microcopy T-893, roll 3, frame 51.

11. Morris M. Gordon, "Report of the Work of the Fulton County Agent—1917," *Extension Service Annual Reports: Kentucky, 1912–1944,* National Archives, Microcopy T-862, roll 2, frame 68; see also E. L. Castile, "Report of Work of the Pittsburg County Agent—1917," *Extension Service Annual Reports: Oklahoma, 1909–1944,* National Archives, Microcopy T-881, roll 2, frame 37; G. R. Bliss, "Scott County Farm Improvement League Annual Report for 1917," *Extension Service Annual Reports: Iowa, 1912–1944,* National Archives, Microcopy T-860, roll 2, p. 3.

12. Allyn H. Tedmon, "War Work of Big Horn County Agent—1917," *Extension Service Annual Reports: Wyoming, 1914–1944,* National Archives, Microcopy T-897, roll 1, frame 2; Nathaniel R. Whitney, *The Sale of War Bonds in Iowa* (Iowa City: State Historical Society of Iowa, 1923), p. 167.

13. "The Middle West's Peace Problems," *Atlantic Monthly* 123, no. 4 (Apr. 1919):555; see also H. G. Tank to Carl Vrooman, Oct. 30, 1917, National Archives, record group 16, "Correspondence of Secretaries of Agriculture," "Farms—Farmers— Farming—1917" file.

14. Whitney, *Sale of War Bonds,* p. 5; an interesting commentary on the relative ineffectiveness of the media in manipulating rural people can be found in S. Wayne Hind to

E. T. Meredith, June 2, 1920, National Archives, record group 16, "Correspondence of Secretaries of Agriculture," "Farms—Farmers—Farming—1920" file; see also N. E. Garber, "War Work of Bucks County Agent—1917," *Extension Service Annual Reports: Pennsylvania, 1914-1944,* National Archives, Microcopy T-883, roll 1, p. 3; A. D. Welton, "Looking Back at the Liberty Loan," *Nation's Business 5,* no. 8 (Aug. 1917):18-19, 49-50.

15. Author Unknown, "How Farmers Led in Oversubscribing Liberty Loan Shown in Final Report," *USDA Weekly News Letter 5,* no. 47 (June 27, 1918):9.

16. Warren H. Wilson, "The Rural Survey and Rural Crisis," *Proceedings of the National Conference of Social Work at the Forty-Fourth Annual Session Held in Pittsburgh, Pennsylvania June 6-13, 1917* (Chicago: National Conference of Social Work, 1917), p. 618; see also William A. Lloyd, "County Agricultural Agent Work Under the Smith-Lever Act, 1914-1924," *USDA, Miscellaneous Circular no. 59, 1926,* p. 54.

17. Remarks of David F. Houston, *Annual Reports, USDA, 1918,* p. 13; remarks of A. C. True, ibid., p. 336; Lester Shephard, "Monona County, War Emergency Report, 1917," *Extension Service Annual Reports: Iowa, 1912-1944,* National Archives, Microcopy T-860, roll 2, frame 4.

18. See L. E. Howard, "Report of the Work of the Mississippi County Agent: Calendar Year 1918," *Extension Service Annual Reports: Arkansas, 1909-1944,* National Archives, Microcopy T-848, roll 3, frame 43; W. T. Snow, "Report of the Work of the Ouachita County Agent: Calendar Year 1918," *Extension Service Annual Reports: Arkansas, 1909-1944,* National Archives, Microcopy T-848, roll 3, frames 43-44.

19. C. H. Wilkes, "Report of Work of the Copiah County Agent: Calendar Year 1917," *Extension Service Annual Reports: Mississippi, 1909-1944,* National Archives, Microcopy T-869, roll 2, frame 35; Dick Lewallen, "Supplementary Narrative Report, Lyman County—1917," *Extension Service Annual Reports: South Dakota, 1913-1944,* National Archives, Microcopy T-888, roll 1, p. 1; Persons J. Crandall, "County Agent Work, Union County—1918," *Extension Service Annual Reports: South Dakota, 1913-1944,* National Archives, Microcopy T-888, roll 2, p. 56.

20. V. M. Emmert, "McPherson County Farm Bureau Annual Report—1918," *Extension Service Annual Reports: Kansas, 1913-1944,* National Archives, Microcopy T-861, roll 3, p. 8; Merton Moore, "Narrative Report of Shawano County Agricultural Representative—1917," *Extension Service Reports: Wisconsin, 1913-1944,* National Archives, Microcopy T-896, roll 1, p. 2; R. G. Hoopingarner, "Narrative Report of Iron County Agent—1917," *Extension Service Annual Reports: Michigan, 1913-1944,* National Archives, Microcopy T-867, roll 2, p. 1; F. S. Sterling, "Narrative Report of Wilkin County Agent—1918," *Extension Service Annual Reports: Minnesota, 1914-1944,* National Archives, Microcopy T-868, roll 4, p. 6.

21. Henry R. Seager and Robert E. Chaddock, "Food Preparedness," *Columbia War Papers,* series 1, no. 6 (New York: Division of Intelligence and Publicity of Columbia University, 1917), p. 3.

22. *Report of the New York State Food Commission for Period October 18, 1917, to July 1, 1918* (Albany: Lyon, 1919), p. 9.

23. E. A. Schubert to Carl Vrooman, May 18, 1917, National Archives, record group 17, "Correspondence of Secretaries of Agriculture," "National Defense (2) Food (May 15-31)" drawer 446; C. W. Scott to Carl Vrooman, May 21, 1917, National Archives, record group 16, "Correspondence of Secretaries of Agriculture," "National Defense (2) Food (May 15-31)" drawer 446.

24. Herbert Quick to David F. Houston, Apr. 11, 1917, National Archives, record group 16, "Correspondence of Secretaries of Agriculture, "National Defense (2) Food (Apr. 1-14)" drawer 441; remarks of W. L. Brown, "Agricultural Advisory Committee: 'Actual Minutes of First Meeting, 30 March 1918,' " Herbert Hoover Archives, Food Administration carton 82 (A), "Agricultural Advisory Committee: 'Actual Minutes of First Meeting, 30 March 1918' " file, sheet 23.

25. Herbert Hoover, "Forward," in Frank M. Surface, *The Stabilization of the Price of Wheat during the War and Its Effect upon the Returns to the Producer* (Washington, D.C.: United States Grain Corp., May 1925), p. 7.

26. Quoted in William Clinton Mullendore, *History of the United States Food Administration, 1917-1919* (Stanford: Stanford University Press, 1941), p. 50.

27. Livermore, *Politics Adjourned,* pp. 170-172; Harry A. Wheeler to Herbert Hoover, Sept.

28, 1917, Herbert Hoover Archives, Food Administration carton 6-H (12), "Illinois: Harry A. Wheeler" file; Henry A. Page to the Roller Mills of North Carolina, Apr. 25, 1918, Herbert Hoover Archives, Food Administration carton 6-H (19), "North Carolina" file; "Agricultural Advisory Committee: Reports and Recommendations," April 6, 1918, file, p. 14; U.S., Congress, Senate, Committee on Agriculture and Forestry, *Hearings Relative to Increasing the Production of Grain and Meat Supplies of the United States,* 65th Cong., 2d sess., 1918.

28. *USDA, Yearbook, 1931,* p. 583.

29. Seager and Chaddock, "Food Preparedness," p. 17.

30. The farm work force, not counting operators or working sons, declined four percent in 1917 alone. See Daniel J. Ahearn, Jr., *The Wages of Farm and Factory Laborers, 1914-1944* (New York: Columbia University Press, 1945), p. 110.

31. Anna Larrabee to R. A. Pearson, Jan. 29, 1918, National Archives, record group 16, "Correspondence of Secretaries of Agriculture," "Army and Navy—1918" drawer 72; E. T. Robbins to Carl Vrooman, Feb. 23, 1918, National Archives, record group 16, "Correspondence of Secretaries of Agriculture," "Army and Navy—1918" drawer 72, p. 1; W. T. Drury to David F. Houston, Apr. 8, 1918, National Archives, record group 16, "Correspondence of Secretaries of Agriculture," "Army and Navy—1918" drawer 73.

32. L. F. Harvey, "Special Supplementary Report for New Haven County, 1917," *Extension Service Annual Reports: Connecticut, 1913-1944,* National Archives, Microcopy T-851, roll 1, p. 2; J. W. Haw, "Annual Narrative Report, Cavalier County Agent—1918," *Extension Service Annual Reports: North Dakota, 1912-1944,* National Archives, Microcopy T-879, roll 2, frames 14-18; Edward Johnson, "Handling the 1918 Wheat Harvest in Kansas," *USDA, Circular 121, 1918,* pp. 4-5.

33. Author Unknown, "Names Agriculture Advisers for District Draft Boards," *USDA Weekly News Letter* 6, no. 10 (Oct. 9, 1918):1; Frederick W. Williamson, *Origin and Growth of Agricultural Extension in Louisiana, 1860-1948* (Baton Rouge: Louisiana State University, 1951), p. 74.

34. R. E. Brossard, "Work of the County Agents and Emergency Demonstration Agents with Special Reference to Conditions Brought About by the War—Bonneville County, July 1–December 1, 1917," *Extension Service Annual Reports: Idaho, 1913-1944,* National Archives, Microcopy T-857, roll 1, p. 3; R. F. O'Donnell, "War Emergency Report—1917: Iowa-Cerro Gordo County," *Extension Service Annual Reports: Iowa, 1912-1944,* National Archives, Microcopy T-860, roll 2, p. 1; A. H. Beckhoff, "Lyon County Agent Annual Report—1918, *Extension Service Annual Reports: Iowa, 1912-1944,* National Archives, Microcopy T-860, roll 3, p. 9; Thorstein Veblen, "Memorandum: Farm Labor and the I.W.W.," Herbert Hoover Archives, Alonzo E. Taylor Collection, Food Administration carton 175, "Veblen, Thorstein" file, pp. 6-8.

35. *Annual Reports, USDA, 1919,* pp. 377-378; Benjamin H. Hibbard, "Agricultural Changes during the World War," in Louis Bernard Schmidt and Earle Dudley Ross, eds., *Readings in the Economic History of American Agriculture* (New York: Macmillan, 1925), pp. 504-528.

36. John H. Fay, "Narrative Report of the County Agent from Middlesex County, 1917," *Extension Service Annual Reports: Connecticut, 1913-1944,* National Archives, Microcopy T-851, roll 1, pp. 9-10; H. S. Brossard, "Annual Report Yellowstone County Farm Bureau—1918," *Extension Service Annual Reports: Montana, 1914-1944,* National Archives, Microcopy T-871, roll 3, p. 16; Reynold M. Wik, *Henry Ford and Grass-roots America* (Ann Arbor: University of Michigan Press, 1972), p. 93.

37. George E. Farrell, "Boys' and Girls' 4-H Club Work Under the Smith-Lever Act, 1914-1924," *USDA, Miscellaneous Circular no. 85, 1926,* p. 19.

38. Edward Wiest, *Agricultural Organization in the United States* (Lexington: University of Kentucky, Apr. 1923), p. 243; see also A. E. Jones, "Annual Report for Jewel County—1918," *Extension Service Annual Reports: Kansas, 1913-1944,* National Archives, Microcopy T-861, roll 3, p. 1.

39. "Narrative Report of Work of Dallas County Agent—1918," *Extension Service Annual Reports: Iowa, 1912-1944,* National Archives, Microcopy T-860, roll 3, p. 8. The patriotic appeal was the key to agent organizational success in some areas; see Nelson G. Malin, "Narrative Report—Dubuque County—1918," *Extension Service Annual Reports: Iowa, 1912-1944,* National Archives, Microcopy T-860, roll 3, p. 1.

40. R. E. F. Washington, "Report of Work of the Charles City County Agent—1917," *Extension Service Annual Reports: Virginia, 1908-1914,* National Archives, Microcopy T-893, roll 2, frame 41; D. Watson Atkinson, "Narrative Report, Delaware County—1917," *Extension Service Annual Reports: Pennsylvania, 1914-1944,* National Archives, Microcopy T-883, roll 1, p. 14; Noel N. Rhodes, "Annual Report Madison County Farm Bureau—1918," *Extension Service Annual Reports: Nebraska, 1913-1914,* National Archives, Microcopy T-872, roll 3, frame 50; Robert L. Morlan, *Political Prairie Fire* (Minneapolis: University of Minnesota Press, 1955), pp. 202-203.

41. Cowgill C. Blair, "The Farmers' Viewpoint," *Review of Reviews* 55, no. 6 (June 1917):630; remarks of Iowa Representative Gilbert Haugen, U.S., Congress, House, *Congressional Record,* 65th Cong., 1st sess., 1917, 55, pt. 2:2035; Paul T. Schooley, "Report of Work of the Albemarle County Agent—1917," *Extension Service Annual Reports: Virginia, 1908-1944,* National Archives, Microcopy T-893, roll 2, frame 46.

42. Albert F. Lawrence, "Summary of Work of the Carver County Farm Bureau—1918," *Extension Service Annual Reports: Minnesota, 1914-1944,* National Archives, Microcopy T-868, roll 3, p. 10; see also Ethel Angel, "Extension Work with Women, Ransom and La Moure Counties—1918," *Extension Service Annual Reports: North Dakota, 1912-1944,* National Archives, Microcopy T-879, roll 2, frame 10; J. F. Thomas, "Annual Narrative Report of Franklin County Agent—1918," *Extension Service Annual Reports: Iowa, 1912-1944,* National Archives, Microcopy T-860, roll 3, p. 3.

43. U.S., Congress, Senate, *Congressional Record,* 65th Cong., 2d sess., 1918, 56, pt. 10:9795; ibid., p. 10075; see also remarks of North Dakota Senator Porter McCumber, ibid., p. 9786.

44. U.S., Congress, House, *Congressional Record,* 65th Cong., 2d sess., 1918, 56, pt. 7:6799; see also the remarks of Texas Representative Hatton W. Summers, North Dakota Representative Patrick Norton, and Iowa Representative James W. Good, U.S., Congress, House, *Congressional Record,* 65th Cong., 1st sess., 1917, 55, pt. 2:2038, 2039, 2049.

45. In some places their opponents used the draft to punish agents. In the Draft District of Southern Iowa the draft board classified county agents "unskilled farm labor" and began drafting them; Ralph K. Bliss to R. A. Pearson, Feb. 5, 1918, National Archives, record group 16, "Correspondence of Secretaries of Agriculture," "Army and Navy—1918" drawer 72.

46. U.S., Congress, House, *Congressional Record,* 66th Cong., 2d sess., 1918, 56, pt. 7:6800; William S. Kenyon to R. A. Pearson, May 23, 1918, National Archives, record group 16," "Correspondence of Secretaries of Agriculture," "Army and Navy—1918" drawer 74; see also the remarks of Michigan Representative James C. McLaughlin and Indiana Representative William E. Cox, U.S., Congress, House, *Congressional Record,* 66th Cong., 2d sess., 1918, 56, pt. 7:6803, 6806.

47. H. H. Boone, "Manuscript Report for 1919, Walla Walla County," *Extension Service Annual Reports: Washington, 1913-1944,* National Archives, Microcopy T-894, roll 3, frame 40; F. E. Longmire, "Annual Report of Grundy County Farm Adviser—1918," *Extension Service Annual Reports: Illinois, 1914-1944,* National Archives, Microcopy T-858, roll 2, p. 12.

48. "County Agricultural Agent Work Under the Smith-Lever Act, 1914 to 1924," *USDA Miscellaneous Circular no. 59, 1926,* pp. 17-18; see also Franklin M. Reck, *The 4-H Story* (Ames, Ia.: National Committee on Boys and Girls Club Work, 1951), p. 155; Russell Lord, *The Agrarian Revival* (New York: American Association for Adult Education, 1939), p. 101.

49. A. G. Davis, "Merrimack County Agent Report—1918," *Extension Service Annual Reports: New Hampshire, 1914-1944,* National Archives, Microcopy T-874, roll 1, frame 16; George L. Winright, "Narrative Report, McCook County—1918," *Extension Service Annual Reports: South Dakota, 1913-1944,* National Archives, Microcopy T-888, roll 2, p. 15; Malinda H. Woodworth, "Monthly Report of District I Home Demonstration Agent," June 1918, *Extension Service Annual Reports: California, 1913-1944,* National Archives, Microcopy T-849, roll 2, p. 2; on ignorance of emergency agents see Henry C. Wallace, *Our Debt and Duty to the Farmer* (New York: Century, 1925), p. 48.

50. W. A. Lloyd, "What Should Be the Relationship of the County Agent to the Farm Bureaus," *Proceedings of the Thirty-Third Annual Convention of the Association of*

American Agricultural Colleges and Experiment Stations Held at Chicago, Illinois, November 12-14, 1919 (Burlington, Vt.: Free Press, 1919), p. 298; see also *Annual Reports, USDA, 1917,* p. 350; Thomas Cooper, "Report of the Director of Agricultural Extension—1917," *Extension Service Annual Reports: North Dakota, 1912-1944,* National Archives, Microcopy T-879, roll 1, p. 3.

51. "Extension Problems of Reconstruction," *Proceedings of the Thirty-Second Annual Convention of the Association of American Agricultural Colleges and Experiment Stations Held at Baltimore, Maryland, January 8-10, 1919* (Burlington, Vt.: Free Press, 1919), p. 247.

52. Edith S. Parrott, "An Abridged Report of the Home Demonstration Work of South Carolina—1917," *Extension Service Annual Reports: South Carolina, 1909-1944,* National Archives, Microcopy T-887, roll 1, p. 7.

53. U.S., Congress, Senate, Committee on Agriculture and Forestry, *Food Production Act: Hearing on H.R. 11945,* 65th Cong., 2d sess., 1919, p. 28; see also Raymond A. Pearson, "War Agriculture," *The Business of Agriculture During the War and After* (Washington: USGPO, 1918), p. 20; H. R. Tolley, "Efficiency of U.S. Agriculture Is Increasing," *USDA, Yearbook, 1926,* p. 319.

54. Mullendore, *United States Food Administration,* p. 77.

55. U.S., Congress, Senate, Committee on Agriculture and Forestry, *Food Production Act: Hearing on H.R. 11945,* 65th Cong., 2d sess., 1919, p. 21.

56. Wilson, "The Rural Survey and the Rural Crisis," p. 618. See also Kenyon Butterfield, "The Morrill Act Institutions and the New Epoch," *Proceedings of the Thirty-First Annual Convention of the Association of American Agricultural Colleges and Experiment Stations Held at Washington, D.C., November 14-16, 1917* (Burlington, Vt.: Free Press, 1918), pp. 43-59; Kenyon L. Butterfield, *The Farmer and the New Day* (New York: Macmillan, 1919), p. 15.

57. "The Farmer and Child Welfare Work," *Proceedings of the National Conference of Social Work at the Forty-Sixth Annual Session Held in Atlantic City, New Jersey June 1-8, 1919* (Chicago: Rogers and Hall, 1919), p. 30.

58. Vogt, *Introduction to Rural Sociology,* p. 400.

59. N. D. Showalter, *A Handbook for Rural School Officers* (Boston: Houghton Mifflin, 1920), p. 194.

60. Author Unknown, "Farming Methods Advance Twenty Years during War," *USDA Weekly News Letter* 6, no. 48 (July 2, 1919):1.

61. National Industrial Conference Board, *The Agricultural Problem in the United States* (New York: National Industrial Conference Board, 1926), p. 56; James H. Shideler, *Farm Crisis, 1919-1923* (Berkeley: University of California Press, 1957), p. 38.

62. G. F. Warren and F. A. Pearson, "Wholesale Prices in the United States for 135 Years, 1797 to 1932," in *Wholesale Prices for 213 Years, 1720 to 1932,* Cornell University Agricultural Experiment Station *Memoir 142* (Ithaca: Cornell University Agricultural Experiment Station, Nov. 1932), p. 46.

63. Shideler, *Farm Crisis,* p. 39; editorial, "Ignorance That Is Malicious," *Orange Judd Farmer,* 68, no. 7 (Feb. 14, 1920):6.

64. E. D. Ball, "The Need of a Food Supply for an Increasing Population," United States House of Representatives, *Report of the National Agricultural Conference, January 23-27, 1922,* Document no. 195 (Washington: USGPO, 1922), pp. 99-106; W. R. Beattie, "The City Home Garden," *USDA Farmers' Bulletin 1044,* p. 4; editorial, "Is It Deliberate?" *Orange Judd Farmer* 68, no. 7 (Feb. 14, 1920):6.

65. David F. Houston, "To the Farmers and the Agricultural Forces of the United States," *USDA Weekly News Letter* 6, no. 15 (Nov. 13, 1918):2; E. G. Nourse, "The Revolution in Farming," *Yale Review* 8, no. 1 (Oct. 1918):90-105; H. Ida Curry, "The Status of Social Work in Rural Communities," *Proceedings of the National Conference of Social Work at the Forty-Fifth Annual Session Held in Kansas City, Missouri May 15-22, 1918* (Chicago: Rogers and Hall, 1918), pp. 83-91; Elliott Dunlap, "Community Councils: Their Present Work: Their Future Opportunity," *Proceedings of the First National Country Life Conference, Baltimore 1919* (Ithaca: National Country Life Association, 1919), pp. 36-46.

66. Theodore M. Beal, "Annual Report of Franklin County Agricultural Agent—1921," *Extension Service Annual Reports: Indiana, 1912-1944,* National Archives, Microcopy T-859, roll 8, p. 1; see also Harriet A. Ackerly, "Narrative Report of Home Demon-

stration Agent of Cheshire County—1918," *Extension Service Annual Reports: New Hampshire, 1914-1944,* National Archives, Microcopy T-874, roll 1, pp. 2-3.

67. Alfred Charles True, *A History of Agricultural Extension Work in the United States, 1785-1923, USDA Miscellaneous Publication no. 15, 1928,* p. 150.

68. *Journal of Proceedings of the National Grange of the Patrons of Husbandry Fifty-First Annual Session St. Louis, Missouri 1917* (Springfield, Mass.: National Grange Monthly, 1917), p. 29; see also K. S. Harlow, "Why Farmers Need Organization," *Pacific Rural Press* 96, no. 3 (July 20, 1918):61.

69. Editorial, "A Platform for Farm Progress," *Country Gentleman* 83, no. 52 (Dec. 28, 1918):12; editorial, "The Farmer and the War," *Farmers' Open Forum* 3, no. 3 (Nov. 1917):8; Liberty Hyde Bailey, "The Place of the Farmer in the Body Politic," *Annual Report of the Secretary of the Connecticut State Board of Agriculture, 1918* (Hartford: State of Connecticut, 1918), pp. 77-78.

70. Thomas J. Smart, "The Problem of Rural Education," *School and Society* 10, no. 254 (Nov. 8, 1919):544.

71. Joseph W. Alsop, "Our Agriculture Problems," *Annual Report of the Secretary of the Connecticut State Board of Agriculture, 1919-1920* (Hartford: State of Connecticut, 1920), p. 50; remarks of Indiana Senator Jim Watson at the Fourth Annual New Jersey Agricultural Convention, *New Jersey Department of Agriculture Bulletin no. 19* (Trenton: New Jersey Department of Agriculture, Feb. 1919), p. 269. Even moderate farm spokesmen seem to have been somewhat radicalized during the war. See Clarence Poe, "More about Russia: How to Understand Conditions Since 'Red Sunday,' " *Progressive Farmer* 34, no. 16 (Apr. 19, 1919):693. The only serious study I found on rural political radicalism and urban political conservatism is Stuart A. Rice, "A Note on the Census Categories, 'Urban' and 'Rural,' " *Journal of the American Statistical Association* 19, no. 145 (Mar. 1924):79-81.

72. John J. Lacey, *Farm Bureau in Illinois* (Bloomington, Ill.: Illinois Agricultural Association, 1965), p. 63.

73. Russell Lord, *The Wallaces of Iowa* (Boston: Houghton Mifflin, 1947), p. 204.

74. Editorial, "The Farm Bureaus in Nebraska," *Nonpartisan Leader* 9, no. 24 (Dec. 15, 1919):7; C. B. Cook, "Annual Narrative Report, Oakland County—1919," *Extension Service Annual Reports: Michigan, 1913-1944,* National Archives, Microcopy T-867, roll 5A, p. 1.

75. R. A. Pearson to the Iowa State Board of Education, January 1, 1919, National Archives, record group 16, "Correspondence of Secretaries of Agriculture," "Extension Work—1919" drawer 338; see also E. E. Hupp, "Annual Report of Pend Oreille County Agent—1920," *Extension Service Annual Reports: Washington, 1913-1944,* National Archives, Microcopy T-894, roll 5, frame 5; *Journal of Proceedings of the National Grange of the Patrons of Husbandry Fifty-Third Annual Session Grand Rapids, Michigan, 1919* (Springfield, Mass.: National Grange Monthly, 1919).

76. Peter A. Speek, *A Stake in the Land* (New York: Harper, 1921), pp. 130-131.

77. Peter Roberts, "Americanization and County Work," *Rural Manhood* 11, no. 3 (Mar. 1920):102. Many were concerned that native farmers were being driven from the land. See J. Madison Gathany, "What's the Matter with the Eastern Farmer? Our Agricultural Plight," *Outlook* 126, no. 3 (Sept. 15, 1920):107.

78. Vogt, *Introduction to Rural Sociology,* p. 267. See also the remarks of H. W. Foght in the "Proceedings of the First National Conference on Rural School Consolidation," *Bulletin of the Iowa State Teachers College* 20, no. 4 (June 1920):42; Marvin S. Pittman, *Successful Teaching in Rural Schools* (New York: American, 1922), p. 145.

79. Harold Waldstein Foght, *The Rural Teacher and His Work* (New York: Macmillan, 1920), p. 176.

80. Robert C. Shaw, "Progress in Consolidation in Pennsylvania," *Proceedings of the Sixty-Sixth Annual Meeting of the National Education Association Held at Minneapolis, Minnesota, July 1-6, 1928* (Washington: National Education Association, 1928), p. 497; Harold Waldstein Foght, "Rural Education," *United States Bureau of Education Bulletin,* no. 7 (1919), p. 20, estimates a wartime rural teacher shortfall of 27,000.

81. George Schultzberg, "Consolidation of Schools," *Sierra Educational News* 14, no. 3 (Mar. 1918):134; see also Author Unknown, "Consolidation as a War Measure," *School Life* 1, no. 1 (Aug. 1, 1918):12.

82. Remarks of Lawrence L. Hill, *Addresses and Proceedings of the Fifty-Sixth Annual*

Meeting of the National Education Association Held at Pittsburgh, Pennsylvania, June 29-July 6, 1918 (Chicago: National Education Association, 1918), p. 347; remarks of Minnesota Representative Sydney Anderson, U.S., House, Committee on Agriculture, *Food Production Act: Hearings,* 65th Cong., 2d sess., 1919, p. 94.

83. Author Unknown, "The Teacher Shortage and Inexperienced Teachers," *School Life* 1, no. 3 (Sept. 1, 1918):9; United States Bureau of Education, *Report of the Commissioner of Education for the Year Ended June 30, 1919* (Washington: USGPO, 1919), p. 90. The Bureau of Education estimated that the teacher shortage forced the closure of 18,279 schools and that 41,900 more were taught by "low standard" teachers. See United States Bureau of Education, *Report of the Commissioner of Education for the Year Ending June 30, 1920* (Washington: USGPO, 1920), p. 40; remarks of Rural School Supervisor E. A. Duke, State of Oklahoma *Seventh Biennial Report of the State Superintendent of Public Instruction Together with the Fourth Report of the State Board of Education, 1918* (Oklahoma City: Oklahoma Department of Education, 1918), p. 42.

84. Calvin Kendall, "An Open Letter from the Commissioner of Education of New Jersey to Boards of Education, Superintendents and Supervising Principals," *Extension Service Annual Reports: New Jersey, 1913-1944,* National Archives, Microcopy T-875, roll 1, Apr. 12, 1917; John Dewey, "Enlistment for the Farm," *Columbia War Papers,* series I, no. 1 (New York: Division of Intelligence and Publicity of Columbia University, 1917); editorial, "Discarding School Books for Farming," *Survey* 38, no. 3 (Apr. 21, 1917):68-69.

85. Flora Melissa Byrd, "Annual Report of Home Demonstration Work for Women and Girls, Bradley County—1919," *Extension Service Annual Reports: Tennessee, 1910-44,* National Archives, Microcopy T-889, roll 3, frame 4; see also editorial, "Farm Life and Labor," *Independent* 99, no. 3690 (Aug. 30, 1919):278-279. Social division did not result from the war in all cases, and there were instances in which the war contributed to rural unity. See Adolph Schock, *In Quest of Free Land* (Assen, Neth.: Royal Vangorcum, 1964), pp. 168-169.

86. Shideler, *Farm Crisis,* p. 19; Constance D'Arcy Mackay, "Imaginative Recreation in Rural Districts: Commercial Recreation," *Playground* 14, no. 1 (Apr. 1920):31. Despite material gains in the countryside, moreover, farmers still did not approach the standards of comfort enjoyed by their urban counterparts. See E. G. Nourse, "Harmonizing the Interests of Farm Producer and Town Consumer," *Journal of Political Economy* 28, no. 8 (Oct. 1920):633.

87. The USDA optimistically estimated that 75-90 percent of farm-boy soldiers were returning to the land, but it admitted that few who had gone to the cities were returning. See Author Unknown, "Soldiers Return to Farms, Department Surveys Show," *USDA Weekly News Letter* 6, no. 43 (May 28, 1919):2. See also John R. Foster to E. T. Meredith, Feb. 17, 1920, National Archives, record group 16, "Correspondence of Secretaries of Agriculture," "Cost of Living—1920" file, and testimony of J. R. Howard, U.S., Congress, Senate, Committees of Agriculture and Forestry, *High Cost of Living in the United States: Joint Hearings on,* 66th Cong., 1st sess., 1919, pt. 1:9.

88. Cook, "Oakland County—1919," *Extension Service Annual Reports: Michigan,* p. 2; and G. H. Dacy, "Who Shall Work the Farms?" *Scientific American* 124, no. 10 (Mar. 5, 1921):195, both indicate that postwar discontent and wanderlust infected areas near the cities particularly. But an Oklahoma agent reported that it required strenuous efforts on his part to keep one community of Negro farmers from packing up and leaving for Africa. See Levi Walton Presley, "Report of Work of the McIntosh County Negro Agent—1919," *Extension Service Annual Reports: Oklahoma, 1909-1944,* National Archives, Microcopy T-881, roll 5, frame 51.

89. James B. Morman, *The Place of Agriculture in Reconstruction* (New York: Dutton, 1919), p. 183.

90. Franklin K. Lane to Woodrow Wilson, May 31, 1918, in Anne Wintermute Lane and Louise Herrick Hall, *The Letters of Franklin K. Lane* (Boston: Houghton Mifflin, 1922), p. 288; Franklin K. Lane, "Farms for Returned Soldiers," *Scientific American* 119, no. 19 (Nov. 9, 1918):372-373.

91. Franklin K. Lane to E. S. Pillsbury, July 30, 1918, in Lane and Hall, *Letters,* p. 291. See also Elwood Mead, *Helping Men Own Farms* (New York: Macmillan, 1920), p. 198.

92. Elwood Mead, "What an Agricultural Engineer Thinks of Our Farming System," *Outlook* 118, no. 14 (Apr. 3, 1918):534-535. Paul K. Conkin, *Tomorrow a New World:*

The New Deal Community Program (Binghamton, N.Y.: American Historical Association, 1959), makes the point that the main thrust of land settlement was toward renovating agriculture, p. 58.

93. "Farming His Own," *Sunset* 39, no. 5 (Nov. 1918):26.

94. Lemuel Call Barnes, "Christian Opportunity among Soldiers," *Missionary Review of the World* 42, no. 4 (Apr. 1919):272. See also Mead, *Helping Men Own Farms,* p. 2; Elwood Mead, "Farm Settlements on a New Plan," *Review of Reviews* 59, no. 3 (Mar. 1919):277; Alvin Johnson, "Land for the Returned Soldier," *New Republic* 16, no. 203 (Sept. 21, 1918):218-220; Alvin Johnson, "The Land Settlement Community," *New Republic* 17, no. 209 (Nov. 2, 1918):11-13.

95. Author Unknown, "Farm Allotments and Farm Laborer's Allotments in the Durham State Land Settlement" (Sacramento: State Land Settlement Board, May 1918); H. A. Crafts, "The State and the Farmer," *Scientific American* 123, no. 20 (Nov. 13, 1920):494; Wayne C. Nason, "Rural Planning: The Social Aspects of Recreation Places," *USDA Farmers' Bulletin 1388,* 1924, p. 27.

96. Elwood Mead, "Placing Soldiers on Farm Colonies," in Clyde Lyndon King, ed., *The Annals of the American Academy of Political and Social Science* (Philadelphia: American Academy of Political and Social Science, Jan. 1919), p. 63; editorial, "Agrarian Reorganization," *New Republic* 13, no. 168 (Jan. 19, 1918):333-334.

97. Author Unknown, "How California Helps Men Own Farms and Rural Homes" (Sacramento: State Land Settlement Board, June 1920), p. 12; Walter V. Woehlke, "Food First," *Sunset* 45, no. 4 (Oct. 1920):35-38, 76-80; Mead, "Farming His Own," p. 70; Mead, *Helping Men Own Farms,* pp. 129-183.

98. Evelyn Dewey, *New Schools for Old* (New York: Dutton, 1919), p. 170; Mead, *Helping Men Own Farms,* p. 140.

99. "Farm Settlements on a New Plan," p. 272; see also David P. Barrows, "Giving the New Settler a Lift," *Sunset* 38, no. 2 (Mar. 1917):21.

100. Speek, *Stake in the Land,* reports that by June, 1919, fully 23 states had passed bills aimed at getting soldiers land, pp. 91-95. None of these measures approached the elaboration of the California land plan, and few ever had any practical value. Despite a good deal of interest in Congress, no land settlement bill passed that body. See also William E. Smythe, "Making America Over," *Review of Reviews* 60, no. 1 (July 1919):70-73.

101. Remarks of Walter E. Edge, *New Jersey Department of Agriculture Bulletin no. 19,* p. 189; Morman, *Agriculture in Reconstruction,* p. 200.

102. H. G. Niesley to David F. Houston, Feb. 14, 1919, National Archives, record group 16, "Correspondence of Secretaries of Agriculture," "Farm—Farmers— Farming—1919" file; Bill G. Reid, "Agrarian Opposition to Franklin K. Lane's Proposal for Soldier Settlement, 1918-1921," *Agricultural History* 41, no. 2 (Apr. 1967):167-179; remarks of David F. Houston, *Annual Reports, USDA, 1919,* pp. 18-21; David F. Houston, "Address of D. F. Houston, Secretary of Agriculture, before the National Association of Commissioners of Agriculture, Auditorium Hotel, Chicago, Illinois, November 11, 1919," *USDA Circular 146,* p. 6.

103. "Proposals for Soldier Settlement during World War I," *Mid-America* 46, no. 3 (July 1964):186.

104. See Paul K. Conkin's fine article, "The Vision of Elwood Mead," *Agricultural History* 34, no. 2 (Apr. 1960):88-89.

105. "California's Farm Colonies," *Review of Reviews* 64, no. 4 (Oct. 1921):404.

106. "Country Life," *Survey* 41, no. 19 (Feb. 8, 1919):679.

CHAPTER 6

1. Newell Leroy Sims, *The Rural Community* (New York: Scribner's, 1920), p. xx.

2. The best work on agriculture in the twenties is James H. Shideler's fine treatment, *Farm Crisis, 1919-1923* (Berkeley: University of California Press, 1957).

3. Emery N. Ferriss, Joint Committee on Rural Schools, *Rural School Survey of New York State: The Rural High School* (Ithaca: Emery N. Ferriss, 1922), 7:148-149; Theodore H. Eaton, Joint Committee on Rural Schools, *Rural School Survey of New*

York State: Vocational Education (Ithaca: Theodore H. Eaton, 1922), 8:106–109; Author Unknown, "Report of the Special Legislative Commission on Agricultural Education," (Sacramento: California Commission on Agricultural Education, California State Printing Office, 1923), p. 13. Harold Waldstein Foght, *The Rural Teacher and His Work* (New York: Macmillan, 1920), p. 176. The United States Bureau of Education had a rather liberal definition of consolidation, considering any school resulting from the union of as few as two schools to be consolidated. See United States Bureau of Education, *Report of the Commissioner of Education for the Year Ended June 30, 1918* (Washington: USGPO, 1918), p. 52.

4. Newell Leroy Sims, *Elements of Rural Sociology* (New York: Crowell, 1928), pp. 420–422; see Author Unknown, "Rural Public Health Service 1921–1925," *Rural America* 3, no. 9 (Nov. 1925):11.

5. E. L. Kirkpatrick, Helen W. Atwater, and Ilena M. Bailey, "Family Living in Farm Homes," *USDA, Department Bulletin no. 1214, 1924;* Department of Commerce, Bureau of Census, *Abstract of the Fourteenth Census of the United States, 1920* (Washington: USGPO, 1923), p. 749.

6. John M. Freeman, "The Consolidated School Movement in Buchanan County" (Master's thesis, University of Iowa, Aug. 1939), pp. 68–70; C. H. Hamilton, "What the Church Is Doing in Behalf of Rural Living Standards in Virginia," Virginia Polytechnic Institute, "The 1929 Institute of Rural Affairs Proceedings," *Bulletin of Virginia Polytechnic Institute* (Blacksburg: Virginia Polytechnic Institute, Jan. 1930) 23, no. 3:118; George A. Works, Joint Committee on Rural Schools, *Rural School Survey of New York State: A Report to the School Patrons,* vol. 1 (Ithaca: George A. Works, 1922), pp. 192–193.

7. C. J. Galpin, "Discriminations against Rural People," *Rural America* 7, no. 4 (Apr. 1929):5–6; see also E. C. Lindeman, "Some Sociological Implications of the Farm Bureau Movement," *Papers and Proceedings of the Eighteenth Annual Meeting of the American Sociological Society* (Chicago: University of Chicago Press, 1924), p. 186; Horace Boies Hawthorn, *The Sociology of Rural Life* (New York: Century, 1926), p. 434.

8. State of Washington, *Twenty-Sixth Biennial Report of the Superintendent of Public Instruction for the Biennium Ending June 30, 1922* (Olympia: Frank M. Lamborn, Public Printer, 1922), pp. 31–130; Ralph S. Childs, "Rural Municipalities of Tomorrow," American Country Life Association, *Country Community Education: Proceedings of the Fifth National Country Life Conference, Teachers College, Columbia University New York City 1922* (New York: Association Press for the American Country Life Association, 1923), p. 146; Edwin L. Earp, *The Rural Church Movement* (New York: Methodist Book Concern, 1923), p. 97; Edwin V. O'Hara, "A Rural Religious Program As Viewed by a Catholic," *Country Life Bulletin* 2, no. 9 (Nov. 1924):9–16; Robert G. Armstrong, "Wanted—a Technique for the Rural County," *Survey* 69, no. 6 (Dec. 15, 1927):382–383.

9. Dwight Sanderson, "Some Fundamentals of Rural Community Organization," *Journal of Rural Education* 1, no. 1 (Sept. 1921):33; Forest C. Ensign, "Consolidated Schools in Iowa," *American City* 27, no. 6 (Dec. 1922):516; Frank Pierrepont Graves, "Rural Education," *Addresses and Proceedings of the Sixty-Second Annual Meeting of the National Education Association of the United States, Held at Washington, D.C., June 29–July 4, 1924* (Washington: National Education Association, 1924), p. 858.

10. For a view of the potential use of the radio in the countryside see David Sarnoff and Samuel D. Gromer, "Radio from Two Viewpoints," *Monthly Bulletin of the Missouri State Board of Agriculture* (Jefferson City: Missouri State Board of Agriculture, Oct. 1924). As for motion pictures, the USDA early recognized the rural fascination for them and their potential manipulative value. Some early reels with which the USDA attempted to bedazzle farmers were "Should I Buy a Tractor?" "Sir Loin of T-Bone Ranch," "Laying Lumbricus Low," and "Crops and Kilowatts." See the remarks of USDA flick mogul Fred W. Perkins, *Annual Reports, USDA, 1923,* pp. 527–531.

11. Remarks of Commissioner George W. Koiner, *Monthly Bulletin of the Department of Agriculture and Immigration of Virginia* (Richmond: Department of Agriculture and Immigration, May 1925), no. 211, p. 3. See also the remarks of Dwight Sanderson, American Country Life Association, *Farm Income and Farm Life* (New York: Univer-

sity of Chicago, 1927), p. vi; Author Unknown, "Striking Testimony of Ex-Farmers," *Rural America* 7, no. 5 (May 1929):3.

12. Eric Englund, "The Trend of Real Estate Taxation in Kansas, 1910-1923," *Journal of Land and Public Utility Economics* 1, no. 1 (Oct. 1925):447; Whitney Coombs, "Taxation of Farm Property," *USDA Technical Bulletin no. 172, 1930.*

13. See Kenyon L. Butterfield, "The Issues of Farm Life," American Country Life Association, *A Decade of Rural Progress: Proceedings of the Tenth and Eleventh National Country Life Conferences East Lansing, Michigan and Urbana, Illinois 1927 and 1928* (Wheeling, W. Va.: University of Chicago Press for the American Country Life Association, 1928), p. 9; remarks of Secretary of Agriculture Henry C. Wallace, *Annual Reports, USDA, 1923,* p. 11; N. R. Baker, "Financial Support for Rural Schools," *Addresses and Proceedings of the Fifty-Ninth Annual Meeting of the National Education Association of the United States Held at Des Moines, Iowa, July 3-8, 1921* (Chicago: National Education Association, 1921), p. 548; Thomas Nixon Carver, "The Vanishing Farmer," *World's Work* 56, no. 5 (Sept. 1928):510-511.

14. See the perceptive article by Benson Y. Landis, "Social Shortages of Rural Life," *Rural Life* 6, no. 9 (Nov. 1928):2.

15. "Realism and Rural Progress," *Survey* 69, no. 6 (Dec. 15, 1922):381; see also Merwin Robert Swanson, "The American Country Life Movement, 1900-1940" (Ph.D. diss., University of Minnesota, Aug. 1972), pp. 251-288.

16. One of the most important works in the development of an understanding of rural complexity was John Harrison Kolb, "Rural Primary Groups: A Study of Agricultural Neighborhoods," *University of Wisconsin Agricultural Experiment Station Research Bulletin 51* (Madison: Agricultural Experiment Station of the University of Wisconsin and the USDA, Dec. 1921); see also John Harrison Kolb and C. J. Bornman, "Rural Religious Organization," *Agricultural Experiment Station of the University of Wisconsin Research Bulletin 60* (Madison: Agricultural Experiment Station of the University of Wisconsin and the USDA, June 1924); Augustus W. Hayes, *Rural Community Organization* (Chicago: University of Chicago Press, 1921); Howard W. Odum, "Public Welfare and Democracy," American Country Life Association, *Needed Readjustments in Rural Life: Proceedings of the Eighth National Country Life Conference Richmond, Virginia 1925* (New York: University of Chicago Press for the American Country Life Association, 1926), p. 119; Edmund deS. Brunner, Gwendolyn S. Hughes, and Marjorie Patten, *American Agricultural Villages* (New York: George H. Doran, 1927), pp. 68-69.

17. John M. Foote, "A Comparative Study of Instruction in Consolidated and One-Teacher Schools," *Addresses and Proceedings of the Sixty-First Annual Meeting of the National Education Association Held at Oakland-San Francisco, California, July 1-6, 1923* (Washington: National Education Association, 1923), pp. 812-826; Charles E. Myers, "The One-Teacher School, Front and Center," *Journal of Rural Education* (May 1924), condensed in "In Defense of the One-Teacher Schools," *Country Life Bulletin* 2, no. 8 (Oct. 1924):8; H. W. McIntosh and H. E. Schrammel, "A Comparison of the Achievement of Eighth-Grade Pupils in Rural Schools and in Graded Schools," *Elementary School Journal* 31, no. 4 (Dec. 1930):301-306; John Taylor Wheeler, "Determining the Agricultural Constants in a Preparatory Curriculum for High School Teachers of Agriculture in Georgia," *Bulletin of the Georgia State College of Agriculture* 20, no. 418 (Dec. 1931):4.

18. H. C. Krebs, "Vocational Guidance in Rural Schools," *Education* 41, no. 4 (Dec. 1920):253-259; T. H. Eaton, "Teaching for the Sake of Vocational Choice in Rural Communities," *School Review* 31, no. 3 (Mar. 1923):191.

19. John H. Butler, "The Little Red Schoolhouse Reincarnated," *Education* 47, no. 3 (Nov. 1926):151; Albert S. Blankenship, *The Accessibility of Rural Schoolhouses in Texas* (New York: Teachers College, Columbia University, 1926).

20. Agnes DeLima, "Sharing Ideas with the Country School," *Survey* 58, no. 10-12 (Aug. 15-Sept. 15, 1927):550-552; Roscoe Pulliam, "What Is the Future of the Rural School," *School and Society* 27, no. 692 (Mar. 31, 1928):392; Bernice Elliott, "Democratic Spirit in the One-Room School," *Journal of the National Education Association* 20, no. 11 (Nov. 1931):277.

21. William E. Leonard, "The Wheat Farmer of Southeastern Washington," *Journal of Land and Public Utility Economics* 2, no. 1 (Jan. 1926):26.

22. *These Changing Times: A Story of Farm Progress during the First Quarter of the*

Twentieth Century (New York: Macmillan, 1927), p. 135; see also Conrad E. Patzer, *Public Education in Wisconsin* (Madison: John Callahan, State Superintendent of Public Instruction, 1924), p. 205.

23. Editorial, "School Changes," *National Grange Monthly* 24, no. 8 (Aug. 1927):10; William John Cooper, "Educating the Farmer's Children," *School and Society* 30, no. 767 (Sept. 7, 1929):309-312.

24. Frederick A. Conrad, "Agrarian Discontent: A Study of Class Conflict Based on Farmer Movements in the United States, 1860-1930" (Ph.D. diss., Stanford University, 1932), p. 87; James Mickel Williams, *The Expansion of Rural Life* (New York: Knopf, 1926); J. F. Steiner, "An Appraisal of the Community Movement," *Papers and Proceedings of the Twenty-Third Annual Meeting of the American Sociological Society* (Chicago: University of Chicago Press, 1929), p. 23; editorial, "Rural Youth," *New Republic* 49, no. 627 (Dec. 8, 1926):57-58.

25. Sidney Glazer, "The Rural Community in the Urban Age," *Agricultural History* 23, no. 2 (Apr. 1949):131; see also Department of Commerce, *Abstract of the Fifteenth Census of the United States* (Washington: USGPO, 1933), p. 598.

26. "Introduction," Jerry Israel, ed., *Building the Organizational Society: Essays on Associational Activities in Modern America* (New York: Free Press, 1972), p. 10.

27. A. W. Dick, G. R. McElveen, and Lawrence M. Peebles, "Lee County, Economic and Social," *Bulletin of the University of South Carolina,* no. 156 (Feb. 1, 1925), p. 73. See also State of Virginia, *Report of the Commission to Study the Condition of the Farmers of Virginia to the General Assembly of Virginia* (Richmond: Division of Purchase and Printing, 1930), pp. 8-9; E. L. Kirkpatrick, "The Farmer's Standard of Living," *USDA, Department Bulletin no. 1466, 1926,* p. 24.

28. An informative and delightful account of the effect of the automobile on the farmer is Reynold M. Wik's *Henry Ford and Grass-roots America* (Ann Arbor: University of Michigan Press, 1972); in this connection, see Wik, p. 25. See also Edward A. Taylor, "The Relationship of the Open-Country Population of Genesee County, New York, to Villages and Cities," *Cornell University Agricultural Experiment Station Bulletin 583* (Ithaca: Cornell University Agricultural Experiment Station, Feb. 1934), p. 45.

29. *Preface to Peasantry: A Tale of Two Black Belt Counties* (Chapel Hill: University of North Carolina Press, 1936), p. 174.

30. Charles Josiah Galpin, *Empty Churches* (New York: Century, 1925); Elizabeth R. Hooker, *Hinterlands of the Church* (New York: Institute of Social and Religious Research, 1931); H. N. Morse and Edmund deS. Brunner, *The Town and Country Church in the United States* (New York: Doran, 1923), p. 63; Paul H. Landis, "South Dakota Town-Country Trade Relations, 1901-1931," *South Dakota Agricultural Experiment Station Bulletin 274* (Brookings: South Dakota Agricultural Experiment Station and the Bureau of Agricultural Economics of the USDA, Sept. 1932); Brunner, Hughes, and Patten, *Agricultural Villages,* pp. 133-134.

31. Adelaide Evans Harris, "Rural Leaders Who Study Their Jobs," *Survey* 49, no. 2 (Oct. 15, 1922):112-113; Harold C. Hoffsommer, "Relation of Cities and Larger Villages to Changes in Rural Trade and Social Areas in Wayne County, New York," *Cornell University Agricultural Experiment Station Bulletin 582* (Ithaca: Cornell University Agricultural Experiment Station, Feb. 1934), p. 59.

32. Catherine A. Dole, "The Personality of the Rural School Teacher," *Education* 42, no. 9 (May 1922):596; see also California State Grange, *Journal of the Proceedings Fifty-First Annual Session of California State Grange Patrons of Husbandry Held in High School Gymnasium Dinuba, California October 16-19, 1923, Inclusive* (California State Grange, 1923), pp. 10-11, 69; Robert C. Foster, "Public Opinion on Rural Problems," *Rural America* 4, no. 2 (Feb. 1926):9.

33. See John Harrison Kolb and A. F. Wileden, *Rural Organizations Handbook* (Madison: University of Wisconsin Agricultural Experiment Station, n.d.), p. 1.

34. Kenyon Butterfield, "The Place of the Home in the Farmers' Movement," American Country Life Association, *The Rural Home: Proceedings of the Sixth National Country Life Conference St. Louis, Missouri 1923* (New York: University of Chicago Press for the American Country Life Association, 1924), pp. 1-16; L. L. Bernard, "Fundamental Values of Farm Life," A.C.L.A., *Farm Income and Farm Life,* p. 30; Williams, *The Expansion of Rural Life,* pp. 216-231; Hawthorn, *The Sociology of Rural Life,* p. 251; W. G. Mather, Jr., T. H. Townsend, and Dwight Sanderson, "A

Study of Rural Community Development in Waterville, New York," *Cornell University Agricultural Experiment Station Bulletin 608* (Ithaca: Cornell University Agricultural Experiment Station, June 1934).

35. One recent work which explores rural anxiety regarding urban expansion and rural change is Don S. Kirschner, *City and Country: Rural Responses to Urbanization in the 1920's* (Westport, Conn.: Greenwood, 1970); see also Edward L. and Frederick H. Schapsmeier, *Henry A. Wallace of Iowa: The Agrarian Years, 1910-1940* (Ames, Ia.: Iowa State University Press, 1968), p. 51.

36. John F. Sinclair, "Why the Farmer Starves," *Nation* 116, no. 3014 (Apr. 11, 1923):416; Edward Sherwood Mead and Bernhard Ostrolenk, *Harvey Baum: A Study of the Agricultural Revolution* (Philadelphia: University of Pennsylvania Press, 1928), p. 23.

37. David F. Houston, *Eight Years with Wilson's Cabinet* (Garden City: Doubleday, Page, 1926), 2:108; see also C. E. Allred, "How Do the Economic Limitations of the Poorer Agricultural Sections Affect Social Conditions?" A.C.L.A., *Farm Income and Farm Life,* p. 189; Wheeler McMillan, *Too Many Farmers* (New York: Morrow, 1929), pp. 243-251.

38. Hugh J. Hughes, "The Radicalism of the Farmer," *Outlook* 130, no. 15 (Apr. 12, 1922):601; see also remarks of Secretary of Agriculture Jewell Mayes, *Missouri Yearbook of Agriculture: Fifty-Third Annual Report of the Missouri State Board of Agriculture* (Jefferson City: Hugh Stevens Printing, 1921), pp. 3-17.

39. U.S. Department of Commerce, Bureau of the Census, *Fifteenth Census of the United States: 1930, Agriculture,* vol. 4 (Washington: USGPO, 1932), pp. 735, 795, 815.

40. G. F. Warren and F. A. Pearson, "Wholesale Prices in the United States for 135 Years, 1797-1932," Cornell University Agricultural Experiment Station *Memoir 142* (Ithaca: Cornell University Agricultural Experiment Station, 1932), pp. 45-46; Willford Isbell King, *The National Income and Its Purchasing Power* (New York: National Bureau of Economic Research, 1930), pp. 305-308, 152.

41. Cooperation was the solution embraced by many businessmen. See National Industrial Conference Board, *The Agricultural Problem in the United States* (New York: National Industrial Conference Board, 1926), pp. 149-150. See also U.S., Congress, House, *Joint Commission of Agricultural Inquiry: Report of the Agricultural Crisis and Its Causes,* 67th Cong., 2d sess., 1922, pt. 4: 204; Macy Campbell, *Rural Life at the Crossroads* (Boston: Ginn, 1927), p. 11; William Bennett Bizzell, *The Green Rising* (New York: Macmillan, 1926).

42. Remarks of Secretary of Agriculture William M. Jardine, *Report of the Secretary of Agriculture—1925* (Washington: USGPO, 1925), p. 18. See also William M. Jardine, "The Agricultural Problem," *Saturday Evening Post* 199, no. 16 (Oct. 16, 1926):177; John M. Gillette, *Rural Sociology* (New York: Macmillan, 1922), p. 356.

43. Thomas Wilson, "The Effect of the Agricultural Depression on the Meat Packing Industry," U.S., Congress, House, *The National Agriculture Conference: Report on,* 67th Cong., 2d sess., Jan. 23-27, 1922, H. Doc. no. 195, p. 48; see also O. B. Jesness, "Cooperative Marketing," *USDA Farmers' Bulletin 1144, 1920.*

44. U.S., Congress, House, *The Agricultural Crisis and Its Causes,* p. 229.

45. Author Unknown, "What's the Matter with Agriculture," *Orange Judd Farmer* 69, no. 28 (July 23, 1921):3; Herman Steen, *Coöperative Marketing: The Golden Rule in Agriculture* (Garden City: Doubleday, Page, 1923); R. H. Elsworth, "Agricultural Cooperative Associations, Marketing and Purchasing, 1925," *USDA, Technical Bulletin no. 40, 1928.*

46. J. R. Howard and A. C. True, "Memorandum of Understanding between the Executive Committee of the American Farm Bureau Federation and the States Relation Service, USDA, relative to Farm Bureaus and Extension Service," June 27, 1922, National Archives, record group 16, "Correspondence of Secretaries of Agriculture," "Extension Work—1922," drawer 124. For conservative pressure see Utah Senator William H. King to Henry C. Wallace, Nov. 28, 1921, National Archives, record group 16, "Correspondence of Secretaries of Agriculture," "County Agents—1921," file; Homer L. Brinkley, "Annual Narrative Report of Calcasieu Parish Agent—1923," *Extension Service Annual Reports: Louisiana, 1909-1944,* National Archives, Microcopy T-863, roll 12, p. 1.

47. Remarks of Secretary Jardine, *Report of the Secretary of Agriculture—1926*

(Washington: USGPO, 1926), p. 8; H. E. Erdman, "Possibilities and Limitations of Co-operative Marketing," in Clyde L. King, ed., "The Agricultural Situation in the United States," *Annals of the American Academy of Political and Social Science* 117 (Philadelphia: American Academy of Political and Social Science, Jan. 1925):217–226; J. W. Jones, "Membership Relations of Cooperative Associations," *USDA, Circular no. 41, 1928,* p. 22.

48. *Fifteenth Census,* p. 526.
49. A. W. McKay and W. J. Kuhrt, "Management Problems of Cooperative Associations," *USDA, Bulletin no. 1414,* p. 2; see also Wik, *Henry Ford,* p. 135. For an example of successful cooperation see Asher Hobson and J. Burton Chaney, "Sales Methods and Policies of a Growers' National Marketing Agency," *USDA, Bulletin no. 1109, 1923.*
50. H. W. Peck, "The Influence of Agricultural Machinery and the Automobile on Farming Operations," *Quarterly Journal of Economics* 41, no. 3 (May 1927):544.
51. C. B. Williams, "The Responsibility of the Agricultural Experiment Station in the Present Agricultural Situation," *Science* 67, no. 1743 (May 25, 1928):519; see also Bernard M. Baruch, "Some Aspects of the Farmers' Problems," *Atlantic Monthly* 128, no. 1 (July 1921):114.
52. Gladys Lucille Baker, *The County Agent* (Chicago: University of Chicago Press, 1939), pp. 57–60; W. Russell Taylor, "The Attitude of Farmers toward the County Farm Bureau," *Twenty-Third Annual Meeting of the American Sociological Society,* p. 270; Glenn W. Birkett, "A Farmer Speaks Out," *Atlantic Monthly* 134, no. 6 (Dec. 1924):763.
53. Baker, *The County Agent,* p. 23; for local bureau problems see W. F. Delp, " Farm Bureau Work in Greene County—1921," *Extension Service Annual Reports: Missouri, 1914–1944,* National Archives, Microcopy T-870, roll 7, p. 1; and H. A. Christiansen, "Annual Report of Extension Work Agricultural Agent Beaver County—1921," *Extension Service Annual Reports: Utah, 1914–1944,* National Archives, Microcopy T-891, roll 4, p. 15.
54. O. E. Baker, "Population, Food Supply, and American Agriculture" (Washington: USDA, Bureau of Agricultural Economics, 1927), p. 11; Wheeler McMillan, *The Farming Fever* (New York: Appleton, 1924), p. 37; McMillan, *Too Many Farmers,* p. 12.
55. *Fifteenth Census,* pp. 443, 490.
56. Ibid., pp. 504, 891.
57. Dean Albertson, *Roosevelt's Farmer: Claude R. Wickard in the New Deal* (New York: Columbia University Press, 1961), p. 33; by the mid-twenties the family farm contributed only about two-fifths of what the farm family consumed. E. L. Kirkpatrick, "The Farmer's Standard of Living," *USDA, Bulletin no. 1466, 1926,* p. 15.
58. *Culture of a Contemporary Rural Community—Irwin, Iowa* (Washington: USDA, Bureau of Agricultural Economics, Dec. 1942), p. 10.
59. Not surprisingly, the USDA was a prime tub-thumper in the tractor revolution. See Arnold P. Yerkes and L. M. Church, "The Farm Tractor in the Dakotas," *USDA Farmers' Bulletin 1035, 1919;* L. A. Reynoldson and H. R. Tolley, "Changes Effected by Tractors on Corn-Belt Farms," *USDA Farmers' Bulletin 1296, 1922;* L. A. Reynoldson and H. R. Tolley, "Cost of Using Tractors on Corn-Belt Farms," *USDA Farmers' Bulletin 1297, 1922;* M. R. Cooper and J. A. Williams, "Cost of Using Horses on Corn-Belt Farms," *USDA Farmers' Bulletin 1298, 1922;* L. A. Reynoldson and H. R. Tolley, "Shall I Buy a Tractor?" *USDA Farmers' Bulletin 1299, 1922.*
60. *Abstract of the Fifteenth Census,* p. 598; see also Neil M. Clark, "The American Farmer Wakes Up," *World's Work* 53, no. 1 (Nov. 1926):51.
61. Arnold P. Yerkes and L. M. Church, "Tractor Experience in Illinois," *USDA Farmers' Bulletin 963, 1918,* p. 4; N.I.C.B., *Agricultural Problem in the United States,* p. 12.
62. Eastman, *These Changing Times,* p. 35.
63. *Abstract of the Fifteenth Census,* p. 501.
64. W. J. Morphy, "Industrialized Farming: A Sound Investment," National Archives, record group 16, "Correspondence of Secretaries of Agriculture," "Farms—Farmers—Farming—1929" file; Mordecai Ezekiel and Sherman Johnson, "Corporation Farming—the Way Out," *New Republic* 63, no. 809 (June 4, 1930):68; Author Unknown, "Corporate Farming Increases: Kansas, Nervous, Starts Inquiry," *Business*

Week (June 18, 1930), p. 22; Wayne Gard, "Agriculture's Industrial Revolution," *Current History* 34, no. 6 (Sept. 1931):853-857. Although corporate farming continues to be a factor in American agriculture, the large and highly mechanized family farm now predominates. See John L. Shover, *First Majority—Last Minority: The Transforming of Rural Life in America* (DeKalb, Ill.: Northern Illinois University Press, 1976), pp. 160-166.

65. *Fifteenth Census, Agriculture,* vol. 4, p. 309.
66. *Abstract of the Fifteenth Census,* pp. 15, 18, 546. See also Shideler, *Farm Crisis,* p. 81.
67. *Fifteenth Census, 1930, Agriculture,* vol. 4, p. 82.
68. *Abstract of the Fifteenth Census,* p. 546.
69. L. C. Gray, Charles L. Stewart, Howard A. Turner, J. T. Sanders, and W. J. Spillman, "Farm Ownership and Tenancy," *USDA, Yearbook, 1923,* p. 554.
70. J. F. Abel, "Rural Child Labor Versus Rural Education," *School Life* 9, no. 6 (Feb. 1924):130-131; Charles E. Gibbons, assisted by Clara B. Armentrout, *Child Labor among Cotton Growers of Texas* (New York: National Child Labor Committee, 1925), p. 49; Nettie P. McGill, "Children in Agriculture," U.S., Department of Labor Children's Bureau, *Bureau Publication no. 187* (Washington: USGPO, 1929).
71. In 1920 about 61 percent of employed children were engaged in agriculture. Author Unknown, "Child Labor Facts," National Child Labor Committee *Publication no. 337* (New York: National Child Labor Committee, Feb. 1927); Author Unknown, "Child Labor Facts" (New York: National Child Labor Committee, 1931).
72. *The Social Economics of Agriculture* (New York: Macmillan, 1932), p. 447.
73. Remarks of Secretary Jardine, *Report of the Secretary of Agriculture—1927* (Washington: USGPO, 1927), p. 12; S. G. Rubinow, "Putting the Factory on the Farm," *Current History* 30, no. 6 (Sept. 1929):1052, 1069-1074.
74. E. R. McIntyre, "Hic Jacet—the Hick," *Independent* 116, no. 3958 (Apr. 10, 1926): 421-422.
75. *Too Many Farmers,* p. 315.
76. *These Changing Times,* p. 152.
77. Charles D. Lewis, *Rural Intelligence in Relation to Rural Population* (Nashville: George Peabody College for Teachers, 1929), pp. 54-73; Wilson Gee and John J. Corson, III, *Rural Depopulation in Certain Tidewater and Piedmont Areas of Virginia* (Charlottesville: Institute for Research in the Social Sciences, University of Virginia, 1929), p. 27; remarks of Secretary of Agriculture Henry C. Wallace, *Annual Reports, USDA, 1923,* p. 10.
78. "The Special Needs of Farm Youth," American Country Life Association, *Farm Youth: Proceedings of the Ninth National Country Life Conference, Washington, D.C. 1926* (New York: University of Chicago Press for the A.C.L.A., 1927), p. 4.
79. Editorial, "An Urban View of Rural Ideals," *Outlook* 131, no. 15 (Aug. 9, 1922):591-592; editorial, "A Million Farmers Should Leave the Farms," *World's Work* 47, no. 2 (Dec. 1923):130-131; C. D. Kinsman, "An Appraisal of Power Used on Farms in the United States," *USDA, Bulletin no. 1348, 1925,* pp. 1-2.
80. Remarks of Secretary Wallace, *Annual Reports, USDA, 1922,* p. 9; Nat T. Frame, "Larger Objectives of Extension Work," *Rural America* 8, no. 4 (Apr. 1930):4; T. H. Eaton, "Coöperative Extension Work in Agriculture and Home Economics," *The Status of Rural Education: The Thirtieth Yearbook of the National Society for the Study of Education* (Bloomington, Ill.: Public School, 1931), p. 241.
81. William C. Smith, "The Rural Mind: A Study in Occupational Attitude," *American Journal of Sociology* 32, no. 5 (Mar. 1927):771-786; Mark Van Doren, "The Real Tragedy of the Farmer," *Harper's Magazine* 161, no. 3 (Aug. 1930):365-370.

CHAPTER 7

1. "Forward," in Wheeler McMillan, *Too Many Farmers* (New York: Morrow, 1929), p. xi.
2. "Old Ideals Versus New Ideas in Farm Life," *Farmers in a Changing World: The Yearbook of Agriculture—1940* (Washington: USGPO, 1940), p. 161.
3. William L. Wanless, *The United States Department of Agriculture: A Study in*

Administration (Baltimore: Johns Hopkins Press, 1920), p. 113; Edward Wiest, *Agricultural Organization in the United States* (Lexington: University of Kentucky, Apr. 1923), p. 47.

4. "Introduction," Jerry Israel, ed., *Building the Organizational Society: Essays on Associational Activities in Modern America* (New York: Free Press, 1972), p. 1.

5. "Old Ideals Versus New Ideas," p. 166.

6. Earle D. Ross, *Iowa Agriculture: An Historical Survey* (Iowa City: State Historical Society of Iowa, 1951), p. 161; Ulysses Prentiss Hedrick, *A History of Agriculture in the State of New York* (Albany: New York State Agricultural Society, 1933), p. 438.

7. Kenyon L. Butterfield, "The Place of the Home in the Farmers' Movement," American Country Life Association, *The Rural Home: Proceedings of the Sixth National Country Life Conference St. Louis, Missouri 1923* (New York: University of Chicago Press for A.C.L.A., 1924), p. 12; William M. Jardine, "Farmers as Managers," in Clyde L. King, ed., "The Agricultural Situation in the United States," *Annals of the American Academy of Political and Social Science* 117 (Philadelphia: American Academy of Political and Social Science, Jan. 1925):86; Carle C. Zimmerman, "Farm Trade Centers in Minnesota, 1905–1929," *University of Minnesota Agricultural Experiment Station Bulletin 269* (St. Paul: University of Minnesota Agricultural Experiment Station, Sept. 1930), p. 23.

8. *A History of Agriculture in the State of New York,* p. 441.

9. "A Fifty-Year Crisis in Agriculture," *Saturday Evening Post* 196, no. 42 (Apr. 19, 1924):122

10. Lewis F. Carr, *America Challenged* (New York: Macmillan, 1929), p. 102.

11. Carr, *America Challenged,* pp. 300–301; E. C. Young, *The Movement of Farm Population* (Ithaca: Cornell University Agricultural Experiment Station, Mar. 1924), p. 32.

12. Henry A. Wallace, "Standards of Economic Efficiency in Agriculture and Their Compatibility with Social Welfare," A.C.L.A., *Farm Income and Farm Life,* Dwight Sanderson, ed. (New York: University of Chicago Press, 1927), p. 120; John D. Black, *Agricultural Reform in the United States* (New York: McGraw-Hill, 1929), p. 58; Macy Campbell, *Rural Life at the Crossroads* (Boston:Ginn, 1927), p. 27.

BIBLIOGRAPHICAL ESSAY

WHEN I BEGAN my study of agriculture between 1900 and 1920 I was struck by the paucity of secondary treatments of the subject. This scarcity is particularly remarkable in view of the sustained attention historians have lavished on the United States in general during a period that they agree was crucial to the development of modern America. The apparent disinterest of historians in agriculture in the Progressive Era can be explained by their rather patronizing tendency to leave the subject to those stigmatized as "agricultural historians." For their part, agricultural historians have avoided the period because it has not interested them. Agricultural historians have been attracted to times of economic hardship and political unrest, and the rural quiescence which characterized agriculture's Golden Age has rendered it boring to them. For historians of agriculture, the first two decades of this century have served only as an intermission between long and exciting periods of agrarian ferment. One of the few attempts at synthesis, and one of the best, is Paul H. Johnstone's perceptive chapter, "Old Ideals Versus New Ideas in Farm Life," which appeared in the 1940 Yearbook of Agriculture, *Farmers in a Changing World* (Washington: USGPO, 1940). Generally, however, the scholar traveling this road will fail to encounter many of those historiographical mileposts which assure him he is on the right route.

If the historian wishes to tie agricultural developments to the larger society he will be able to compensate for the shortage of specific studies. In my work, Robert H. Wiebe's *The Search for Order* (New York: Hill and Wang, 1967) helped shape my thinking regarding the desire for organization and efficiency in an industrial society, though I found this book less clear and concrete at times than I would have liked. On the drive for efficiency I drew insights from Samuel Haber's *Efficiency and Uplift: Scientific Management in the Progressive Era* (Chicago: University of Chicago, 1964). Also, I found Jerry Israel's edited collection, *Building the Organizational Society: Essays on Associational Activities in Modern America* (New York: Free Press, 1972), and particularly the introductory essay by Samuel P. Hays, useful in emphasizing the organizational impulse in twentieth century America.

In the main, the paucity of secondary treatments of agriculture in this period is reflected in the narrower areas with which I was concerned as well. For example, there is no modern descriptive study of rural society and rural life in this period. Consequently, piecing together an

183

accurate picture of rural America was difficult for me. Even if farmers and their families were articulate, which they were not, people living a life take most aspects of it for granted and do not talk about it. The proceedings of meetings of farm organizations and letters to the editors of agricultural publications reflect rural opinions on public questions and help expose the rural self-image, but they tell us little about the nature of rural society or rural life. Those who did describe rural society must be approached with caution because they were seldom disinterested observers. Novelists, for example, were often either nostalgics or were, as in the case of Hamlin Garland, biased against rural society. Government publications are of some use, but they were usually prescriptive and reflected an urban prejudice. The Children's Bureau, the Public Health Service, and the Bureau of Education undertook studies of aspects of rural society, but the most varied and comprehensive treatment was that of the United States Department of Agriculture. Some of the best governmental publications available, which helped me understand rural society and economics, were W. C. Funk's "What the Farm Contributes Directly to the Farmer's Living," *USDA Farmers' Bulletin 635* (Washington: USGPO, 1914), E. A. Goldenweiser's "The Farmer's Income," *USDA Farmers' Bulletin 746* (Washington: USGPO, 1916), and E. L. Kirkpatrick's "The Farmer's Standard of Living," *USDA Department Bulletin No. 1466* (Washington: USGPO, 1926). I also found a series of four reports based on a survey of the wives of crop reporters, "Social and Labor Needs of Farm Women," "Domestic Needs of Farm Women," "Educational Needs of Farm Women," and "Economic Needs of Farm Women," *USDA Reports No. 103, No. 104, No. 105,* and *No. 106* (Washington: USGPO, 1915), interesting, but the size and nature of the sample made me somewhat skeptical of their value. Township and county social surveys by rural sociologists are useful to the historian because they allow him to glimpse some aspects of rural life, but they are equally interesting in exposing the attitudes and concerns of rural sociologists. Some of the best early social surveys include Paul L. Vogt's "A Rural Survey in Southwestern Ohio," *Miami University Bulletin,* series XI, no. 8 (April 1913); "A Rural Life Survey of Greene and Clermont Counties, Ohio," *Miami University Bulletin,* series XII, no. 11 (July 1914); Fred C. Ayer and Herman N. Morse, *A Rural Survey of Lane County, Oregon* '(Eugene: University of Oregon Extension Division, 1916); Carl W. Thompson and G. P. Warber, *Social and Economic Survey of a Rural Township in Southern Minnesota* (Minneapolis: University of Minnesota, April 1913); and Lewis H. Haney and George S. Wehrwein, editors, "A Social and Economic Survey of Southern Travis County," *Bulletin of the University of Texas,* no. 65 (November 20, 1916). I also exploited the most concerted effort at rural social surveying, the investigations undertaken by the Department of Church and Country Life of the Board of Home Missions of the Presbyterian Church in the U.S.A. between 1911 and 1915. A number of surveys were done and most are very good, though the best for my purposes were the Tennessee, Indiana, and Pennsylvania studies. Some of the survey work done by the National Child Labor Committee also helped me achieve an understanding of the countryside. As rural sociology matured, it turned its interest away from reform and toward a more scholarly study of the nature of rural society, how it was unique, and how it was changing and responding to change. Hence, some of the social investigations undertaken in the twenties are indispensable to the student of rural life. Anyone who wants to understand the social configuration of the countryside, for example, must read John Harrison Kolb's fine "Rural Primary Groups: A Study of Agricultural Neighborhoods," *University of Wisconsin Agricultural Experiment Station Research Bulletin 51* (December 1921); as well as Charles Josiah Galpin's seminal work, "The Social Anatomy of an Agricultural Community," *University of Wisconsin Agricultural Experiment Station Research Bulletin 34* (May 1915); and Dwight Sanderson and Warren S. Thompson, "The Social Areas of Otsego County," *Cornell University Agricultural Experiment Station Bulletin 422* (July 1923). The twenties and early thirties saw systematic study of rural society by several universities—South Carolina, Cornell, Wisconsin, Tennessee, Virginia, North Carolina, Minnesota, and North Carolina State, among others, undertook useful investigations. Each university tended to be interested in some aspect of rural life slightly different from what another was concerned with, but the higher standards of rural sociology by the twenties make most of these useful to the investigator of rural life. Particularly interesting to me were a series done by North Carolina State, thoroughly examining the white farmers of Wake County, and a series of Cornell bulletins examining the effects of changes in economics, communications, and transportation on the social institutions of the rural New York neighborhood.

The Country Life Movement has enjoyed more scholarly treatment than most of the topics with which I dealt. Students will want to look at William L. Bowers's *The Country Life Movement in America, 1900-1920* (Port Washington, N.Y.: Kennikat, 1974) and Robert Merwin Swanson's "The American Country Life Movement, 1900-1940," (Ph.D. dissertation, University of Minnesota, August 1972). Bowers sees the Country Lifers as middle-class people motivated by status anxiety. I do not accept Bowers's thesis, but I think his book does serve scholars in other ways, particularly by indentifying many of the leaders of the movement. Swanson concentrates on the American Country Life Association and the social side of the movement which the ACLA represented. Primary works which helped me understand the Country Life Movement included Kenyon L. Butterfield's *Chapters in Rural Progress* (Chicago: University of Chicago Press, 1908), Liberty Hyde Bailey's *The Country-Life Movement in the United States* (New York: Macmillan, 1911), and Sir Horace Plunkett's *The Rural Life Problem of the United States* (New York:

Macmillan, 1910). A number of influential national publications, particularly the *Outlook,* the *Independent,* and the *World's Work,* were also concerned with the Country Life Movement and gave me valuable insights regarding the movement and the tremendous urban interest in it. Of course, I also used the *Report of the United States Country Life Commission* (Washington: USGPO, 1909), and some of the many proceedings of state and local country life conferences held during the period before World War I. For the Country Life Movement in the twenties the best sources are the *Proceedings* of the American Country Life Association and the Association's organ, *Rural America.*

Rural sociologists assumed an increasingly important part in the Country Life Movement and produced a large volume of work. Rural sociology is studied by Swanson, whose work is cited above, by Edmund deS. Brunner, *The Growth of a Science* (New York: Harper and Brothers, 1957), and by Lowry Nelson, *Rural Sociology: Its Origin and Growth in the United States* (Minneapolis: University of Minnesota Press, 1969). A good monograph, preferably by an intellectual historian, is needed to probe rural sociology in its formative years. It was my finding that rural sociologists, particularly in their work before the 1920s, were most interesting as primary sources in and of themselves, and I used them as such. Some of their most important works in this period were Thomas Nixon Carver's *Principles of Rural Economics* (Boston: Ginn, 1911), John M. Gillette's *Constructive Rural Sociology* (New York: Sturgis and Walton, 1916), Paul L. Vogt's *Introduction to Rural Sociology* (New York: Appleton, 1917), Charles Josiah Galpin's *Rural Life* (New York: Century, 1918), John Phelan's edited collection, *Readings in Rural Sociology* (New York: Macmillan, 1920), and Newell Leroy Sims's *The Rural Community* (New York: Charles Scribner's Sons, 1920). By the 1920s rural sociology had matured to the point that its practitioners were avoiding open prescription. The best works done in the twenties include a pair of fine, thoughtful volumes by James Mickel Williams, *Our Rural Heritage* (New York: Knopf, 1925) and *The Expansion of Rural Life* (New York: Knopf, 1926). Other useful books are Horace Boies Hawthorn's *The Sociology of Rural Life* (New York: Century, 1926) and Carl C. Taylor's *Rural Sociology* (New York: Harper, 1926). I also studied the *Proceedings* of the National Conference of Charities and Correction, the *Proceedings* of the Academy of Political Science in the City of New York, the *Proceedings* of the American Sociological Society, the *Annals* of the American Academy of Political and Social Science, the *American Journal of Sociology,* and the *Survey,* all of which are filled with useful information on the concerns of rural social scientists and social workers.

I found that the evidence on the involvement of businessmen and bankers in agriculture was relatively sparse. Indeed, a good monograph is needed on business involvement in agriculture in the early years of the century, one which could possibly revolve around the shadowy National

Soil Fertility League, a business-supported organization active in the campaign to industrialize agriculture. There are a number of good books on the role of the railroads in pressing change in the countryside, but here the secondary work abruptly ends. For my purposes the *Nation's Business,* the *Financier, Moody's Magazine,* the *Journal of the American Bankers Association,* and the *Proceedings* of that organization were all useful. And in the twenties the *Business Week, Business,* and the National Industrial Conference Board's study, *The Agricultural Problem in the United States* (New York: National Industrial Conference Board, Inc., 1926), added evidence regarding business opinion and activity. Some of my best evidence of business involvement also came from the newspaper, *Banker-Farmer,* published by B. F. Harris, a remarkable Champaign, Illinois, banker, and many expressions of business opinion can be found at the National Archives, Washington, D.C., in record group 16, the "Correspondence of the Secretaries of Agriculture." Generally speaking, however, their relative reticence makes businessmen and bankers difficult groups to track down.

I also found a shortage of secondary material on the rural church. Fortunately, there were numerous works done on the problems of the country church during the period with which I was concerned. Some of the most important works on rural religion include Warren Hugh Wilson's two volumes, *The Church of the Open Country* (New York: Missionary Education Movement of the United States and Canada, 1911) and *The Evolution of the Country Community* (Boston: Pilgrim Press, 1912); as well as Kenyon Butterfield's *The Country Church and the Rural Problem* (Chicago: University of Chicago Press, 1911); and George Walter Fiske's *The Challenge of the Country* (New York: Association Press, 1912). A volume that was tremendously influential before World War I is one by Charles Otis Gill and Gifford Pinchot, *The Country Church* (New York: Macmillan, 1913), and the role played by the rural YMCA is followed in one of the Association's organs, *Rural Manhood.* The twenties saw the publication of a number of thoughtful books on the problems of rural religion. Some of the best are H. N. Morse and Edmund deS. Brunner, *The Town and Country Church in the United States* (New York: Doran, 1923); C. Luther Fry, *Diagnosing the Rural Church* (New York: Doran, 1924); Charles Josiah Galpin, *Empty Churches* (New York: Century, 1925); and Elizabeth R. Hooker, *United Churches* (Garden City: Doubleday, Doran, 1928), which examines the problem of consolidated country churches.

Rural education is another area in which I was able to counter a scarcity of secondary materials with a wealth of published primary work. Some of the best sources are government publications, and I began with A. C. True's "Some Problems of the Rural Common School," *Yearbook of the United States Department of Agriculture—1901* (Washington: USGPO, 1902), which usefully outlines the problems of rural education from the urban perspective and sets the terms of the debate over it.

Many state educational publications are also useful, but the publications of the United States Bureau of Education are essential because they reflect governmental ideas about education and embrace a national perspective. Some of the most important of these are A. C. Monahan, "The Status of Rural Education in the United States," *United States Bureau of Education Bulletin No. 515* (1913); Fletcher B. Dresslar, "Rural Schoolhouses and Grounds," *United States Bureau of Education Bulletin No. 585* (1914); A. C. Monahan, "Consolidation of Rural Schools and Transportation of Pupils at Public Expense," *United States Bureau of Education Bulletin No. 604* (1914); Katherine M. Cook and A. C. Monahan, "Rural School Supervision," *Bureau of Education Bulletin No. 48* (1916); and Katherine Cook, "Rural Education," *Biennial Survey of Education, 1920–1922* (Washington: USGPO, 1923), vol. 1. The finest state publication on rural education is the exhaustive, multivolumed *Rural School Survey of New York State,* undertaken by the special state-appointed Joint Committee on Rural Schools in the early twenties.

The rural school drew the attention of many leading educators. Harold Waldstein Foght's *The American Rural School* (New York: Macmillan, 1910) captured nationwide renown, and was soon followed by other, more complete examinations of rural school problems by urban-oriented educators. Among the best of these are Mabel Carney's *Country Life and the Country School* (Chicago: Row, Peterson, 1912), J. D. Eggleston and Robert W. Bruère's *The Work of the Rural School* (New York: Harper, 1913), George Herbert Betts and Otis E. Hall's *Better Rural Schools* (Indianapolis: Bobbs-Merrill, 1914), and Elwood P. Cubberley's two important volumes, *The Improvement of Rural Schools* (Boston: Houghton Mifflin, 1912), and *Rural Life and Education* (Boston: Houghton Mifflin, 1914). Also very useful in tracing the evolution of the debates over rural education were the *Proceedings* of the National Education Association throughout the period, as well as professional journals like *Elementary School Teacher, Educational Review, Education, School Life, Journal of Rural Education, Journal of the National Education Association,* and *School and Society.*

The involvement of the United States government in agriculture is important and easy to trace. The USDA's *Yearbooks* and *Annual Reports* are rich sources of information throughout the period, as are the dozens of bulletins published by the department every year. The rise and progress of agricultural extension is particularly easy to follow because it has been examined more completely by historians than most of the subjects I have discussed. A classic treatment is Alfred Charles True, *A History of Agricultural Extension Work in the United States, 1785–1923, USDA Miscellaneous Publication No. 15* (Washington: USGPO, 1928), a rather dry narrative which contains a large amount of useful information. Roy V. Scott's excellent monograph, *The Reluctant Farmer* (Urbana: University of Illinois Press, 1970), fully covers pre–Smith-Lever extension efforts, and the *Proceedings* of the Association of American

Agricultural Colleges and Experiment Stations also contain valuable discussions of extension and its problems. The best source for post-Smith-Lever extension developments is still Gladys Lucille Baker's *The County Agent* (Chicago: University of Chicago, 1939). The federal government's extension goals and efforts are well chronicled in the publications of the USDA. Some of the more interesting documents are Carl Vrooman's "Meeting the Farmer Halfway," *Yearbook of the United States Department of Agriculture—1916* (Washington: USGPO, 1917); William A. Lloyd's "County Agricultural Agent Work under the Smith-Lever Act, 1914–1924," *USDA Miscellaneous Circular No. 59* (Washington: USGPO, 1926); and George E. Farrell's "Boys' and Girls' 4-H Club Work under the Smith-Lever Act, 1914–1924," *USDA Miscellaneous Circular No. 85* (Washington: USGPO, 1926). David F. Houston's *Eight Years with Wilson's Cabinet* (Garden City: Doubleday, Page, 1926) delineates both long- and short-term federal extension aims. Regarding the relationship between extension and the farm bureaus, Grant McConnell's classic, *The Decline of Agrarian Democracy* (Berkeley: University of California Press, 1953), remains preeminent. In contrast to McConnell, I believe that the USDA allowed the American Farm Bureau Federation significant de facto power in the making of agricultural policy precisely because the Farm Bureau embraced the same ends for agriculture in which the USDA believed. It has appeared at times that the Farm Bureau directs the USDA, but it has moved it precisely in the direction in which the USDA has wanted agriculture to go. Despite my disagreement with the emphasis of McConnell's thesis, however, his book is a milestone in agricultural history and in the history of American corporatism. There are other useful treatments of extension and the farm bureaus. One of the more analytical of these is M. C. Burritt's contemporary investigation, *The County Agent and the Farm Bureau* (New York: Harcourt, Brace, 1922). Scholars who wish to become deeply involved in the study of agricultural extension must use the *Extension Service Annual Reports*. I found these county agent reports, which are available at the National Archives, to be the single most useful source I encountered. The reports are concerned mainly with production, and because of their progress orientation they must be used with discrimination, but they contain a wealth of information on the progress of the extension program in the countryside and on rural society, politics, and attitudes. They are particularly valuable for the information they contain about the countryside during World War I, information which is unavailable elsewhere. I cannot overstress the value of this largely untapped source of information on rural America.

Because their interest is drawn to agrarian discontent, historians have developed a substantial body of work on agriculture during the twenties. In the field of economics James H. Shideler's *Farm Crisis, 1919–1923* (Berkeley: University of California Press, 1957) is preeminent, and it also makes significant points about the social effects of the price collapse. Two recent books on the important Wallace family which provided me with insights on the Wallaces and on the USDA are Edward L. and Frederick H. Schapsmeier's *Henry A. Wallace of Iowa: The Agrarian Years, 1910–1940* (Ames: Iowa State University Press, 1968), and Donald L. Winters's *Henry Cantwell Wallace as Secretary of Agriculture, 1921–1924* (Urbana: University of Illinois Press, 1970). I also found two very different treatments of rural society in the twenties valuable. The first is Don S. Kirschner's *City and Country: Rural Responses to Urbanization in the 1920's* (Westport, Connecticut: Greenwood, 1970), a fine analytical work dealing with rural social and economic change and urban-rural conflict in Iowa and Illinois. The second is Reynold M. Wik's *Henry Ford and Grass-roots America* (Ann Arbor: University of Michigan Press, 1972), a breezy, enjoyable, well-written survey of Ford's relationship with the countryside which also sheds some light on the social and economic importance of the automobile to rural people. I also found a number of books written in the twenties useful for helping me understand the shifting terms of debate regarding farmers and rural problems. Some of the best of these include Wheeler McMillan's *The Farming Fever* (New York: Appleton, 1924) and *Too Many Farmers* (New York: William Morrow, 1929), Henry C. Wallace's *Our Debt and Duty to the Farmer* (New York: Century, 1925), Macy Campbell's *Rural Life at the Crossroads* (Boston: Ginn, 1927), John D. Black's *Agricultural Reform in the United States* (New York: McGraw-Hill, 1929), and Ellis Lore Kirkpatrick's *The Farmer's Standard of Living* (New York: Century, 1929). The *Proceedings* of the American Country Life Association and its organ, *Rural America,* also contain a great deal of material on rural social stasis and social change in the twenties.

The foregoing essay is merely a brief sketch of the field, emphasizing the sources most useful to me. A large, almost staggering, amount of source material is available, and a great many topics should be exploited. In my research I found gaps in the secondary literature that could and should be filled. Rural education, rural religion, World War I in the countryside, the role of business in agriculture, the immigrant on the farm, and the functional significance of the rural neighborhood are a few of the worthy topics historians have overlooked. As I noted earlier, there has been a great deal of work done on agrarian discontent, for reasons that are both understandable and justifiable. But most of these studies, interesting as they are, are concerned primarily with the aberrant and tell us little about the nature of rural society and rural people. It is in the field of social history where agricultural historians should and, I believe, will make their most valuable contributions in the future.

INDEX